COLLECTED WORKS OF RENÉ GUÉNON

STUDIES IN FREEMASONRY
AND THE COMPAGNONNAGE

RENÉ GUÉNON

STUDIES IN FREEMASONRY AND THE COMPAGNONNAGE

Translators

Henry D. Fohr
Cecil Bethell
Michael Allen

SOPHIA PERENNIS

HILLSDALE NY

Originally published in French as
Études sur la Franc-Maçonnerie et le Compagnonnage [2 vols]
© Éditions Traditionnelles 1964
English translation © Sophia Perennis 2004
First English Edition 2004
All rights reserved

Series editor: James R. Wetmore

For information, address:
Sophia Perennis, P.O. Box 611
Hillsdale NY 12529
sophiaperennis.com

Library of Congress Cataloging-in-Publication Data

Guénon, René
[Études sur la franc-maçonnerie et le compagnonnage. English]
Studies in Freemasonry and the Compagnonnage / René Guénon;
translators Henry D. Fohr, Cecil Bethell, Michael Allen.— 1ˢᵗ english ed.

p. cm.
"Originally published in French as Études sur la Franc-Maçonnerie
et le Compagnonnage. Éditions Traditionnelles, 1964."
ISBN 0 900588 88 8 (pbk: alk. paper)
ISBN 0 900588 51 9 (cloth: alk. paper)
1. Freemasonry—France—History.
2. Guilds—France—History I. Title.
HS 603.G8513 2004
366'.1'09440902—dc22   2004019338

CONTENTS

EDITORIAL NOTE

THE PAST CENTURY HAS WITNESSED an erosion of earlier cultural values as well as a blurring of the distinctive characteristics of the world's traditional civilizations, giving rise to philosophic and moral relativism, multiculturalism, and dangerous fundamentalist reactions. As early as the 1920s, the French metaphysician René Guénon (1886–1951) had diagnosed these tendencies and presented what he believed to be the only possible reconciliation of the legitimate, although apparently conflicting, demands of outward religious forms, 'exoterisms', with their essential core, 'esoterism'. His works are characterized by a foundational critique of the modern world coupled with a call for intellectual reform; a renewed examination of metaphysics, the traditional sciences, and symbolism, with special reference to the ultimate unanimity of all spiritual traditions; and finally, a call to the work of spiritual realization. Despite their wide influence, translation of Guénon's works into English has so far been piecemeal. The *Sophia Perennis* edition is intended to fill the urgent need to present them in a more authoritative and systematic form. A complete list of Guénon's works, given in the order of their original publication in French, follows this note.

René Guénon had a lifelong preoccupation with Freemasonry. In his search for an operative initiatic path in the Western world, he explored many groups—occult, neo-Gnostic, Theosophical—claiming to be initiatory, ultimately rejecting them all, with the single exception of the Craft. His relation to Freemasonry, however, was far from simple; mostly before World War I, for example, he contributed articles to both Masonic and anti-Masonic publications, though he continued to review books on Masonry and refer to Masonic lore in his own works until the end of his life. Recognizing that the symbolism and ritual employed by Masonry was for the most part both traditional and esoteric, he labored to discover, define, or create a Freemasonic initiation that would be compatible with Catholic Christianity, as it supposedly was when the Masonic guilds designed and built the great cathedrals of Europe. However, the thick overgrowth of pseudo-esoterism obscuring that 'original' Freemasonry, not to mention the various rationalist, anti-clerical, illuminist, and even revolutionary strands to be found within the Masonic tradition, ultimately forced him to abandon his project. Nonetheless, this record of Guénon's struggle to come to terms with an initiatory lineage fallen on hard times is of real relevance to all now seeking a spiritual affiliation in the darkness prevailing in our time.

For this edition, the chapters and articles contained in the two volumes of the French original have been rearranged in accordance with their content, and book and article reviews have been selected with the anglophone reader in mind.

Guénon often uses words or expressions set off in 'scare quotes'. To avoid clutter, single quotation marks have been used throughout. As for transliterations, Guénon was more concerned with phonetic fidelity than academic usage. The system adopted here reflects the views of scholars familiar both with the languages and Guénon's writings. Brackets indicate editorial insertions, or, within citations, Guénon's additions. Wherever possible, references have been updated, and English editions substituted.

The translation is based on the work of Henry Fohr (edited by his son Samuel Fohr), Cecil Bethell, and Michael Allen. The text was checked for accuracy and further revised by Marie Hansen. A special debt of thanks is owed to Cecil Bethell, who revised and proofread the text at several stages and provided the index. Cover design by Michael Buchino and Gray Henry, based on a drawing of Sagittarius from the Denderah Zodiac ceiling, Upper Egypt, now in the Louvre, by Guénon's friend and collaborator Ananda K. Coomaraswamy.

THE WORKS
OF RENÉ GUÉNON

LIST OF ORIGINAL SOURCES

V.I. = Le Voile d'Isis, E.T. = Études Traditionnelles

1   *La Gnose* Oct. 1911
2   *E. T.* July–Dec. 1948
3   *La Gnose* July–Aug. 1911
4   *V.I.* Jan. 1927
5   *E. T.* Dec. 1946
6   *La Gnose* April 1910
7   *La Gnose* March 1910
8   *La Gnose* May 1910
9   *E. T.* July–Aug. 1948
10 *V.I.* June 1930
11 *V.I.* Oct. 1928
12 *E. T.* Oct. 1947

13 *E. T.* Jan.–Feb. 1951
14 *Regnabit* Feb. 1926
15 *E. T.* May–June 1936
16 *V.I.* Jan. 1930
17 *V.I.* Dec. 1929
18 *Vers l'Unité* March 1927
19 *E. T.* June 1952
20 *E. T.* Sept. 1952
21 *La France Antimaçonnique*
    April–July 1914
22 *V.I.* Jan. 1927
23 *La Gnose* Jan. 1912

1

SCIENTIFIC IDEAS
AND THE MASONIC IDEAL

THE FIRST ARTICLE of the Constitution of the Grand Orient of France states that

> Freemasonry, considering metaphysical ideas to pertain exclusively to the domain of the individual judgment of its members, refuses to make any dogmatic assertions.

We do not doubt that such a declaration should have excellent practical results, but from a somewhat less contingent point of view it would have been much better to avoid the expression 'metaphysical ideas', using instead religious and philosophical, or even scientific and social, ideas. This would have been the most rigorous application of the principles of 'mutual tolerance' and 'liberty of conscience', in virtue of which 'Freemasonry admits no distinction of belief or opinion among its adepts', according to the terms of the Constitution of the Grand Lodge of France.

If Masonry is to be faithful to its principles, it must accord equal respect to all religious and philosophical beliefs, and to all scientific or social opinions, whatever they might be, on the sole condition that they be held sincerely. Religious dogmatism or scientific dogmatism: the one is no better than the other; and it is moreover perfectly certain that the Masonic spirit necessarily excludes all dogmatism even when it is 'rationalist', and that by very reason of the particular nature of its symbolic and initiatic teaching.[1] But

1. See chapter 2, 'The Great Architect of the Universe', and chapter 6, 'Masonic Orthodoxy'.

what has metaphysics to do with dogmatic assertions of any kind? We see no relation between them, and are willing to dwell further on this point.

Indeed, in a general sense what is dogmatism if not the purely sentimental and very human tendency to present one's own individual ideas (whether these pertain to a man or to a collectivity), with all the relative and uncertain elements they inevitably entail, as if they were incontestable truths? It is but a short step from this to the desire to impose these so-called truths on others, and history shows well enough how many times this step has been taken; nevertheless, on account of their relative and hypothetical—and therefore in a large measure illusory—character, such ideas constitute 'beliefs' or 'opinions', and nothing more.

It becomes clear, then, that where there is a certitude excluding any hypothesis and any sentimental consideration (which so often tend, and always for the worst in this regard, to encroach upon intellectual ground) there can be no question of dogmatism. Such is the case with mathematical certitude, which leaves no room for 'belief' or 'opinion' and is completely independent of all individual contingencies; assuredly, no one would dream of contesting this, not even the positivists. But aside from pure mathematics, does the least possibility of the same certitude exist in the scientific domain? We think not, but it matters little to us, for by way of recompense there still remains everything that falls outside the domain of science, and that constitutes, precisely, metaphysics. Indeed, true metaphysics is none other than the complete synthesis of certain and immutable knowledge, which stands apart from and transcends everything contingent and variable; consequently, we cannot consider metaphysical truth to be anything other than axiomatic in its principles and theorematic in its deductions, and therefore just as rigorous as mathematical truth, of which it is the unlimited prolongation. Understood thus, metaphysics contains nothing that might offend even the positivists, and they in turn cannot without illogicality refuse to admit that there exist outside the present limits of their comprehension demonstrable (and even, for others than themselves, perfectly demonstrated) truths having nothing in common with dogma, since it is on the contrary in the essential nature of dogma to be incapable of demonstration, which is its way of being outside of if not beyond all discussion.

If metaphysics is indeed as we have just described it, we are then bound to believe that this could not be what was meant by the phrase 'metaphysical ideas' in the text we initially quoted, a text that F∴ A. Noailles, in an article on 'La Morale laïque et scientifique', published in *L'Acacia* (June–July 1911), offers as 'incontestable proof of an exclusively secular scientific view of things.' We shall of course not contradict the author on this point so long as he is careful to specify that the view in question must be scientific only regarding what pertains to the scientific domain, but it would be an error for one to wish to extend this point of view and method beyond its particular domain, to things to which it can no longer in any way be applied. If we insist on the need to set forth profound distinctions between the different domains in which human activity, through no less differing means, is exercised, this is because these fundamental distinctions are too often neglected, with the resulting strange confusions, notably in regard to metaphysics. These confusions must be dispelled, together with the prejudices they entail, and this is why we think the present considerations not altogether inopportune.

If therefore the expression 'metaphysical ideas' has been applied to anything other than true metaphysics (and this indeed seems to be the case) then we are merely faced with a material error hinging entirely upon the meaning of terms, and we have no desire to imagine it was ever anything more. The mistake is quite easily explained by the complete ignorance into which the modern West as a whole has fallen in regard to metaphysics. It is therefore excusable on account of the very circumstances that made it possible, circumstances that, moreover, equally provide an explanation for many other related errors. And so we shall leave this point, and return to the distinctions made above. We have already sufficiently explained the subject of religious doctrines,[2] and as for philosophical systems (be they spiritualist or materialist), we believe we have also said

2. See 'La Religion et les religions', *La Gnose*, September–October 1910, p219, n10. — See also Matgioi's articles on 'L'erreur métaphysique des religions à forme sentimentale', *La Gnose*, July–August 1910, p177, n9 and 1911, p77, n3.

clearly enough what we think of them;[3] we shall therefore deal no further with them here, limiting ourselves to that which more particularly concerns scientific and social conceptions.

In the article we already mentioned, F∴ Noailles distinguishes between

> truths of faith, which are of the domain of the unknowable, and which as such one can either accept or not, and scientific truths, successive and demonstrable contributions of the human mind, which each man's reason can test, revise, and make his own.

First of all, let us recall that if it is indisputable that there are at present things unknown to human beings, we should by no means suppose that they are on that account 'unknowable'.[4] For us, so-called 'truths of faith' can only be simple objects of belief, and their acceptance or rejection can consequently only be a result of entirely sentimental preferences. As for 'scientific truths', which are quite relative and always subject to revision inasmuch as they are induced from observation and experimentation (it goes without saying that we exclude here those truths that are entirely mathematical, as these have a wholly other source), we think that by reason of their very relativity such truths are only demonstrable in a certain measure and not in a rigorous, absolute fashion. Moreover, when science claims to depart from the domain of strictly immediate experience, are the systematic conceptions to which it gives rise themselves then fundamentally exempt from sentimentalism? We do not think so,[5] nor do we see that faith in scientific hypotheses should itself be any more legitimate (nor, for that matter, any less excusable on account of the conditions that produce them) than faith in religious or philosophical dogmas.

This is because there can indeed also exist veritable scientific dogmas that hardly differ from other kinds of dogma except in the order of questions to which they relate; and metaphysics, such as we understand it (and to understand it otherwise would be not to

---

3. See chapter 2, 'The Great Architect of the Universe'.
4. Ibid.
5. On this point, refer again to chapter 2.

understand it at all) is as independent of the one as it is of the other. To find examples of scientific dogmas we need only refer to another article recently published in *L'Acacia* by F∴ Nergal with the title 'Les Abbés Savants et Notre Idéal Maçonnique'. In this article the author complains, though with all due courtesy, of the interference of the Catholic Church, or rather of certain of its representatives, in the domain of the so-called positive sciences, and then discusses the possible consequences of this interference; but it is not this question that interests us. What we wish to note is his manner of presenting mere hypotheses as indubitable, universal truths (though in a restricted sense, it is true) [6] even though the relativity of their probability is itself often far from having been demonstrated; besides, they can in any case only correspond at the very most to special and strictly limited possibilities. This illusion in regard to the range of certain conceptions is not unique to F∴ Nergal, whose good faith and sincere conviction would moreover never be called into question by those who know him; but it is shared (so we might be led to believe) no less sincerely by nearly all contemporary scholars.

There is one point, however, on which we are in perfect agreement with F∴ Nergal: he declares that 'science is neither religious nor anti-religious, but a-religious [*a* privative],' and it is indeed obvious that it could not be otherwise, since science and religion do not apply to the same domain. But if this is so, and if one recognizes as much, then one must not only lay aside any reconciliation of science and religion, which is something that could only be accomplished by a bad theologian[7] or a faulty scholar with narrow views. One must equally renounce the opposition of the two and not find contradictions and incompatibilities between them when they do not exist, since their respective points of view have nothing in common that would allow any comparison in the first place. This would hold true even for the 'science of religions', if such a science really exists, keeping strictly to scientific ground, and above all not serving merely as a pretext for an exegesis of Protestant or

6. Ibid.
7. This was, moreover, the real reason for Galileo's trial.

modernist tendencies (which, moreover, amount to almost the same thing). Until proof is given to the contrary, we shall allow ourselves formally to doubt the value of its results.[8]

Another point on which F∴ Nergal is sorely deluded concerns the possible result of research on the 'filiation of beings'. Even were one or another of the multiple hypotheses that have been proposed on this subject one day proved irrefutably and thereby lost its hypothetical character, we do not really see how this could embarrass a given religion (of which we are certainly not a defender) unless its representative authorities (and not only some esteemed individuals who nonetheless have no mandate) should imprudently and clumsily set forth a position, which no one had asked of them, on the solution to this scientific question that in no way falls within their competence.[9] And even in this case it would always be permissible for their 'faithful', without ceasing to be such, to take no more account of their opinion in this regard than they would of any other individual opinion, since in acting thus the authorities would manifestly have overstepped their prerogative, which relates only to matters pertaining directly to their 'faith'.[10] As for metaphysics (and we say this in order to give an example of the complete separation of the two domains, metaphysical and scientific), it does not have to deal with the question at all, as all interest in it is removed in virtue of the theory of the multiplicity of the states of the being, which allows one to envisage everything in an aspect of simultaneity as well as, and at the same time as, of succession, reducing the ideas of 'progress' and 'evolution' to their proper value as purely relative and contingent notions. On the subject of the 'descent of man', the only interesting observation that could be made from our point of view is that if

---

8. See 'La Religion et les religions', *La Gnose*, September–October 1910, p 219, n 10. On the other hand, we do not believe that Loisy can still be considered Catholic anymore. — Finally, we must ask ourselves what 'the mother of *Brahama*' [*sic*] might be; we have never found anything of the sort in the Hindu Theogony.

9. Is it not said, in the Vulgate Bible itself, that 'God hath left the World to the disputes of men'?

10. This is in strict conformity with the definition of the Catholic dogma of 'papal infallibility', even understood in its most literal sense.

man is spiritually the principle of all of Creation, then materially he must be the result of it,[11] for 'what is below is like that which is above, but inversely so,' (and again it would go beyond and entirely distort our thought to wish to interpret this in a 'transformist' sense).

We shall not dwell further on the above, adding only this: F∴ Nergal concludes by saying that 'science can only have one goal, a more perfect knowledge of phenomena.' We shall simply say that its goal can only be 'the knowledge of phenomena', without any question of 'more or less perfect'. Science, being thus eminently relative, can of necessity only attain to truths no less relative, and it is integral knowledge alone that is 'truth', just as the 'ideal' is not 'the greatest perfection possible for the human species' alone; it should be the Perfection that lies in the Universal Synthesis of all species, of all humanities.[12]

It now remains to clarify the matter of social conceptions, and we shall immediately say that by such an a expression we do not only mean political opinions, which are obviously out of the question. It is not without purpose, indeed, that Masonry forbids all discussion on this subject, and, without being reactionary in the slightest, one is quite able to assert that 'Republican Democracy' is not the social ideal of all Masons everywhere in the two Hemispheres. But in this category of social conceptions we also include here those that concern morality, for it is not possible to consider the latter as anything other than a 'social art', as F∴ Noailles so aptly put it in the article already cited; thus we would not, as he does, go so far as to 'leave the field open to all metaphysical speculation' in a domain in which metaphysics has no relevance. Indeed, despite what philosophers and moralists have said, as soon as it is a question of social relations, it can only be a matter of considerations based on interest, and on an interest moreover that resides in a practical and purely material

11. This is why all traditions agree in considering him to be formed from a synthesis of all of the elements and all of the kingdoms of Nature.

12. Tradition, indeed, does not only admit the plurality of inhabited worlds, but also the plurality of humanities filling these worlds (see Simon and Théophane, *Les Enseignements secrets de la Gnose*, pp 27–30); we shall have occasion to return to this question elsewhere.

utility, or in a preference of a sentimental order, or, as is in fact most often the case, in a combination of the two. Here, therefore, everything relates solely to individual assessments, and for a given collectivity the question is reduced to searching for and finding a common ground that might reconcile the diversity of these multiple appraisals, which correspond to as many different interests. If conventions are needed to make social life tolerable, or even simply possible, one should at least be frank enough to acknowledge that they are only conventions which in themselves contain nothing absolute, and which must vary incessantly with the circumstances of time and place upon which they entirely depend. Within these limits, which precisely mark its relative character, morality, limited to 'searching for rules of action given that men live in societies' (these rules inevitably being modified according to the form of the society), will have a perfectly established value and an undeniable utility. But it must not claim anything more, just as no religion in the Western sense of the word can boast of establishing anything more than belief pure and simple, on pain of departing from its role, as all too often happens. And in virtue of its sentimental aspect, morality itself, however 'secular' or 'scientific' it may be, will always contain a portion of belief, since in his current state the human individual, with very rare exceptions, is such as to be unable to pass beyond it.

But must the Masonic ideal then be founded on like contingencies? And must it depend upon the individual tendencies of each man and each segment of humanity? We do not think so. On the contrary, we hold that in order truly to be the 'Ideal', this ideal must remain outside and beyond all opinions and beliefs, as well as all parties and sects and systems and particular schools, for there is no other way to 'tend toward universality' than to 'lay aside that which divides in order to preserve that which unites'; and this opinion must assuredly be shared by all who intend to labor, not toward the vain raising of a 'Tower of Babel', but toward the effective realization of the Great Work of Universal Construction.

2

THE GREAT ARCHITECT
OF THE UNIVERSE

TOWARD THE END of an earlier article[1] we alluded to certain contemporary astronomers who sometimes depart from their own field
to indulge in digressions bearing the marks of a philosophy that can
without injustice be called entirely sentimental since it is essentially
poetic in expression. Now to say sentimentalism is always to say
anthropomorphism, of which there are many kinds; and the particular kind in question here manifests itself first as a reaction against
the geocentric cosmogony of the revealed, dogmatic religions, and
ends in the narrowly systematic concept of scholars who, on the one
hand, wish to limit the Universe to the measure of their own present
understanding,[2] and on the other, to beliefs that are at the very least
(again by reason of the entirely sentimental character of belief
itself) just as singular and irrational as those they claim to replace.[3]
In what follows we shall return to both sets of beliefs, products of

1. See 'Le Symbolisme de la Croix', *La Gnose*, 2nd year, no. 6, p166. — Here is the
passage in question: 'If it is impossible for us to accept the narrow point of view of
geocentrism, we nevertheless cannot approve of the sort of scientific lyricism, or
what could be called such, that seems especially dear to certain astronomers, who
never tire of speaking of "infinite space" and "eternal time", which are pure absurdities; here again we can only see, as we shall show elsewhere, another aspect of the
tendency towards anthropomorphism.'

2. 'Man is the measure of all things,' a Greek philosopher has said; but it is quite
evident that this must not be understood of contingent, individual man, but of
Universal Man.

3. In keeping with notions suggested directly by astronomy, let us cite as an
example the strange theory of the migration of the individual being through various planetary systems, an error completely analogous to that of reincarnation (on
which see *La Gnose*, 2nd year, no. 3, p94, n1: 'A limitation of universal Possibility is

the same mentality; but it is well to note that they are sometimes found together, and it is hardly necessary to recall by way of example the famous 'positivist religion' instituted by Auguste Comte toward the end of his life. Let it not be thought however that we bear the least hostility toward the positivists; on the contrary, when they are in fact strict positivists,[4] and despite the fact that their positivism inevitably remains incomplete, they hold an entirely different place in our regard than do the modern, doctrinaire philosophers who label themselves monists or dualists, spiritualists or materialists.

But to return to our astronomers, one of those best known to the greater public (it is for this reason alone that we cite him rather than some other with higher scientific credentials) is Camille Flammarion, who, even in those of his works that seem purely astronomical, includes such statements as the following:

> If worlds died forever, and if suns, once extinguished, never shone again, it is probable that there would no longer be stars in the sky.

> And why?

> Because creation is so ancient that its past can be considered eternal.[5] Since the period of their formation, the innumerable suns of space have had ample time to be extinguished. Relative to the eternity of the past, only new suns shine. The first have been

---

in the proper sense of the word an impossibility; we shall see elsewhere that this excludes reincarnationist theory as also the "eternal return" of Nietzsche, or the simultaneous repetition in space of supposedly identical individuals, as Blanqui imagined.'). For an exposition of this idea, see, besides the works of Flammarion, Figuier's *Le Lendemain de la Mort ou la Vie future selon la Science.*

4. But the positivist, if he wants to be logically consistent, can of course never adopt an attitude of negation, whatever form it might take; in other words, he cannot be systematic, since negation implies limitation, and *vice versa.*

5. The notion of a so-called temporal eternity composed of successive periods of duration and seemingly divided into two halves, the one past and the other future, is a singular one; in reality, it is only a matter of the indefinitude of duration, to which human immortality corresponds. We shall later have occasion to return to this idea of a divisible pseudo-eternity and to the conclusions some contemporary philosophers have wished to draw from it.

extinguished. The idea of succession is thus imposed on our minds.[6]

Whatever the private beliefs each of us has acquired in his consciousness regarding the nature of the Universe, it is impossible to grant the former theory of a creation enacted once and for all.[7] Is not the very idea of God synonymous with the idea of a Creator? As soon as God exists, he creates; if he had only created once, there would no longer be suns in the immensity of space, nor planets drawing round about their light, their heat, their electricity and life.[8] Creation must thus necessarily be perpetual.[9] And if God did not exist, the antiquity, the eternity, of the Universe would stand out with even greater prominence.[10]

The author states that the existence of God is 'a question of pure philosophy and not of positive science,' which does not prevent him elsewhere from trying to demonstrate,[11] if not scientifically then at least by scientific arguments, the same existence of God, or, we should rather say, of a god, and what is more, of a god that could scarcely be called luminous[12] since he has only the aspect of a Demiurge. The author himself states this by affirming that for him 'the idea of God is synonymous with that of a Creator,' and when he speaks of creation he is always concerned with the physical world alone, that is, with the contents of space that the astronomer

6. It is almost superfluous to draw attention to the many pure hypotheses crowded into these few lines.

7. In the name of what principle, one might ask, is this impossibility proclaimed, when it is a question of belief (the word he uses), that is, something that relates solely to individual conscience?

8. From this sentence it clearly follows that for the author God has a beginning and is subject to time as well as to space.

9. But perpetual, which implies only indefinite duration, is by no means synonymous with eternal; and antiquity, be it ever so great, has no relation to eternity.

10. *Astronomie populaire,* pp 380–381.

11. *Dieu dans la Nature,* or 'Le Spiritualisme et le Materialisme devant la Science moderne'.

12. We know that the word for God [French, *Dieu*] is derived from the Sanskrit *Deva,* which means 'luminous'. Here it is of course a question of spiritual light and not of the physical light that is only its symbol.

explores with his telescope.[13] Incidentally, here are scholars who hold themselves to be atheists simply because this is the only way they can conceive of the Supreme Being, and because they find this conception repugnant to reason (which at least testifies in their favor); but Flammarion is not of their number since he, on the contrary, misses no opportunity to profess his deistic faith. Even in the text at hand, he proceeds shortly after the passage just cited (through considerations taken moreover from an entirely atomist philosophy) to formulate this conclusion: 'Life is universal and eternal.'[14] He claims to have arrived at this through positive science alone (by means of how many hypotheses!). But it is rather singular that this very conclusion has long been dogmatically asserted and taught by Catholicism as pertaining exclusively to the domain of faith.[15] If science and faith were in such perfect agreement, was there really need to reproach religion so acrimoniously on account of the few annoyances Galileo had to suffer from the hands of its representatives, for having taught the rotation of the Earth and its revolution around the Sun, opinions contrary to the geocentrism then supported by an exoteric (and erroneous) interpretation of the Bible, but of which the most ardent defenders (for they still exist) are perhaps no longer found among the faithful of the revealed religions?[16]

Seeing Flammarion combine sentimentalism with science under

13. Indeed, modern science only admits, at least in principle, that which can be subjected to examination by one or more of the five bodily senses; from this narrowly specialized point of view the rest of the Universe is considered purely and simply non-existent.

14. *Astonomie populaire*, p387.

15. We shall return to this question of 'eternal life', but here can observe that this so-called eternalization of a contingent, individual existence is but the consequence of a confusion between eternity and immortality. Moreover, in a certain measure this error may be excused more easily than that committed by spiritists and other psychics who believe immortality can be demonstrated 'scientifically', which is to say experimentally, although experience obviously can prove nothing more nor better than the survival of some elements of individuality after the death of the corporeal, physical element. We should add that from the point of view of positive science even this simple survival of *material* elements is still far from firmly established, despite the claims of various schools of neo-spiritualists.

16. We are alluding here in particular to certain occultist groups, whose theories are moreover not serious enough to merit the briefest presentation; this simple

the pretext of 'spiritualism' in this way, we should not be surprised that he soon arrives at an 'animism' which, like that of a Crookes, a Lombroso (at the end of his life), or a Richet (so many examples of the failure of experimental science in the face of a mentality long since formed by the influence of anthropomorphic religion in the West), differs from ordinary spiritism only in form so that 'scientific' appearances might be saved. But what would be even more astonishing—if one did not believe that the idea of an individual, and still further, a 'personal' God, could satisfy all mentalities, or even all sentimentalities—would be to find the very same 'scientific philosophy' on which Flammarion constructs his neo-spiritualism, presented in nearly identical terms in the writings of other scholars, although used on the contrary to justify a materialist conception of the Universe. Of course, we can grant no more legitimacy to the one than to the other, for the spiritism and the 'vitalism' or 'animism' of the one are as foreign to pure metaphysics as are the materialism and 'mechanism' of the other, and the conceptions of the Universe held by both are equally limited, although in different ways,[17] for they take what in reality is only spatial and temporal indefinitude as infinity and eternity. 'Creation develops in infinity and in eternity,' Flammarion writes, and we know the restricted sense in which he uses the word 'creation'. But let us leave this and proceed without further delay to that which has occasioned the present article.

∴

The March 1911 issue of *L'Acacia* carries an article by F∴ M.-I. Nergal on 'La question du Grand Architecte de l'Univers', a question already treated[18] in the same periodical by the late F∴ Ch.-M.

indication will certainly suffice to put our readers on guard against ravings of this sort.

17. Curious remarks could be made regarding the various limitations of the Universe as conceived of by modern scholars and philosophers; it is a question that we shall perhaps one day address.

18. In 1908.

Limousin and F∴ Oswald Wirth. We ourselves said a few words about them over a year ago.[19]

Now, if Flammarion can be seen as an example of the neo-spiritualist tendencies of certain contemporary scholars, F∴ Nergal can very well be taken as an example of the materialist tendencies of certain others. Indeed, he himself clearly affirms as much, rejecting all terms that (like 'monist', notably) might give rise to any equivocation; and we know that, in reality, true materialists are very few in number. Again, it is difficult for them always to preserve a strictly logical attitude, for while they believe themselves to be of rigorously scientific minds, their conception of the Universe is merely a philosophical view like any other, and a good number of sentimental elements enter into its construction. Some go so far in the direction of granting (at least in practice) a preponderance to sentimentalism over intellectuality that we can find cases of a veritable materialistic mysticism. Indeed, is not the concept of an absolute morality (or what is called such) an eminently mystical and religious notion when it exercises so strong an influence on the mentality of the materialist that it leads him to admit that, even were there no rational motive for being a materialist, he would remain one all the same solely because it is 'nobler' to 'do good' without any hope of possible recompense? This, assuredly, is one of those 'reasons' that reason does not know, but we believe F∴ Nergal himself grants too great an importance to moral considerations to deny all value in such an argument.[20]

Be that as it may, in the article just mentioned, F∴ Nergal defines the Universe as 'the totality of worlds revolving through the infinites [*sic*].' Might we not believe we were listening to Flammarion? It was precisely on such an assertion that we took leave of the latter, and if we take note of this before all else, it is simply to make manifest the similarity of certain ideas in men who, by reason of their respective

19. See the chap. 6, 'Masonic Orthodoxy'.

20. In the same article in question here, F∴ Nergal speaks of 'the ideal of beauty and of sentiment, which have in view the sincerity of strong and profound convictions founded upon the methods and disciplines of science,' a sincerity he opposes to that of 'the spiritualism of F∴ G…, the natural fruit of his literary education.'

individual tendencies, nonetheless come to diametrically opposed philosophical conceptions.

For us, the question of the Great Architect of the Universe, which is closely linked to the preceding considerations, seems well worth revisiting frequently, and since F∴ Nergal desires that his article garner response, we shall offer some reflections it has suggested to us, and this, of course, without any dogmatic claims, since such would be foreign to the interpretation of Masonic symbolism.[21]

We have already said that for us the Great Architect of the Universe constitutes solely an initiatic symbol, to be treated as any other symbol, so that before all else one must seek to form a rational idea of it,[22] which is to say that this conception can have nothing in common with the God of anthropomorphic religions, the notion of which is not only irrational but is even anti-rational.[23] However, although we think 'each can attribute to this symbol the significance of his own philosophical [or metaphysical] conception,' we are far from comparing it to an idea as vague and insignificant as Herbert Spencer's 'Unknowable', or in other words to 'that which science cannot attain'; and it is quite certain that, as F∴ Nergal rightly says, 'although no one contests the existence of the unknown,[24] absolutely nothing authorizes us to claim as some have done that this unknown represents a mind, a will.' Doubtless, the 'unknown retreats,' and can do so indefinitely; it is therefore limited, which amounts to saying that it constitutes only a fraction of Universality, and consequently such a conception could not correspond to that of the Great Architect of the Universe, which, in order to be truly universal, must imply every particular possibility contained within the harmonious unity of Total Being.[25]

21. See chap. 6, 'Masonic Orthodoxy' (quotation from the *Rituel interpretatif pour le Grade d'Apprenti*).

22. Ibid.

23. What we say here of anthropomorphism applies equally to sentimentalism in general and to mysticism in all its forms.

24. This, of course, in relation to human individualities considered in their current state; but 'unknown' does not necessarily mean 'unknowable': nothing is unknowable when everything is envisaged from the point of view of Universality.

25. As we have pointed out on several occasions, it must not be forgotten that the material possibility is only one of these particular possibilities, and that there

F∴ Nergal is again right to say that often 'the expression the Great Architect only corresponds to an absolute void, even for those who adhere to it,' but it is hardly likely that this was the case for those who created it, for they must have wanted to inscribe on the front of their initiatic edifice something other than an expression devoid of meaning. To rediscover their train of thought, it obviously suffices to ask oneself what the expression signifies in itself, and precisely from this point of view we find it all the more appropriate to the way it is used, since it corresponds admirably to the whole of Masonic symbolism, which it dominates and illumines as the ideal conception presiding over the construction of the Universal Temple.

The Great Architect is, indeed, not the Demiurge, but something greater, even infinitely greater, for it represents a much loftier concept: he draws the ideal plan,[26] which is realized in act, that is, manifested in its indefinite (but not infinite) development through the individual beings contained (as particular possibilities, at once the elements and the agents of this manifestation) within its Universal Being; and it is the collectivity of these individual beings envisaged as a whole that in reality constitutes the Demiurge, the artisan or craftsman of the Universe.[27] This conception of the Demiurge, which we have already presented in another study, corresponds in the Kabbalah to *Adam Protoplastes* (first former),[28] while the Great Architect is identical to *Adam Qadmon*, or Universal Man.[29]

---

exist an indefinite number of others, each equally subject to an indefinite development within its manifestation, that is, in passing from potency to act (see in particular 'La Symbolisme de la Croix', 2nd year, nos. 2–6).

26. 'The Architect is the one who conceives of the building, who directs its construction,' F∴ Nergal himself says, and on this point too we are in perfect agreement; but if it can be said in this sense that he truly is the 'author of the work', it is nevertheless evident that he is not materially (or, in a more general sense, formally) its 'creator', since the architect who draws the plan must not be confused with the craftsman who executes it. From another point of view this is precisely the distinction between speculative and operative Masonry.

27. See 'Le Demiurge', *La Gnose*, 1st year, nos. 1–4 [*Miscellanea*, pt.1, chap.1].

28. And not 'first formed', as the Greek term *Protoplastes* has sometimes incorrectly been rendered by a translation that is manifestly contrary to its real meaning.

29. See 'Le Demiurge', *La Gnose*, 1st year, no. 2, pp 25–27 [*Miscellanea*, pt.1, chap.1].

This will suffice to mark the profound distinction that exists between the Great Architect of Masonry on the one hand and on the other hand the gods of the various religions, who are only so many aspects of the Demiurge. Moreover, it is incorrect to identify, as does F∴ Nergal, the anthropomorphic God of exoteric Christians with *Jehovah,* or יהוה, the Hierogram of the Great Architect of the Universe himself (the idea of which, despite this nominal designation, remains much more indefinite than the author even suspects), or with *Allah,* another Tetragram, the hieroglyphic composition of which quite clearly designates the Principle of Universal Construction.[30] Such symbols are by no means personifications, even less so since it is forbidden to represent them through just any figures.

On the other hand, it follows from what has just been said that the substitution of various formulas for the former expression, 'To the Glory of the Great Architect of the Universe' (or 'of the Sublime Architect of the Worlds' in the Egyptian Rite), is in reality only its replacement with equivalent expressions, such as 'To the Glory of Humanity,' where humanity is understood in its totality as constituting Universal Man;[31] or again 'To the Glory of Universal Freemasonry,' since Freemasonry, in the universal sense of the term, is identified with integral Humanity seen in the light of the (ideal) accomplishment of the Great Work of Construction.[32]

30. Indeed, the four Arabic letters that form the name *Allah* are, respectively, the symbolic equivalents of the ruler, the square, the compasses, and the circle, the latter being replaced by the triangle in the Masonry that makes us of an exclusively rectilinear symbolism.

31. It goes without saying that each individual will in fact construct for himself a more or less limited notion of integral Humanity in accordance with the current breadth of his intellectual perception (what might be called his 'intellectual horizon'), but for our part we must consider the formula solely in its true and complete sense, detached from all of the contingencies determining individual conceptions.

32. We should observe that the first precept of the Masonic Code is precisely formulated as follows: 'Honor the G∴ A∴ of the U∴ ', and not 'Worship the G∴ A∴ of the U∴ ', in order to avoid even the slightest appearance of idolatry. Such would indeed only be an appearance, since, as the considerations we have set forth here prove, the formula implying worship would be sufficiently justified by the doctrine of the 'Supreme Identity', which, seen in this light, can be expressed in a (literal)

We could expand much further on this subject, as it lends itself by nature to indefinite development, but in order to conclude practically we shall only remark that atheism in Masonry is and can only be a mask, which no doubt in the Latin countries and particularly in France temporarily had its utility—one could almost say its necessity, and that on account of various reasons we need not investigate here—but today it has become rather dangerous and compromising for the outward prestige and influence of the Order. Nevertheless, this is not to say that one must on that account, in imitation of the pietist influence that still dominates Anglo-Saxon Masonry, demand of the institution a profession of deistic faith, implying a belief in a personal and more or less anthropomorphic God. May such a thought be far from our mind; what is more, if such a declaration were ever demanded in any initiatic Fraternity, we would certainly be the first to refuse to subscribe to it. But the symbolic formula of recognition of the G∴ A∴ of the U∴ contains nothing of the sort; it is sufficient, all the while allowing everyone perfect freedom of personal convictions (a character it shares moreover with the Islamic formula of Monotheism),[33] and from the strictly Masonic point of view one cannot reasonably ask for anything more or anything other than this simple affirmation of Universal Being, which so harmoniously crowns the edifice of the Order's ritual symbolism.

---

numeric equation well known in the Muslim Kabbalah. According to the Koran itself, Allah 'commanded the angels to worship Adam, and they worshiped him; the proud Iblis refused to obey, and [this is why] he was numbered with the infidels' (II:32). — Another question, connected to the former, and one that holds interest both from the ritual and historical point of view, would be to determine the significance and original value of the symbol of the G∴ A∴ of the U∴, researching whether regularity dictates that one say: 'To the Glory of the G∴ A∴ of the U∴', following the prevalent usage within French Masonry, or instead, in accordance with the English formula, 'In the Name of the G∴ A∴ of the U∴' (I.T.N.O.T.G. A.O.T.U.).

33. 'Theism' must not be confused with 'deism', for the Greek Θεός carries with it a much more universal significance than the God of modern exoteric religions; we shall moreover have occasion to return to this point later.

not positively indicated anywhere, it even seems that this substitute was later lost in turn.[3] Among the Persians, for whom the *haoma* is the same thing as the Hindu *soma*, this second loss is on the contrary mentioned expressly: the white *haoma* could only be gathered on *Alborj*, that is, on the polar mountain representing the primordial abode; it was later replaced by the yellow *haoma*, just as, in the region where the ancestors of the Iranians settled, there was another *Alborj* which was nothing more than an image of the first; but this yellow *haoma* was later lost in turn and only its memory remained. And while on this subject it bears recalling that in other traditions wine also substitutes for the 'draught of immortality'; moreover, this is why it is generally taken as a symbol of the hidden or guarded doctrine, namely, esoteric and initiatic knowledge, as we have explained elsewhere.[4]

We come now to another form of the same symbolism, which, moreover, may correspond to actual historical events; but it should be apparent that as regards historical facts, it is their symbolic value alone that interests us. Generally, each tradition has as its normal means of expression a certain language, which thereby takes on the character of a sacred language, and if that tradition happens to disappear, it is natural that the corresponding sacred language should be lost at the same time. Even if something of it does survive outwardly, it is no more than a kind of 'corpse', since its profound meaning is no longer truly known. Such must have been the case in the first instance with the primeval language through which the primordial tradition was expressed, which is why in traditional narratives we find numerous allusions to such a primeval language and to its loss. And let us add that when a particular sacred language known in our day is sometimes identified with the primeval language itself, it must be understand that it is really a substitute, and consequently that it takes its place for the adherents of the

---

3. It is therefore perfectly vain to look for the plant that produced the *soma;* thus are we always tempted, independently of any other consideration, to be grateful to an orientalist who, in speaking of the *soma*, spares us the conventional 'cliché' of the *asclepias acida?*

4. *The King of the World*, chap. 6.

traditional form concerned. According to certain accounts connected with it, however, it would seem that the primeval language subsisted up to an epoch which, however distant it may appear to us, is nonetheless far removed from primordial times. Such is the case of the biblical story of the 'confusion of tongues', which, although it is possible to connect it with a determined historical period, can scarcely correspond to anything but the beginning of the *Kali-Yuga*. Now, it is certain that far earlier than this, particular traditional forms already existed, each of which had its own sacred language, so that the persistence of the unique language of the origins must not be taken literally but rather in the sense that, until then, consciousness of the essential unity of all traditions had not yet disappeared.[5]

In certain cases, instead of the loss of a language, mention is made of the loss of a word only, such, for example, as a divine name characterizing a certain tradition and representing it as it were synthetically; and the substitution of a new name for the former will mark then the passage from that tradition to another. Sometimes mention is also made of partial 'losses' occurring at certain critical periods in the course of the existence of one traditional form, and when these were restored by the substitution of some equivalent, this signified that a readaptation of the tradition in question was then necessitated by circumstances; in the opposite case, they indicate a more or less serious diminishment of that tradition which cannot later be remedied. To confine ourselves to the best known example, we will cite only the Hebraic tradition, where we find both of these cases. After the Babylonian captivity, a new type of writing had to be substituted for the one that had been lost,[6] and, given the hieroglyphic value of the characters of a sacred language, this

5. We could note in this connection that what is designated as the 'gift of tongues' (see *Perspectives on Initiation*, chap. 37) is related to knowledge of the primeval language understood symbolically.

6. We hardly need point out how unlikely this would be if taken literally, for how could a short period of 70 years suffice to account for the loss from memory of the ancient characters? But it is certainly not unreasonable that this should have happened in the age of traditional readaptations in the sixth century before the Christian era.

change was bound to imply some modification in the traditional form itself, that is to say a readaptation.[7] Moreover, at the time of the destruction of the Temple of Jerusalem and the dispersion of the Jewish people, the true pronunciation of the tetragrammatic Name was lost; the name *Adonai* was substituted, but it was never regarded as the real equivalent of the one that could no longer be pronounced. Indeed, the regular transmission of the exact pronunciation of the principal divine name,[8] designated *ha-Shem* or the Name par excellence, was essentially linked to the continuation of the priesthood, whose functions could be exercised only in the Temple of Jerusalem; from the time this latter no longer existed the Hebraic tradition became irremediably incomplete, as is sufficiently proved by the cessation of sacrifice, that is to say of what constituted the most 'central' part of the rites of that tradition; just so, the Tetragram used to occupy within the tradition a truly 'central' position with respect to the other divine names; and it was effectively the spiritual center of the tradition that was lost.[9] It is obvious that in such an example, the historical fact, which is in no way questionable as such, cannot be separated from the symbolic significance that is its essential raison d'être and without which it would be completely unintelligible.

The notion of something lost, symbolized under various forms, is to be found in the very exoterism of the various traditional forms, as we have just seen; and one could even say more precisely that it refers above all to this exoteric aspect, for it is evident that this is where that the loss took place and is truly effective, and also that in a way it can be considered definitive and irremediable, since it is effectively so for the generality of terrestrial humanity as long as the present cycle lasts. There is something which, on the contrary, belongs properly to the esoteric and initiatic order: the search for that lost something, or, as was said in the Middle Ages, its 'quest';

---

7. It is very probable that changes in the form of the Chinese characters, which occurred several times, should also be interpreted in this way.

8. That transmission is exactly comparable to that of a *mantra* in the Hindu tradition.

9. The term *diaspora* or 'dispersion' (in Hebrew *galūth*) defines very well the state of a people whose tradition is deprived of its normal center.

and this is easily understood, since the first part of initiation, which corresponds to the 'lesser mysteries', has indeed as its essential goal the restoration of the primordial state. We should note that, just as the loss actually took place gradually and in several stages before arriving finally at the present state, so the search will always have to be made gradually, by passing once again in inverse order through those same stages, that is to say by reascending as it were the course of the historical cycle of humanity, from one state to an earlier state, on up to the primordial state itself; and the degrees in the initiation to the 'lesser mysteries'[10] will naturally correspond to these different stages. We should immediately add that the successive substitutions which we mentioned can likewise be taken up in inverse order, which explains why in certain cases what is given as the 'rediscovered word' may in reality still be only a 'substituted word' representing one or another of the intermediary stages. It should be quite evident that anything communicable outwardly cannot truly be the 'lost word', that it is always only a more or less inadequate symbol for it, as is every expression of transcendent truths; and this symbolism is often very complex by reason of the multiplicity of meanings attached to it, just as are the degrees included in its application.

In Western initiations there are at least two well-known examples (which of course is not to say that they are always well understood by those who speak of them) of the search in question, and these can be taken respectively as types of the two principal forms of symbolism we have indicated: the 'quest for the Grail' in the chivalric initiations of the Middle Ages, and the 'search for the lost word' in Masonic initiation. As for the first, A. E. Waite has rightly pointed out that it contains many more or less explicit allusions to substituted formulas and objects; moreover, can it not be said that the 'Round Table' itself is after all only a 'substitute', since although it is destined to receive the Grail, this reception never actually takes place? This does not mean that the 'quest' can never be fulfilled, as some might too easily be tempted to believe, but only that, even if it can be so for some few, it cannot be so for an entire collectivity, even when the latter possesses the most incontestable initiatic

---

10. On this point see *Perspectives on Initiation*, chap. 39.

character. As we have seen elsewhere,[11] the 'Round Table' and its Knighthood present all the characteristics of the constitution of an authentic spiritual center; but let us repeat that every secondary spiritual center, being only an image or reflection of the supreme center, can really only play the role of 'substitute' with respect to the latter, just as every particular traditional form is properly only a 'substitute' for the primordial tradition.

Coming now to the 'lost word' and the search for it in Masonry, we must note that, at least in the present state of things, this subject is shrouded in obscurity. We certainly cannot claim to dispel it entirely, but the few remarks we will make may perhaps suffice to dispel what might at first be seen as contradictions. The first thing to be noted is that the grade of Master as it is practised in *Craft Masonry* emphasizes the 'loss of the word', which is there presented as a consequence of the death of Hiram, although there seems to be no explicit indication regarding a search for it, and is even less a question of the 'word found'. This may well seem odd, since, as the final grade constituting Masonry properly speaking, Mastership must necessarily correspond, at least virtually, to the perfection of the 'lesser mysteries', without which its very designation would be unjustified. It is true that one could reply that initiation at that grade is in itself properly only a starting-point, which is after all quite normal; but it would still be necessary that this initiation comprise something permitting one to 'prime', so to speak, the search that constitutes the subsequent task which is to lead to the effective realization of Mastership—and despite appearances, we think such is really the case. The 'sacred word' of the grade is obviously a 'substituted word', and moreover is only given as such; but this 'substituted word' is of a very particular sort: it has been distorted in so many different ways to the point of becoming unrecognizable,[12] and it has received various interpretations presenting some additional interest through their allusions to certain symbolic

11. *The King of the World*, chaps. 4 and 5.
12. These deformations have even furnished two so-called distinct words, one 'sacred word' and one 'password', interchangeable according to the different rites, but are really one only.

elements of the grade, but none of these can be justified by any Hebraic etymology whatsoever. Now, if this word is restored to its correct form, its meaning is seen to be altogether different from those usually attributed to it; this word is really nothing but a question, and the answer to that question would be the true 'sacred word' or 'lost word' itself, that is, the true name of the Great Architect of the Universe.[13] Once the question is asked, the search is indeed been 'primed', as we have just said; it will then be up to each one, if he is capable, to find the answer and to reach effective Mastership through his own inner work.

Another point to consider is that in conformity with Hebraic symbolism the 'lost word' is generally likened to the tetragrammatic Name; but if taken literally this would obviously be an anachronism, for it is well known that at the time of Solomon and the construction of the Temple the pronunciation of the Name had not been lost. However, we would be wrong to think that this anachronism posed any real difficulty, for here we are not concerned with the 'historicity' of facts as such, which from our point of view matters little in itself, for the Tetragrammaton is only being considered for the value it holds traditionally. In a certain sense it too may very well have been only a 'substituted word' since it properly belongs to the Mosaic revelation, and thus could not really go back as far as the primordial tradition, any more than could the Hebrew language itself.[14] If we emphasize this point, it is above all to draw attention to the more important fact that in Judaic exoterism the word substituted for the Tetragrammaton, whose pronunciation had been lost, was another divine name, *Adonai*, also formed of four letters but considered as less essential; indeed, there is something that implies resignation to a loss judged irreplaceable, to be only remedied only

13. We need not investigate whether the multiple distortions of the word itself or its meaning were deliberate, which would doubtless be a difficult task given the lack of precise information regarding the circumstances in which they were in fact produced; but what is in any case certain is that they have the effect of entirely concealing what can be considered the most essential point of the grade of Master, which they have thus made a sort of enigma, apparently without any possible solution.

14. On the 'first name of God', according to certain initiatic traditions, see *The Great Triad*, chap. 25.

in the measure still allowed by present conditions. In Masonic initiation, on the contrary, the 'substituted word' is concerned with restoring the possibility of finding the 'lost word' again, and therefore of restoring the state preceding its loss. This is one of the fundamental differences between the exoteric and the initiatic points of view, expressed symbolically in a rather striking way.[15]

But before going any further, a digression is necessary so that what follows may be clearly understood. Masonic initiation essentially relating to the 'lesser mysteries', as do all the craft initiations, reaches its completion with the grade of Master since complete realization of this grade implies the restoration of the primordial state; but we might well wonder what the meaning and role of what are called the high grades of Masonry can be, some for just this reason having insisted on their being no more than vain and useless 'superfluities'. Here we must first distinguish between grades[16] linked directly with Masonry on the one hand,[17] and on the other, grades that can be considered vestiges or memories[18] of other ancient Western initiatic organizations that have been grafted onto Masonry as it were or 'crystallized' around it. When all is said and done, the purpose of these last grades (assuming one does not consider them as having a merely 'archeological' interest, which would obviously be an altogether insufficient justification from the initiatic point of

---

15. We point out incidentally that in the grade of Master there is not only a 'substituted word' but also a 'substituted sign': if the 'lost word' is identified symbolically with the Tetragrammaton, certain indications suggest correlatively that the 'lost sign' should be that of the benediction of the *Kohanim*. Here again it is unnecessary to see this as the expression of a literal historical fact, for in reality this sign has never been lost; but one could legitimately ask whether, when the Tetragrammaton was no longer pronounced, it could effectively conserve all its ritual value.

16. Naturally, we leave aside here the all too numerous grades in certain 'systems' that have only a rather fanciful character and obviously reflect only the particular conceptions of their authors.

17. One cannot however strictly say that they are an integral part of it, with the single exception of the *Royal Arch*.

18. We add here the word 'memories' in order to avoid any discussion on the more or less direct filiation of these grades, which would risk taking us too far, especially as concerns organizations related to various forms of chivalric initiation.

view), is the conservation in the only way still possible after their disappearance as independent forms, of what can still be preserved of these initiations. There would certainly be much to say about this 'conserving' role of Masonry and the possibility it offers of compensating to a certain extent for the absence of initiations of another order in the present-day Western world, but this lies wholly outside the subject under consideration, for it is only the first case, that of the grades whose symbolism is more or less directly connected to Masonry proper, that concerns us here.

These grades can generally be considered as constituting extensions or developments of the grade of Master, for although in principle the latter is incontestably sufficient unto itself, the fact that it is so difficult to draw out from this grade all that it implicitly contains justifies the existence of these later developments.[19] Thus it is a matter of an aid offered those who wish to actualize what they still only possess virtually; this is at least the fundamental intention of these grades, whatever reservations one might justifiably entertain as to the degree of practical effectiveness of such aid, of which the least one can say is that in most cases it is, unfortunately, diminished by the fragmentary and too often altered aspect under which the corresponding rituals are presented. But here we need only concern ourselves with the principle involved, which is independent of such contingent considerations. In truth, moreover, if the grade of Master were more explicit, and if all admitted to it were truly qualified, these developments would find their place within it, and there would be no need to make them the object of other grades nominally distinct from the former.[20]

---

19. We should also add, at least as a subsidiary reason, the reduction of the seven grades of ancient Operative Masonry to three: since all the grades were not known to the founders of Speculative Masonry, serious gaps arose which, in spite of certain subsequent 'renewals', could not be entirely fulfilled within the framework of the present-day three symbolic grades. There are some high grades which seem primarily to have been attempts to remedy this defect, although one cannot say whether they have fully succeeded, as they lack the true operative transmission which would have been indispensable for it.

20. By the very fact that he possesses 'the plenitude of Masonic rights', the Master notably has the right of access to all knowledge comprised in the initiatic form

Now, the point we have been aiming at is that among the high grades in question, a certain number place greater emphasis on the 'search for the lost word', that is to say on what, following what we have explained, constitutes the essential work of Mastership. Some grades even offer a 'word found', implying, it seems, the successful completion of their search; but in reality this 'word found' is never anything but a new 'substituted word', and given what we have said it is easy to understand that it could not be otherwise, since the true 'word' is strictly speaking incommunicable. This is especially the case with the grade of *Royal Arch*, the only grade that should be regarded as strictly Masonic, and whose direct operative origin is beyond doubt: it is the normal complement, as it were, of the grade of Master, with a perspective opening onto the 'greater mysteries'.[21] Since in this grade the term representing the 'word found' appears in a much altered form, as do so many others, it has given rise to various suppositions as to its meaning; but according to the most authoritative and plausible interpretation it is in reality a composite word formed from the union of three divine names drawn from as many different traditions. This is interesting from at least two points of view, first, in its obvious implication that the 'lost word' is indeed considered to be a divine name, and then, in that the association of these different names can only be explained as an implicit affirmation of the fundamental unity of all traditional forms. But it goes without saying that such a compounding of names derived from several sacred languages remains an entirely exterior juxtaposition and could in no way adequately symbolize a restoration of the primordial tradition itself, and that in consequence it is really no more than a 'substituted word'.[22]

to which he belongs; this is quite clearly expressed in the ancient conception of 'Master of all grades', which seems completely forgotten today.

21. We refer the reader to what we have already said on this subject, especially in our study 'La pierre angulaire' (issues of April-May) [see 'The Cornerstone', *Symbols of Sacred Science*, chap. 45].

22. It must be understood that what we are saying here relates to the *Royal Arch* of the English Rite, which despite the similarity of title has only a slight relation to the grade called *Royal Arch of Enoch*, a version of which became the 13th degree of the Ancient and Accepted Scottish Rite in which the 'word found' is represented by

Another though very different type of example is the Scottish grade of Rosicrucian, in which the 'word found' is presented as a new Tetragrammaton intended to replace the ancient one that had been lost; in fact these four letters, which are moreover only initials and do not form a word, cannot here express anything other than the situation of the Christian tradition vis-à-vis the Hebraic tradition, or the replacing of the 'Old Law' by the 'New Law', and it would be difficult to say that they represent a state closer to the primordial state, unless this were meant in the sense that Christianity has accomplished a 'reintegration' opening certain new possibilities for the return to the latter, which, moreover, is in a way true for every traditional form founded at a certain age as conforming more particularly with the conditions of that age. It is worth adding that other interpretations are naturally superimposed upon the simply religious and exoteric meaning, these interpretations being chiefly of an Hermetic order, which are certainly not without interest in themselves. But aside from leading us away from a consideration of the divine names essentially inherent in the 'lost word', this derives far more from Christian Hermeticism than from Masonry properly speaking, and whatever may be the affinities between the one and the other, they nevertheless cannot be considered identical, for if they make use of the same symbols to a certain extent, they nonetheless proceed from initiatic 'techniques' differing greatly in many respects. Moreover, the 'word' of the Rose-Cross grade obviously refers to the point of view of one specific traditional form, which in any case is far removed from a return to the primordial tradition that lies beyond all particular forms. In this respect, as in many others, the grade of *Royal Arch* certainly has more reason to declare itself as the *nec plus ultra* of Masonic initiation.

We think we have said enough about the different 'substitutions', and in bringing this study to a close we must now return to the grade of Master in order to seek the solution to another enigma that

---

the Tetragrammaton itself, inscribed on a gold plate deposited in the 'ninth vault'. Moreover, the attribution of this deposit to Enoch constitutes an obvious anachronism as concerns the Hebraic Tetragrammaton, but it can be taken as indicating an intention to go right back to the primordial, or at least 'antediluvian', tradition.

presents itself on that subject: how is it that the 'loss of the word' is presented as resulting from the death of Hiram alone, whereas according to the legend itself others must also have possessed it? Indeed, we have here a question that perplexes many Masons who reflect on symbolism, and some even go so far as to see in it an improbability which seems altogether impossible to explain in an acceptable way, while as we shall see, it is really something altogether different.

The question we asked at the end of the preceding part of this study can be formulated more precisely as follows: at the time of the construction of the Temple, the 'word' of the Masters was, according to the very legend of the grade, in the possession of three individuals who had the power to communicate it: Solomon; Hiram, King of Tyre; and Hiram-Abi. If this be granted, how can the latter's death suffice to bring about the loss of that word? The answer is that in order to communicate it regularly and in ritual form, the cooperation of the 'three first Grand-Masters' was necessary, so that the absence or disappearance of a single one of them rendered that communication impossible, this being as necessary as are all three sides to a triangle; and despite what those may think who are not sufficiently in the habit of drawing certain symbolic correspondences, this is no mere comparison or more or less imaginary and baseless relationship. Indeed, an operative Lodge can only be opened with the cooperation of three Masters,[23] who have in their possession three batons the respective lengths of which are in the proportion 3 to 4 to 5. Only when these three batons are brought together and positioned in the form a Pythagorean right triangle can the opening of works commence. That being so, it is easy to understand, similarly, that a sacred word may be formed of three parts, such as three syllables,[24] each of which can only be transmitted by one of three

23. Here the Masters are those who possess the 7th and last operative degree, to which the legend of Hiram first belonged; moreover, this is why the latter was not known by the 'accepted' Companions who on their own initiative founded the Grand Lodge of England in 1717 and who naturally could not transmit anything more than what they had themselves received.

24. The syllable is the element that is really irreducible in the spoken word; moreover, it is to be noted that the 'substituted word' is, in its different forms, itself

Masters, so that in the absence of one of them the word as well as the triangle remains incomplete and can no longer be validly accomplished, a point we will shortly return to.

And let us point out in passing another case with a similar symbolism, at least with respect to what interests us at present. In certain Middle-Eastern guilds, the chest containing the 'treasure' was provided with three locks, the keys to which were entrusted to three different officers, so that all three had to be present to open the chest. Naturally, those who consider things superficially will see herein no more than a precaution against a possible breach of trust, but as is always the case, this quite outward and profane explanation is entirely insufficient, and even admitting that it may be legitimate in its own order, this in no way prevents the same fact from having an altogether profound symbolic meaning, which constitutes all its real value. To think otherwise is tantamount to completely misunderstanding the initiatic point of view; furthermore, the key itself has a symbolism important enough to justify what we have said here.[25]

To return to the right triangle mentioned above, it can be said that, as we have seen, the death of the 'third Grand-Master' leaves it incomplete. In a certain sense and independently of its own proper significance considered as a square, this corresponds to the form of the square of the Venerable One, which has unequal sides, normally in the ratio of 3 to 4, so that they may be considered the two sides of the right-angle of this triangle, the hypotenuse of which

---

always composed of three syllables, which are enunciated separately in its ritual pronunciation.

25. We cannot dwell here on the various aspects of the symbolism of the key, and especially on its axial character (see what we said about this in *The Great Triad*, chap. 6), but we must at least point out that in ancient Masonic 'catechisms' language is represented as the 'key of the heart'. The connection between language and the heart symbolizes that of 'Thought' and 'Word', that is, according to the Kabbalistic meaning of these terms, envisaged principially, that of the interior and exterior aspects of the Word. From this also results, among the ancient Egyptians (who moreover used wooden keys having precisely the form of a tongue), the sacred character of the persea tree, the fruit of which takes the form of a heart and the leaf that of a tongue (cf. Plutarch, *Isis et Osiris*, 68; translation by Mario Meunier, p198).

is then absent, or, if one wishes, 'implied'.[26] And it should be noted that the reconstitution of the complete triangle, such as is portrayed in the insignia of the *Past Master*, implies, or at least ought theoretically to imply, that the latter has succeeded in accomplishing the restoration of what was lost.[27]

As for the sacred word that can only be communicated by the cooperation of three persons, it is quite significant that this characteristic is found precisely in the one who, at the grade of *Royal Arch*, is considered to represent the 'word found' and whose regular communication is effectively possible only in this way. The three persons themselves form a triangle, and the three parts of the word, which are then the three syllables corresponding to as many divine names in the different traditions 'pass' successively so to speak from one to the other of the sides of this triangle until the word is entirely 'correct and perfect'. Although it is really only a 'substituted' word, the fact that the *Royal Arch* is the most 'authentic' of all the higher grades in respect of its operative filiation, also gives this mode of communication an incontestable importance in confirming the interpretation of what in this respect remains obscure regarding the grade of Master such as it is practiced today.

In this connection we will add another observation concerning the Hebraic Tetragrammaton: since the latter is one of the divine names most often identified with the 'lost word', there must be in it something corresponding to what we have just discussed, for insofar as the same characteristic is truly essential, it must exist in some manner in everything that represents this word with any adequacy. By this we mean that in order for the symbolic correspondence to be exact, the pronunciation of the Tetragrammaton had to be trisyllabic; but since on the other hand it was naturally written with four letters, it could be said that, according to numerical symbolism, 4 here relates to the 'substantial' aspect of the word (insofar as the

26. As a curiosity we point out in this connection that in mixed Masonry, or *Co-Masonry*, it has been deemed wise to give equal sides to the square of the Venerable One in order to represent the equality of man and woman, which has not the slightest relation to its true meaning; this is a good example of the incomprehension of symbolism and of the fanciful innovations that are its inevitable consequence.

27. Cf. *The Great Triad*, chaps. 15 and 21.

latter is written or spelled in conformity with the writing which plays the role of a corporeal 'support') and 3 to its 'essential' aspect (insofar as it is pronounced integrally by the voice which alone gives it 'spirit' and 'life'). It follows that although it cannot be regarded as the true pronunciation of the Name, which is no longer known to anyone owing to the fact that it has three syllables, the form *Jehovah* (the very antiquity of which, insofar as it is an approximate transcript in Western languages, might already give us food for thought), because it has three syllables, at least represents it far better than the purely fanciful form *Yahweh* invented by the modern exegetes and 'critics', and which, having only two syllables, is manifestly unsuited for a ritual transmission like the one involved here.

Much more could of course be said on all this, but we must end these already overlong considerations, which, let us repeat, are only intended to shed a little light on some aspects of the very complex subject of the 'lost word'.

4

THE BUILDERS
OF THE MIDDLE AGES

AN ARTICLE BY Armand Bédarride published in the May 1929 issue of *Symbolisme*, 'Les Idées de nos Précurseurs', provides the occasion for some useful reflections. The subject of the article, is the guilds of the Middles Ages insofar as they have transmitted something of their spirit and traditions to modern Masonry.

In this connection, let us first note that the distinction between 'Operative Masonry' and 'Speculative Masonry' should be taken in quite another sense than that normally attributed to it. Indeed, it is often thought that 'Operative' Masons were mere workers or artisans and nothing else, and that the more or less profound meaning of their symbolism only occurred quite late, following the admission to the guild organizations of people unfamiliar with the art of building. This however is not the opinion of Bédarride, who cites a great many examples, notably from religious monuments, of figures with an incontestably symbolic character. He speaks in particular of the two columns of Würtzbourg cathedral, 'which prove,' he says, 'that Masons of the fourteenth century practiced a philosophical symbolism.' This is correct on condition, it goes without saying, that he means 'Hermetic philosophy' and not 'philosophy' in the current sense, which is wholly profane, and has never made the least use of any symbolism. Such examples could be multiplied indefinitely, since the very plans of the cathedrals are eminently symbolic, as we have already observed on other occasions; and we might add that in addition to the common medieval symbols of which modern Masons have preserved some memory—

though hardly understanding their significance any longer—there are many others of which they have not the least notion.[1]

In our opinion one must go against the current way of thinking and consider 'Speculative Masonry' as being in many ways merely a degeneration of 'Operative Masonry'. The latter was indeed truly complete in its own order, possessing both theory and corresponding practice, and in this respect its name can best be understood as alluding to the 'operations' of the 'sacred art', of which building in accordance with the traditional rules was one application. As for 'Speculative Masonry', which moreover arose at a time when the building guilds were in full decline, its name indicates clearly enough that it is confined to 'speculation' pure and simple, that is to say to a theory lacking any realization. Surely, it would require an odd twist to regard this as 'progress'. If again there had only been a diminution, the harm would not have been as great as it is in reality; but as we have frequently said, there has been a real deviation since the start of the eighteenth century, when the Grand Lodge of England was established, this being the starting-point of all modern Masonry. We shall not dwell further at present, although we do wish to make the point that if one really wants to understand the spirit of the medieval builders, these observations are quite essential, for otherwise the conception one might form of them would be false or at least very incomplete.

Another idea no less important to rectify is that the use of symbolic forms was imposed for reasons of mere prudence. We do not contest that such reasons did sometimes exist, but this is only the most outward and least interesting aspect of the question. We have spoken of them in connection with Dante and the 'Fedeli d'Amore',[2] and can reiterate it all the more as regards the building guilds since fairly close ties have been maintained between all these organizations which seem so different in character but which all

1. We recently had occasion to observe on the Strasbourg cathedral and on other edifices of Alsace a large number of stone-cutters' marks dating from different periods, from the twelfth up to the beginning of the seventeenth century. Among these marks were some quite curious ones, notably the *swastika* on one of the turrets of the spire of Strasbourg, to which Bédarride refers.

2. See *Voile d'Isis*, Feb. 1929. [Chap. 4 of *Insights into Christian Esoterism*. ED.]

participated in the same traditional knowledge.[3] Now it is precisely symbolism that is the normal mode of expression for knowledge of this order, this being its true raison d'être in all times and in all countries, even in cases where there was no reason to conceal things, and this quite simply because there are things which by their very nature cannot be expressed otherwise than under this form.

The error too often made in this connection, of which we find an echo in Bédarride's article, seems to derive from two chief causes, the first being that the medieval Catholicism is generally rather poorly understood. It should not be forgotten that just as there is an Islamic esoterism, so also at the time was there a Catholic esoterism also, by which we mean an esoterism taking as its basis and support the symbols and rites of the Catholic faith, being superimposed on the latter without in any way opposing it; and there is no doubt that certain religious Orders were no strangers to this esoterism. If the tendency of most present-day Catholics is to deny the existence of such things, this proves only that they are no better informed in this respect than are the rest of our contemporaries.

The second cause of error is that it is believed that what lies hidden behind the symbols in question are almost exclusively social or political ideas,[4] whereas in reality it is a matter of something quite different. In the eyes of those who possess certain knowledge, ideas of this order could after all have only a very secondary importance, that of one possible application among many others. We will even add that wherever they came to assume too great a role and became predominant, they have invariably been a cause of degeneration and deviation.[5] Is this not precisely what has caused modern Masonry to lose its understanding of what it still preserves of the ancient symbolism and traditions of which, in spite of all its insufficiencies, it still seems to be sole heir in the present Western world? If the more

3. To this day, the Companions of the 'Rite of Solomon' have preserved the memory of their link with the 'Order of the Temple'.

4. This way of seeing things is in large part shared by Aroux and Rossetti in their interpretation of Dante, and it is also to be found in many passages from Eliphas Lévi's *History of Magic*.

5. The example of certain Islamic organizations, in which political preoccupations have as it were stifled the original spirituality, is very clear in this respect.

or less licentious satirical figures sometimes found in their works is adduced as evidence of the social preoccupations of the builders, we simply reply that these figures were intended primarily to put off the profane, who stop at outer appearances and do not see that they conceal what is most profound. Nor is this something specific to builders, for certain writers, Boccacio and Rabelais in particular, and many others besides, have worn the same mask and employed the same means. And it must be acknowledged that this stratagem has worked well, since in our day doubtless more than ever before, the profane are still taken in by them.

If we wish to get to the bottom of things, we must see in the symbolism of the builders the expression of certain traditional sciences related to what can in general be called 'Hermeticism'. But in speaking here of 'sciences' it should not be thought that we mean something comparable to profane science, almost the only science known to modern people. Such an identification conforms to the mentality of Bédarride, who speaks of 'the changing form of the positive knowledge of science'—an observation that applies clearly and exclusively to profane science—and who, taking purely symbolic images literally, believes he finds therein 'evolutionist' and even 'transformist' ideas, ideas which stand in absolute contradiction to all traditional teachings. In several of our works we have developed at length the essential difference between sacred or traditional science and profane science, and although we cannot repeat it all here, we thought it well at least to draw attention to this important point.

In closing, let us add that it is not without reason that among the Romans Janus was both the god of initiation into the mysteries and the god of the artisans' guilds; nor is it without reason that the builders of the Middle Ages kept the two solstitial festivals. This same Janus then becomes in Christianity the two Saint Johns, of winter and summer;[6] and when we once know the connection of Saint John with the esoteric side of Christianity, do we not then immediately see that, making due allowance for circumstances and 'cyclical laws', what is involved is the same initiation into the mysteries that is in question?

6. See *Symbols of Sacred Science*, chaps. 37 and 38. ED.

5

MASONS
AND CARPENTERS

AMONG CRAFT INITIATIONS there has always been a sort of quarrel over precedence between masons and stone-cutters, and carpenters; and if we consider this not from the present-day relationship of these two professions in the building trade, but if from the standpoint of their respective antiquity, it is quite certain that the carpenters can in fact claim priority. Indeed, as we have noted on other occasions, structures were generally built in wood before being built in stone, and this is why, notably in India, no trace of them is found beyond a certain age, wooden buildings obviously being less durable than those of stone; in addition, the use of wood among sedentary peoples corresponds to a state of lesser fixity than that of stone, or to put it another way, a lesser degree of 'solidification', which accords with the fact that it has to do with an early stage in the course of the cyclical process.[1]

Simple as this observation may seem, it is not without importance for an understanding of certain aspects of traditional symbolism, in particular the fact that in the most ancient texts of India all comparisons referring to the symbolism of construction are drawn from the carpenter, his tools, and his labor; and *Vishvakarma*, the 'Great Architect' himself, is also designated by the name *Tvashtri*, literally the 'Carpenter'. It goes without saying that the role of the

---

1. See what we have said on this subject in *The Reign of Quantity and the Signs of the Times*, especially chaps. 21 and 22. Naturally, the change in question cannot be regarded as having been produced simultaneously among all peoples, but there are always corresponding stages in the course of the life of each people.

architect (*Sthapati*, who moreover was originally the master carpenter) is in no way altered by that, since aside from the adaptation required by the nature of the materials used, it is always from the same 'archetype' or from the same 'cosmic model' that he must draw his inspiration, whether in the construction of a temple, a house, a chariot, or a ship (and in these last cases, the craft of the carpenter has never lost anything of its initial importance, at least until the quite modern use of metals, which represent the final degree of 'solidification').[2] It is obvious also that whether or not certain parts of a building are executed in wood or in stone changes nothing but the outer form, at least of their symbolic meaning; in this respect, for example, it matters little whether the 'eye' of the dome, that is, its central opening, is covered by a piece of wood or by a stone worked in a certain way, both constituting equally and in an identical sense the 'crowning' of the edifice, according to what we have said in previous studies;[3] and this is all the more true of the parts of the framework retained even after stone was substituted for wood as the primary building material—such as the beams which, starting from the 'eye' of the dome, represent the solar rays with all their symbolic correspondences.[4] It can be said therefore that the crafts of carpenter and mason, both deriving in the final analysis from the same principle, furnish two equally appropriate languages for the expression of the same higher truths. The only difference is one of secondary adaptation, as is always the case with translation from one language into another. Of course when one is dealing with

2. It is understood that professions like those of cartwright and cabinet-maker must be regarded as only particular forms or later 'specializations' of that of carpenter, which in its most general and at the same time most ancient meaning includes everything having to do with the working of wood.

3. See *Symbols of Sacred Science*, chaps. 39–44. ED.

4. Even if these beams were replaced later still in certain cases by 'ribs' of stone (we are thinking especially of the Gothic vaults), this changes nothing in the symbolism. — In English, the word *beam* means both 'ray' and 'girder', and as Coomaraswamy has noted on various occasions, this double meaning has nothing fortuitous about it. It is unfortunately untranslatable into French, where however one does commonly speak of 'rays' or 'spokes' of a wheel, which in relation to the latter's hub play the same role as do the beams in question with respect to the 'eye' of the dome.

a particular established symbolism, as in the case of the traditional texts from India alluded to above, it is necessary to know precisely to which of these two languages it properly relates, in order to fully understand its meaning and value.

A particularly important point in this connection is that the Greek word *hyle* originally meant 'wood', but at the same time designated the substantial principle, or *materia prima*, of the cosmos, and, by derivation from the former, all *materia secunda*, that is to say all that which in a relative sense plays a role analogous to that of the substantial principle of all manifestation.[5] Moreover, this symbolism according to which the world's substance is likened to wood is quite common in the most ancient traditions, and in line with what we have just said regarding building symbolism, it is easy to understand the reason for this. Indeed, since it is from 'wood' that the elements of cosmic construction are drawn, the 'Great Architect' must be regarded above all as a 'master carpenter', as he effectively is in such a case, and as it is natural that he be so, when the human builders, whose art from the traditional point of view essentially 'imitates' that of the 'Great Architect', are themselves carpenters.[6] As concerns the Christian tradition more particularly, it is not without importance to note, as Coomaraswamy has already done, that this

5. It is rather curious that in Spanish the word *madera*, derived directly from *materia*, still designates wood, and even more particularly wood used for the framework.

6. It is perhaps not without interest to note that in the 22nd degree of Scottish Masonry, which according to Hermetic interpretation represents 'the preparation of the materials necessary for the "Great Work"', these materials are represented not by stones, as in the grades that properly constitute Masonic initiation, but by construction wood. One might see in this grade, whatever may in fact be its historical origin, a sort of 'vestige' of the initiation of the carpenters, all the more so as the ax, which is its symbol or chief attribute, is essentially a carpenter's tool. — Moreover, we must note that the symbolism of the ax is here quite different from the much more enigmatic symbolism with which, in *Craft Masonry*, the 'pointed cubic stone' is associated, and which we explained in 'Le hiéroglyphe du Pôle in the May 1937 issue. Let us recall also the symbolic relationship that the ax has, generally, with the *vajra* (cf. our article 'Les pierres de foudre' in the May 1929 issue, and 'Les armes symboliques', in the Oct. 1936 issue). [The articles referred to above now form chaps. 15, 25, and 26 of *Symbols of Sacred Science* ('A Hieroglyph of the Pole', 'Thunderbolts', and 'Symbolic Weapons') ED.]

makes clear why Christ had to appear as the 'son of a carpenter'. As we have often said, historical facts are in the final analysis merely the reflection of realities of another order, and it is that gives them all their value; here is a much deeper symbolism than is ordinarily thought (if indeed the great majority of Christians even entertain however vaguely the notion that there may be any symbolism whatever). Even if it only be an apparent filiation, it is still required by the coherence of the symbolism, since it is a matter of something in keeping with the external order of manifestation only, and not with the principial order. It is exactly the same in the Hindu tradition, where *Agni*, insofar as he is the *Avatāra* par excellence, has *Tvashtri* as his adoptive father when he is born in the Cosmos; and how could it be otherwise when that Cosmos itself is nothing else, symbolically, than the very work of the 'master carpenter'?

6

MASONIC ORTHODOXY

SO MUCH HAS BEEN WRITTEN on the subject of Masonic regularity, and so many different and even contradictory definitions given, that far from being resolved, the problem has perhaps only become more confused. The question itself seems to have been badly framed, for regularity is always taken to be based on purely historical considerations, on the real or supposed proof of an uninterrupted transmission of authority from some more or less distant period. Now we would of course have to admit that from this point of view a degree of irregularity could easily be found in the origins of all the Rites practiced today, but we think this a far less important point than some have for various reasons wished to imagine, for we see true regularity as residing essentially in Masonic orthodoxy. And this orthodoxy consists above all in faithfully following tradition, in carefully preserving the symbols and ritual forms that express and as it were clothe it, and in resisting every innovation that smacks of modernism. We have intentionally used the word modernism here to designate a tendency—all too widespread within Masonry as well as everywhere else—characterized by a misuse of criticism, a rejection of symbolism, and a negation of everything that constitutes esoteric and traditional science.

We do not wish to say, however, that in order to remain orthodox Masonry must enclose itself in a narrow formalism, or that ritualism must be something absolutely immutable, to which nothing could either be added or taken away without this amounting to a sort of sacrilege; such would be proof of a dogmatism completely foreign and even contrary to the spirit of Masonry. By no means does tradition exclude evolution or progress; rituals therefore can and must be modified whenever necessary, in order that they might be adapted to the varying conditions of time and place, but naturally only insofar as such modifications do not affect any essential point. Changes in details of ritual matter little, provided that the initiatic teaching which emerges suffers no distortion; and the multiplicity of rites need present no serious drawback—it could perhaps even offer certain advantages—however unfortunate it has in fact all too often proved itself to be, serving only as a pretext for dissension between rival Orders and thereby compromising the unity of universal Masonry, which though ideal, if one wishes, is nevertheless real.

It is especially regrettable that so many Masons display complete ignorance of symbolism and its esoteric interpretation, and forsake the initiatic studies without which ritualism becomes nothing more than a collection of ceremonies devoid of meaning, as in exoteric religions. From this point of view, there exist today certain truly unpardonable cases of negligence, particularly in France and Italy; we may cite as an example the Masters who have ceased to wear their apron, which is in reality the true Masonic garb, the cord merely being its ornament, as T∴ Ill∴ F∴ Dr Blatin recently showed so well in a paper that must still be fresh in the minds of the FF∴. Even more serious is the absence or oversimplification of the initiatic ordeals, and their replacement with the recitation of virtually insignificant formulas. In this regard we can do no better than reproduce the following lines, which also give an apt general definition of symbolism:

Masonic Symbolism is the sensible form of a philosophical synthesis of a transcendent or abstract order. Concepts represented by the Symbols of Masonry cannot lead to any dogmatic teaching; they escape concrete formulas of spoken language and cannot be translated into words. They are, as is most rightly said, Mysteries veiled from profane curiosity, Truths that the mind can only grasp after judicious preparation. This preparation for understanding of the Mysteries is staged allegorically in Masonic initiations by the ordeals of the three fundamental grades of the Order. Contrary to what one might imagine, these trials are in no way meant to draw forth the courage or moral qualities of the newly elect; they represent a teaching the thinker must discern, then meditate upon throughout the course of his initiatic career.[1]

From this it will be seen that Masonic orthodoxy, as we have defined it, is linked to the entirety of its symbolism taken as a complete and harmonious whole, and not to such and such a particular symbol, or even to a formula such as A∴ L∴ G∴ D∴ G∴ A∴ D∴ L∴ U∴, which some have wished to make the distinguishing mark of Masonic regularity, as if this alone could constitute a necessary and sufficient condition; indeed, its suppression in French Masonry since 1877 has often been criticized. Here let us take this occasion to protest strongly against a campaign more ridiculous than odious that for some time now has been waged in France against French Masonry by people affecting rather dubious Masonic qualities, all on behalf of a so-called spiritualism that has nothing to do with this case; if these people, to whom we do not wish to give the honor of mentioning by name, believe that their methods will assure the success of the pseudo-Masonry which they vainly attempt to disseminate under various labels, they are strangely mistaken.

We do not wish to address here the question of the G∴ A∴ of the U∴ here, at least for the moment. In the last issue of *L'Acacia* this question was the subject of a most interesting discussion between FF∴ Oswald Wirth and Ch.-M. Limousin, but, unfortunately, the discussion was interrupted by the death of the latter, whose passing was a cause of mourning for all of Masonry. Be that as it may, we shall only remark that the symbol of the G∴ A∴ of the U∴ does not express a dogma, and that properly understood it can be accepted by all Masons regardless of philosophical opinion, without by any means requiring on their part the recognition of the existence of any God, as is all too often supposed. It is regrettable that French Masonry should be mistaken on this subject, but in all fairness it must be recognized that it has thereby only shared in a rather common error. Should this confusion be dispelled, all Masons would

---

1. *Rituel interprétatif pour le Grade d'Apprenti*, edited by the *Groupe Maçonnique d'Etudes Initiatiques*, 1893.

understand that, instead of suppressing the G∴ A∴ of the U∴, a rational idea must be sought for it, and that in this regard it should be treated like any other initiatic symbol, as F∴ Oswald Wirth has said, with whose conclusions we entirely agree.

We can only hope that the day will come, and that it is not far off, when agreement will be established once and for all on the fundamental principles of Masonry and the essential points of traditional doctrine. All branches of universal Masonry, certain of which have deviated, will then return to true orthodoxy, and all will unite together at last to labor toward the realization of the Great Work, which is the integral accomplishment of Progress in every domain of human activity.

7

GNOSIS AND FREEMASONRY

'GNOSIS,' said T∴ Ill∴ F∴ Albert Pike, 'is the essence and marrow of Freemasonry.' Here Gnosis must be understood to mean that traditional knowledge which constitutes the common basis of all initiations, the doctrines and symbols of which have been transmitted from the most distant antiquity down to the present day through all the secret Fraternities, the long chain of which has remained unbroken.

Esoteric doctrines can be transmitted only through initiation, and every initiation necessarily comprises several successive phases, to which there correspond as many different grades. These grades and phases can always be reduced to three, considered as marking the three ages of the initiate or the three periods of his education and are characterized by the three words birth, growth, and production, respectively. Here is what F∴ Oswald Wirth says on the subject:

> The goal of Masonic initiation is to illumine men, that they might be taught to work usefully, in full conformity with the very purpose of their existence. Now in order to illumine men, it is first necessary to rid them of all that might keep them from seeing the Light. They are therefore submitted to certain purifications intended to eliminate heterogeneous residues, themselves the causes of the opacity of the layers that serve as so many protective shells for the spiritual kernel of man. As soon as they are made clear, their complete transparence allows the rays of outward Light to penetrate to the conscious center of the initiate. Then his entire being is progressively saturated by Light until he

is Illumined in the highest sense of the word; he is thereafter known also as an adept, himself transformed into a radiant focus of Light.

Masonic initiation is thus made up of three distinct phases, consecrated successively to the discovery, assimilation, and propagation of Light. These phases are represented by the three grades of Apprentice, Fellow, and Master, corresponding to the triple mission of the Masons, which consists first in searching for, then possessing, and finally being able to spread the Light. The number of these grades is absolute: there can be only three, no more, no less. The invention of various systems known as high grades rests solely on an equivocation, by which the initiatic grades, strictly limited in number to three, are confused with the degrees of initiation, the multitude of which is necessarily indefinite.

The initiatic grades correspond to the triple program pursued through Masonic initiation. They carry in their esoterism a solution to the three questions of the Sphinx's riddle: Where do we come from? What are we? Where are we going? and they thereby correspond to all that can interest men. They are immutable in their fundamental character, and in their trinity they form a complete whole, to which nothing can either be added or taken away: Apprenticeship and Fellowship are the two pillars supporting Mastery.

As to the degrees of initiation, they allow the initiate to penetrate more or less deeply into the esoterism of each grade. From this there results an indefinite number of different ways of entering into possession of the three grades of Apprentice, Fellow, and Master. It is possible to possess their outward form only, the uncomprehended letter; in Masonry, as everywhere, there are in this regard many called but few chosen, for it is only given to the true initiate to grasp the inner spirit of the initiatic grades. What is more, not everyone will achieve the same results; more often than not, an initiate will scarcely emerge from esoteric ignorance, and will never advance in a decided manner toward integral Knowledge, toward perfect Gnosis.

Perfect Gnosis, which in Masonry is symbolized by the letter G∴ within the Blazing Star, applies simultaneously to the program of intellectual discovery and to the moral training of the three grades of Apprentice, Fellow, and Master. With Apprenticeship, it aims to penetrate the mystery of the origin of things; with Fellowship, to unveil the secret of man's nature; and with Mastery, to reveal knowledge of the future destiny of beings. Moreover, it teaches the Apprentice to increase his interior strength to its highest level; it shows the Fellow how to attract surrounding forces to himself; and it instructs the Master to reign as sovereign, subjecting nature to the scepter of his intelligence. It must not be forgotten in all this that initiatic Masonry relates to the Great Art, the Sacerdotal and Royal Art of the ancient initiates.[1]

Without wishing to enter here into the quite complicated question of Masonry's historical origins, let us simply recall that in the form in which it is currently known, modern Masonry resulted from a partial fusion of the Brotherhood of the Rose-Cross, which had preserved gnostic doctrine since the Middle Ages, with the ancient building guilds of the Masons, whose tools had moreover already been used as symbols by the Hermetic philosophers, as can particularly be seen in a figure like Basil Valentine.[2]

But laying aside the restricted point of view of Gnosticism for the time being, we must stress above all the fact that the goal of Masonic initiation, as of all other initiations, is the attainment of integral Knowledge, which is Gnosis in the true sense of the word. It is precisely this knowledge that, properly speaking, constitutes the Masonic secret, which is why this secret is essentially incommunicable.

To conclude, and in order to avoid all ambiguity, we shall observe that for us Masonry cannot and must not be bound to any particular philosophical opinion, that it is no more spiritualist than materialist, no more deist than atheist or pantheist in the ordinary sense of all these terms, for it must only be Masonry pure and simple. In

---

1. 'L'Initiation Maçonnique', an article published in *L'Initiation*, fourth year, January 1891.

2. On this subject, see *Le Livre de l'Apprenti*, by F∴ Oswald Wirth, pp 24–29 of the new edition.

entering the Temple, each member must divest himself of his profane personality, laying aside all that is foreign to the fundamental principles of Masonry, on which all must be united in order to labor together on the Great Work of universal Construction.

8

THE MASONIC
HIGH GRADES

IN A PREVIOUS ARTICLE we saw that Masonic initiation comprises three successive phases, and that there can thus be only three grades, representing these three phases; from this it would seem to follow that the systems of high grades are completely useless, at least in theory, since in their entirety the rituals of the three symbolic grades describe the complete cycle of initiation. However, since Masonic initiation is in fact symbolic, it produces Masons who are only symbols of true Masons, simply outlining for them the course of the steps they must take in order to arrive at real initiation. It is this goal that, at least originally, was the aim of the various systems of high grades, which seem to have been instituted precisely in order to realize in practice the Great Work that symbolic Masonry teaches in theory.

It must be recognized, however, that very few of these systems actually achieve their proposed goal; in most cases, one meets with points of incoherence, lacunae, and superfluities, and the initiatic value of certain rituals appears quite meager, especially when compared to that of the symbolic grades. These failings are all the more conspicuous the greater number of degrees the system contains, and if such is already the case with the Scottish Rites of 25 and 33 degrees, what of those Rites having 90, 97, or even 120 degrees? This multiplicity of degrees is all the more useless in that one is obliged to confer them successively. In the eighteenth century everyone wanted to invent a system for himself, always, of course, grafted onto symbolic Masonry, merely elaborating the fundamental principles thereof, which were all too often interpreted in accordance with the author's personal conceptions, as is the case with nearly all the Hermetic, Kabbalistic, and philosophical Rites, as well as with the Orders of Knighthood and Illuminism. This is what gave birth to the tremendous diversity of rites, many of which were never written down, and it is virtually impossible to untangle the history of them all. Everyone who has tried to find order in this chaos has had to give it up, or for whatever reasons has at least preferred to give more or less fanciful and sometimes even completely fabulous explanations for the origins of the high grades.

We shall not relate here all the so-called historical assertions we have come across in the writings of various authors; but what is in any case certain is that contrary to the frequent claim, the knight Ramses was in no way the inventor of the high grades, and if he was responsible for them, he was so only indirectly, those who conceived of the Scottish Rite having been inspired by a speech he gave in 1737, in which he linked Masonry both to the Mysteries of antiquity and, more recently, to the religious and military Orders of the Middle Ages. But Ramses is no more the author of the rituals of the Scottish grades than Elias Ashmole is of the symbolic grades, to mention another widely held opinion, shared by Ragon and other historians.

> Elias Ashmole, a learned antiquarian and an adept of Hermeticism and secret disciplines then in vogue, was received as a Mason on October 16, 1646 at Warrington, a small town in Lancaster County. He returned to the lodge after thirty-five years, on March 11, 1682, for the second and last time in his life, as he himself bears witness in his journal, which he kept daily with scrupulous meticulousness.[1]

We do not think, moreover, that initiatic rituals in general can be considered the work of one or more particular individuals, but that they came together progressively through a process it would be impossible for us to describe, since it defies definition. Those of some of the more insignificant high grades, by contrast, present all the characteristics of a contrived and artificial composition, pieced

---

1. Oswald Wirth, *Le Livre de l'Apprenti*, p30 of the second edition.

together by an individual mentality. Without dwelling further on considerations of no great interest, it will suffice to envisage the various systems as so many manifestations of the creative tendency of men not content with pure theory, but who, in wishing to pass to the practical, all too often forget that real initiation must necessarily be in large part personal.

We have simply wished to say here what we think of the institution of high grades and their reason for being. We consider them of an incontestable practical utility, but on condition—a condition that is unfortunately but rarely realized, especially today—that they truly fulfill the goal for which they were created. For that, it would be necessary for the Lodges of these high grades to be reserved for philosophical and metaphysical studies, which are overly neglected in symbolic Lodges. One should never forget the initiatic character of Masonry, which latter, whatever has been said, is not and cannot be either a political club or an association of mutual support. Doubtless, it is not possible to communicate that which is in its essence inexpressible, which is why true secrets are their own defense against indiscretion; but one can at least provide keys that will allow each to obtain real initiation through his own efforts and personal meditation, and, following the constant Tradition and practice of initiatic Temples and Colleges of every age and every country, one can also place those who aspire to initiation in the most favorable conditions for its realization, and furnish them with that aid without which it would be nearly impossible for them to attain this realization. We shall not pursue this subject further, judging that we have said enough to give a glimpse of what the Masonic high grades could be if, instead of wishing to suppress them altogether, one were to make of them true initiatic centers, charged with transmitting esoteric science and preserving in its integrity the sacred store of orthodox tradition, one and universal.

9

FEMININE INITIATION
AND CRAFT INITIATIONS

IT HAS OFTEN been pointed out to us that in the traditional Western forms still extant today there seems to be no opportunity for women as regards an initiatic order, and many wonder what may be the reason for this state of affairs, which although certainly most regrettable would doubtless be quite difficult to remedy. Besides, this should give pause to those who imagine that the West has granted woman a privileged position which she has never had in any other civilization. This may perhaps be true in certain respects, but primarily only in the sense that in modern times she has been taken out of her normal role by being granted access to functions that ought to belong exclusively to men, this being yet another case of the disorder of our time. From other more legitimate points of view, on the contrary, Western women are in reality much more disadvantaged than they are in Eastern civilizations, where notably it has always been possible for them to find a suitable initiation as soon as they possesses the requisite qualifications; thus it is, for example, that Islamic initiation has always been accessible to women, which, let us note in passing, suffices to reduce to nothing some of the absurdities often heard in Europe on the subject of Islam.

To return to the Western world, it goes without saying that we are not speaking here of antiquity, when there were most certainly feminine initiations, and when some initiations were even exclusively feminine, others being exclusively masculine. But how was it in the Middle Ages? It is certainly not impossible that women were admitted at that time into organizations possessing an initiation connected with Christian esoterism, and this is even quite probable,[1] but since there has been no trace of such organizations for quite some time, it is very difficult to speak of them with certainty and precision, and in any case it is likely that they provided only very limited possibilities. As for chivalric initiation, it is more than obvious that by its very nature it could not in any way be suitable for women, the same holding true for trade initiations, or at least for the most important among them, those which in one way or another have continued right up to our time. The true reason for the absence of any feminine initiation in the contemporary West is that all the initiations it retains are based essentially on trades the exercise of which pertains exclusively to men; and as we said above, this is why one does not very well see how this regrettable gap could be filled, unless it proves possible some day to realize a possibility that we shall presently consider.

We are well aware that certain of our contemporaries believe that in cases where the effective exercise of the trade has disappeared, the exclusion of women from the corresponding initiation has thereby lost its raison d'être; but this is veritable nonsense, for the basis of such an initiation is in no way altered on that account, and as we have already explained,[2] such an error implies a complete misunderstanding of the significance and the real extent of initiatic qualifications. As we said, the connection with the trade, entirely independent of its outward exercise, necessarily remains inscribed in the very form of that initiation and in what characterizes and constitutes it essentially as such, so that it could not in any case be valid for anyone unsuited to exercise the trade in question. Naturally, it is Masonry that we have particularly in view here, since, as concerns the Compagnonnage, the exercise of the trade has not ceased to be considered an indispensable condition; moreover, we

---

1. A case like that of Joan of Arc seems very significant in this respect, in spite of the many enigmas surrounding it.

2. *Perspectives on Initiation* chap. 14.

do not know any other example of such a deviation as is found in 'mixed Masonry', which for that reason will never be admissible as 'regular' by anyone who understands even a modicum of the true principles of Masonry. Basically, the existence of this 'mixed Masonry' (or *Co-Masonry* as it is called in English-speaking countries) quite simply represents an attempt to transport into the initiatic domain itself, one that in particular ought to be exempt from it, the 'egalitarian' idea which, in refusing to see the differences of nature that exist among beings, ends up attributing to women a role that is properly masculine, and clearly lies at the root of all the contemporary 'feminism'.[3]

Now, the question to be considered is this: why are the trades included in the Compagnonnage exclusively masculine, and why do no feminine occupations seem to have given rise to a similar initiation? The question is really quite complex, and we do not claim to resolve it entirely here. Leaving aside research into the historical contingencies that may have arisen in this regard, we shall say only that there may be certain difficulties involved, a chief one being due perhaps to the fact that from the traditional point of view feminine occupations must normally have to do with the interior of the house and not with what lies outside, as with masculine trades. However, such a difficulty is not insurmountable, and could be gotten round by special provisions in the constitution of an initiatic organization; and on the other hand, there are doubtless feminine trades perfectly capable of supporting an initiation. A clear example is weaving, the particularly important symbolism of which we have discussed in one of our works.[4] However, this trade is one that can be practiced by both men and women. As an example of a more exclusively feminine trade we might mention embroidery, which is

---

3. It is understood of course that we are here speaking of a Masonry into which women are admitted under the same conditions as men, and not of the former 'Masonry of adoption' which had as its aim only to give satisfaction to women who complained of being excluded from Masonry, by conferring upon them a semblance of initiation which, although altogether illusory and of no real value, at least did not share the claims or the disadvantages of 'mixed Masonry'.

4. *The Symbolism of the Cross*, chap. 14.

directly related to the symbolism of the needle, of which we have also spoken on various occasions, as well as to that of the *sūtrātmā*.[5] From this perspective it is clear, at least in principle, that the possibilities for a feminine initiation are by no means negligible; but we say 'in principle' because under present conditions there is unfortunately no authentic transmission that can realize these possibilities. It cannot be too often repeated, since it seems always to be lost to sight, that aside from such a transmission there can be no valid initiation, for the latter cannot in any way be constituted by individual initiatives, which, whatever they may be, can by themselves only end in pseudo-initiation since the supra-human element, that is to say the spiritual influence, is necessarily lacking in such a case.

Nevertheless, one can perhaps glimpse a solution in recalling that by taking into account their more particular affinities, the trades belonging to the Compagnonnage were always in a position to affiliate themselves with some other trade and to confer on it an initiation that it did not previously possess, and that would then be regular by the very fact that it amounts to an adaptation of a pre-existing initiation. Is there not some trade capable of effecting such a transmission with respect to certain feminine trades? This does not seem absolutely impossible and is perhaps not entirely without precedent,[6] but we must not in any case pretend that there would not then be great difficulties as concerns the necessary adaptation, the latter obviously being a far more delicate matter than an adaptation between two masculine trades: where would we find today men sufficiently competent to realize such an adaptation in a rigorously traditional spirit, who were also wary of not introducing into it the slightest whim, which might risk compromising the validity of the

---

5. See especially 'Encadrements et Labyrinthes in the October–November 1947 issue [translated as 'Frameworks and Labyrinths' in *Symbols of Sacred Science*, chap. 66]. The drawings in question, by Dürer and da Vinci, could be considered—and moreover have been by some—as representing models of embroidery.

6. We have seen mentioned somewhere the fact that in the eighteenth century at least one feminine guild, that of pin-makers, was probably affiliated with the Compagnonnage in this way; unfortunately, we can recall no more precise details on this subject.

initiation transmitted?[7] However that may be, we can naturally formulate nothing more here than a simple suggestion, and it is not for us to proceed further in this direction; but so often do we hear it deplored that no feminine initiation exists in the West that it seemed to us at least worthwhile to indicate what, in that order, seems to constitute the sole possibility that presently exists.

7. The danger would be to attach to the Compagnonnage something having no more real value than the 'Masonry of adoption' of which we have spoken above; yet those who instituted the latter at least knew what to expect, whereas under our hypothesis those who would want to institute a feminine companionic initiation without taking into account certain necessary conditions, would, because of their incompetence, be the first to delude themselves.

10

PILGRIMAGES

THE RECENT APPEARANCE in *Le Voile d'Isis* of a remarkable article by Grillot de Givry on places of pilgrimage brings us back to a question we have already considered in these pages, as we are reminded in Clavelle's introduction to this article.

Let us note first of all that the Latin word *peregrinus*, from which 'pilgrim' comes, means both 'traveler' and 'stranger', and this simple observation already points to some rather curious connections. Among the Companions there are on the one hand, those who qualify as 'wayfarers' and others who as 'strangers', corresponding exactly to the two meanings of *peregrinus* (meanings also found in the Hebrew *gershôn*), and on the other hand, the symbolic ordeals of initiation are called 'journeys' even in modern 'speculative' Masonry. In many traditions the various initiatic stages are described as stages of a journey, sometimes an ordinary journey, sometimes a voyage, as we have pointed out on other occasions. This symbolism of the journey is perhaps more widespread than that of war, to which we alluded in an earlier article. Moreover, both symbolisms share a certain connection which is sometimes even expressed outwardly in historical facts. We are thinking especially of the close connection during the Middle Ages between pilgrimage to the Holy Land and the Crusades. And let us add that even in the most ordinary religious language, earthly life, considered as a time of trials, is often likened to a journey, and even qualified more particularly as a pilgrimage—the celestial world, which is the object of this pilgrimage, also being identified symbolically with the 'Holy Land' or 'Land of the Living'.[1]

---

1. Concerning the symbolism of the 'Holy land', we refer to our study *The King of the World* and also to our article published in the special number of *Le Voile d'Isis*

The state of 'wandering', if one may so put it, or of migration, is therefore in general a state of 'probation'; and here again we note that such is in fact its actual characteristic in organizations such as the Compagnonnage. Besides, what is true in this respect for individuals can in certain cases also be so to some degree for peoples taken collectively, a very clear example is this being the Hebrews' wandering for forty years in the desert before reaching the Promised Land. But a distinction must be made here, for this state, which is essentially transitory, must not be confused with the nomadic state normal for certain peoples: even after their arrival at the Promised Land, and up to the time of David and Solomon, the Hebrews remained a nomadic people, but this nomadism obviously did not have the same character as their wandering in the desert.[2] We could even envisage a third case of 'wandering', which could be referred to more exactly as 'tribulation': it is that of the Jews after their dispersion, and in all likelihood also that of the Bohemians; but this would lead us too far afield, and we shall say only that this case is equally applicable to groups and to individuals. One sees by this how complex these things are and how distinctions are to be made among men who appear outwardly identical to the ordinary pilgrims with whom they mingle; and beyond this, sometimes it even happens that initiates who have attained the goal, or even 'adepts', may for special reasons adopt this same guise of 'traveler'.

But to return to pilgrims, we know that their distinctive signs were the scallop shell (so called from Saint-Jacques) and the staff. The latter, which is also closely connected to the walking-stick of the Compagnonnage, is naturally an attribute of the traveler, but it has many other meanings, and perhaps one day we shall devote a special study to this question. As for the scallop shell, it was in certain regions called the 'creusille', a word that must be linked to 'crucible', again recalling the notion of trials, envisaged here more particularly in connection with alchemical symbolism and understood in the

---

The distinction of nomadic people (shepherds) and sedentary (farmers), which goes back to the very origins of terrestrial humanity, has great importance for the understanding of the special characteristics of the different traditional forms.

sense of 'purification', the Pythagorean *catharsis*, which was precisely the preparatory phase of initiation.[3]

Since the scallop shell is regarded as a special attribute of St James, we are led to an observation regarding the pilgrimage to Saint James of Compostello [Santiago de Compostela]. The routes formerly followed by the pilgrims are even today often called 'paths of Saint-Jacques', but this expression has at the same time quite another application: in the language of the peasants, the 'Way of Saint James' is in fact also the 'Milky Way', and this will perhaps seem less unexpected if we note that etymologically Compostello means 'starlit field'. Here we come upon another idea, that of 'celestial voyages', and this moreover in connection with a terrestrial voyage. This is a point on which we cannot dwell at present, but let us at least note that this gives one a sense of a certain correspondence between the geographic location of the places of pilgrimage and the ordering of the celestial sphere itself, and thus that the 'sacred geography' we mentioned is here integrated in a true 'sacred cosmography'.

While on the subject of pilgrimage routes, we should recall that Joseph Bédier had the merit of recognizing the connection between the sanctuaries marking the stages of pilgrimage, and the development of the *chanson de gestes*. This fact could be applied generally, so that the same could be said spread of many legends whose real initiatic import unfortunately almost always goes unrecognized by moderns. Owing to the plurality of meanings, accounts of this kind could appeal simultaneously to the multitude of ordinary pilgrims and... to others; each would understand them according to the measure of his own intellectual capacity, and only a few would penetrate the profound meaning, as is the case for all initiatic teaching. We should also note that because so many kinds of people, including pedlars and even beggars, crossed paths on these routes, a certain solidarity was established among them for reasons no doubt difficult to define, which was expressed in the common adoption of a special conventional language, the 'Scallop argot' or 'pilgrim's tongue'. In one of his recent books Léon Daudet makes the interesting remark

3. We refer here to what we have said in *The King of the World* on the designation of initiates in the different tradition, by terms linked to the idea of 'purity'.

that many words and phrases belonging to this language are found in Villon and Rabelais.[4] In Rabelais' case he also points out that for several years

> he wandered through Poitiers, at that time a province celebrated for the mystery plays and farces performed there and also for its cycles of legends; in *Pantagruel* we rediscover traces of these legends and farces as well as a certain number of specifically Poitevan terms.[5]

We cite this last phrase because, apart from its reference to the legends of which we spoke just now, it raises still another question relevant to our present topic, that of the origins of the theater.[6] In the beginning the theater was on the one hand itinerant, and on the other assumed a religious character, at least as to its outer forms—a religious character that connects it with those pilgrims and others who challenged its appearance. What lends still more importance to this fact is that it is not unique to the Europe of the Middle Ages; the history of the theater in ancient Greece is quite similar, and other examples could be found in most of the countries of the East.

But we must limit ourselves here, and shall raise only one final point regarding the expression 'noble travellers' applied to initiates, or at least to some among them, precisely because of their wanderings. On this point O. V. de L. Milosz[7] wrote:

> Transmitted by oral tradition to initiates of the Middle Ages and of modern times, Noble Traveller is the secret name of initiates of antiquity. The last time that it was pronounced in public was on May 30, 1786, in Paris, at a session of Parliament devoted to the cross-examination of a famous defendant [Cagliostro],

---

4. *Les Horreurs de la Guerre*, pp 145, 147, and 167.

5. Ibid., p 173.

6. See *Perspectives on Initiation*, chap. 28, 'The Symbolism of the Theater'. ED.

7. Oscar Vladislas de Lubicz [1877–1939], of Lithuanian and Jewish origin but educated in France, was a mystical poet, metaphysician, dramatist, Biblical exegete, and novelist, sometimes described as the French Goethe. See *The Noble Traveller: The Life and Writings of O. V. de L. Milosz*, (West Stockbridge, MA: The Lindisfarne Press, 1985). ED.

victim of a pamphleteer, Theveneau de Morande. Initiates' wanderings did not differ from ordinary travels for study except that their itinerary, though apparently haphazard, rigorously coincided with the adept's most secret aspirations and gifts. The most illustrious examples of these pilgrimages are offered to us by: Democritus, who was initiated into the secrets of alchemy by Egyptian priests and by Ostanes, the magus, and into Asiatic doctrines during his stays not only in Persia but also, according to some historians, in India as well; Thales, instructed in the temples of Egypt and of Chaldea; and Pythagoras, who visited all the countries known to the ancients (and, very probably, India and China), whose sojourns were distinguished—in Persia by conversations with Zaratas the magus, in Gaul by his cooperation with the Druids, and in Italy by his speeches at the Assembly of the Elders of Crotona. To these examples it would be proper to add Paracelsus' stays in France, Austria, Germany, Spain and Portugal, England, Holland, Denmark, Sweden, Hungary, Poland, Lithuania, Valachia, Carniola, Dalmatia, Russia and Turkey, as well as the travels of Nicholas Flamel to Spain where Maistre Canches taught him how to decipher the famous hieroglyphic figures of the Book of Abraham the Jew. The poet Robert Browning has defined the secret character of these scholarly pilgrimages in a stanza particularly rich in intuition: 'I see my way as birds their trackless way.... In some time, His good time, I shall arrive: He guides me and the bird.' William Meister's years of travel have the same initiatic meaning.[8]

We wanted to reproduce this entire passage despite its length because of the interesting examples it contains. No doubt one could find many others more or less well-known, but these are particularly characteristic, even if they do not perhaps belong to the same category as those discussed earlier, and which should not be confused with 'study travels', even when these latter are really initiatic and involve special missions of adepts or even of initiates of a lesser degree.

---

8. *The Noble Traveller: The Life and Writings of O. V. de L. Milosz*, op. cit., verse 46, pp338–339. ED.

Returning to the expression 'noble travelers', the point we wish to emphasize is that the epithet 'noble' seems to indicate not just initiation in general but more particularly a *Kshatriya* initiation, or what may be called the 'royal art', according to an expression Masonry still employs. In other words, the initiation concerned does not pertain to the order of pure metaphysics, but to the cosmological order and to the applications attached to it, that is, to everything that in the West has been given the general name 'Hermeticism'.[9] If such is the case, Clavelle was quite right to say that whereas Saint John corresponds to the purely metaphysical point of view of the Tradition, Saint James corresponds rather to the point of view of the 'traditional sciences'; and even without claiming a connection however plausible, with the 'Master James' of the Compagnonnage, many concordant indications do tend to establish that this correspondence is justified. It is really to this domain, which can be called 'intermediary', that all the matters associated with pilgrimages as well as the traditions of the Compagnonnage, or of the Bohemians, refer. Knowledge of the 'lesser mysteries', or of the laws of 'becoming', is acquired in traversing the 'wheel of things'; but knowledge of the 'greater mysteries', being that of immutable principles, requires unmoving contemplation in the 'great solitude' at the fixed point which is the center of the wheel, the fixed point around which the manifested Universe revolves.

9. On the distinction between the two initiations, sacerdotal and royal, see *Spiritual Authority and Temporal Power.*

11

THE COMPAGNONNAGE
AND THE BOHEMIANS

In an article by M.G. Milicent published in the journal *Le Compagnonnage* of May 1926 and reproduced in *Le Voile d'Isis* of November 1927, we find this sentence:

> What surprised me and made me somewhat skeptical, was that C.∴ Bernet told us he presides annually at Saintes-Maries-de-la-Mer over the election of the King of the Bohemians.

We said the same thing a long while ago, although we did not wish to pursue the question at the time; but now that it has been raised publicly we no longer see any reason not to say something about it, and all the more since to do so may cast light on certain points that are not without interest.

In the first place, the Bohemians do not elect a King, but a Queen, and secondly, this election is not repeated every year. What does take place annually, is only the meeting (with or without an election) of the Bohemians in the crypt of the church of Saintes-Maries-de-la-Mer. Moreover, it is quite possible that some not belonging to the Bohemian race may be admitted by reason of their qualities or their functions in order to assist at that meeting and with the rites that take place there. But as to 'presiding over it,' that is quite another matter, and the least we can say about this is that it is extremely unlikely. Since the assertion in question was first made in an interview that appeared some while ago in the *Intransigeant*, we would like to think whatever is incorrect in it may quite simply be ascribed to the journalist who, as very often happens, could have exaggerated in order to arouse the curiosity of his readers, who would be as ignorant as he concerning such questions and consequently incapable of perceiving his errors. We do not intend to dwell longer than necessary on this point, since for us the true interest of the matter lies rather in the more general question of the connections that may exist between the Bohemians and the guild organizations. In his article, Milicent continues, saying

> that the Bohemians practice the Jewish rite, and that there could be connections with the C∴ stonemasons' Strangers of the Duty of Liberty.

The first part of this expression seems to contain another inaccuracy, or at least an ambiguity: it is true that the Queen of the Bohemians bears the name or rather the title of *Sarah*, which is also given to the saint whom they recognize as their patroness and whose body lies in the crypt of Saintes-Maries; and it is also true that this title, the feminine form of *Sar*, is Hebrew and means 'princess'. But is this enough to justify speaking here of a Jewish rite? Judaism properly belongs to a people among whom religion is closely bound up with race; now the Bohemians, whatever their origin may be, certainly have nothing in common with the Jewish race; but despite this might there not still be ties due to certain affinities of a more mysterious order?

In speaking of the Bohemians it is essential to make a distinction that is all too often forgotten: there are in reality two kinds of Bohemians, who seem entirely foreign to one another and even treat one another as enemies. They do not have the same ethnic characteristics, do not speak the same language, and do not ply the same trades. There are the oriental Bohemians, or *Zingaris*, who are for the most part exhibitors of bears and coppersmiths, and there are the southern Bohemians, or *Gypsies*, called 'Caraques' in Languedoc and Provence, who are almost exclusively horse traders, as it is only these last who meet in Saintes-Maries. In a curious study entitled *The Bohemians of Saintes-Maries-de-la-Mer*, the Marquis of Baroncelli-Javon points out numerous traits which this people have in common with the America Indians, and on the basis of these comparisons and also by the interpretation of their own traditions, he does not hesitate to attribute to them an Atlantean origin; and even if this is only an hypothesis, it is nonetheless quite worth noting. But here is something else we have not seen referred to anywhere and which is no less extraordinary: just as there are two kinds of Bohemians, so are there also two kinds of Jews, *Ashkenazim* and *Sephardim*, for whom we could make similar comments as concerns differences of physical traits, language, and aptitudes, and who do not always have the most cordial relations either, each claiming to be the sole representative of pure Judaism, whether by race or tradition. Even in point of language there is a striking similarity. Neither the Jews nor the Bohemians really have a complete language of their own, at least for everyday use; they use the languages of the regions where they live, mixing in certain words special to them, Hebrew words for the Jews, and for the Bohemians, words deriving also from an ancestral language and representing its last vestiges; this particularity can be explained moreover by the conditions of peoples forced to live dispersed among strangers. But what is more difficult to explain is that the regions traversed by the oriental Bohemians and the southern Bohemians happen to be precisely the same as those where the *Ashkenazim* and the *Sephardim* live. Would it not be a much too 'simplistic' attitude to see in all this mere coincidence?

These remarks prompt us to think that even if there are no ethnic links between the Bohemians and the Jews, there are perhaps other links which, without further specifying their nature, may be qualified as traditional. Now, this leads us directly to our subject, from which we have only apparently strayed: could not the guild organizations, for which the ethnic question obviously does not arise, also have links of the same order, either with the Jews or with the Bohemians, or with both at the same time? At the moment we do not seek to explain the origins of and the reason for these links, but will have to rest content with drawing attention to a few more particular points. Are not the Companions divided into several rival rites, often more or less hostile to one another? Do not their travels include itineraries following different rites and having different bases? Do they not have a so to speak special language, the basis of which is certainly formed from ordinary language, but which is distinguished from it by the introduction of particular terms, exactly as in the case of the Jews and the Bohemians? Do we not use the term 'jargon' to designate the conventional language in use in certain secret societies, notably the guilds, and do not the Jews sometimes also give the same name to the language they speak? On the other hand, in certain rural areas are not the Bohemians known as 'wayfarers', a name often leading them to be confused with pedlars, and which is, as we know, also applied to the Companions? Finally, could not the legend of the 'wandering Jew' be, like many others, of Companionist origin?

We could doubtless multiply these questions marks, but we think those given suffice, and that research directed along this line could shed light on certain enigmas. If there is good reason, we ourself will perhaps return to the question, bringing other complementary information; but are the Companions of today really interested in everything touching on their traditions?

12

HEREDOM

HAVING RECENTLY SEEN some notes on the word *Heredom* that offer a few explanations as to its real origin but nevertheless suggest no conclusion, it seemed to us that it might not be without interest to collect a few observations on the subject. We know that this enigmatic word sometimes written as *Herodom*, or several other ways that seem to be more or less incorrect) is used to designate for a high Masonic grade, and, by extension, the whole Rite of which this grade constitutes the most characteristic element. At first glance it may seem that *Heredom* is nothing but a slightly altered form of *heirdom*, that is to say 'heritage'. In the 'Royal Order of Scotland' the heritage in question could be that of the Templars who, according to the legend, having taken refuge in Scotland after the destruction of their Order, were said to have been welcomed there by the king Robert Bruce and to have founded the Mother-Lodge of Kilwinning.[1] However, this etymology does not begin to explain everything, and it is quite possible that this meaning was only a secondary accretion resulting from a phonetic similarity with a word the true origin of which was altogether different.

We can say as much of the hypothesis that *Heredom* derived from the Greek *hieros domus*, 'sacred dwelling'; this too is certainly not

---

1. It seems to us quite useless to interpose here the heritage of the Stuarts, as Ragon wished to do; even if it is true that some have made this application, the latter could in any case only be late and occasional, and it would be almost as far off the mark as that by which Hiram, as is also said, would have been considered to represent Charles I of England.

without meaning, and may even be less inclined to lend itself to 'exterior' considerations than a simply historical allusion. However, such an etymology is nonetheless very questionable, and reminds us of another which claims that, because of its Greek form *Hierosolyma*, the name Jerusalem is a hybrid compound which also includes the word *hieros*, whereas in reality it is a case of a purely Hebraic name meaning 'dwelling of peace', or, if we take for its first part a slightly different root (*yara* instead of *yarah*), 'vision of peace'. And this reminds us also of the interpretation given the symbol of the grade of *Royal Arch*, a triple *tau*, which is seen to be formed by the superposition of the two letters 'T' and 'H', giving us the initials of the words *Templum Hierosolymæ*; and for those who entertain this hypothesis, the *hieros domos* in question is also precisely the Temple of Jerusalem. We certainly do not wish to say that comparisons of this type, whether based on the consonance of the words or on the form of the letters and symbols, need necessarily be without meaning or justification, for some are indeed far from lacking interest and have an unquestionable traditional value; but obviously we must be very careful never to confuse these secondary meanings, which may be more or less numerous, with the original meaning, which in the case of a word is the only one to which the name of etymology may properly be applied.

What is perhaps most singular is that *Heredom* has so frequently seen as the name of a mountain in Scotland. Now we need hardly say that no mountain bearing this name has in fact ever existed, either in Scotland or in any other country, but here the idea of the mountain must is associated with 'holy place', which, in a way, brings us full circle to the *hieros domos*. This supposed mountain was not, moreover, always located in Scotland, for such a location would hardly be reconcilable with the assertion found in the ritual of the Adonhiramite Masonry according to which the first Lodge was held in

the deep valley where reign peace, the virtues [or truth], and union, the valley existing between the mountains Moriah, Sinai, and *Heredom* [*sic*].

Now, if we go back to the ancient rituals of Operative Masonry, which certainly constitute a surer and traditionally more authentic 'source',[2] we must note something that makes this last assertion even stranger, that the three sacred mountains were Sinai, Moriah, and Tabor. These 'high places' were represented in certain cases by the places occupied by the three chief officers of the Lodge, so that the very location of the latter could in effect be likened to a 'valley' located between these three mountains. The latter correspond quite clearly to the three successive 'revelations', of Moses, David, and Solomon (we know that Moriah is the hill in Jerusalem on which the Temple was erected), and of Christ. The association of these three can easily be understood, but where, when, and how could the curious substitution of *Heredom* for Thabor have come about (a substitution which is in any case incompatible with the identification of *hieros domos* with the Temple of Jerusalem, since it is expressly distinguished from Mt Moriah)? Since we do not have the necessary facts at our disposal we will not undertake to resolve this enigma, but did want at least to draw attention to it.

To return to the origin of the word *Heredom*, it is important to note that in the 'Royal Order of Scotland' it is customary to write certain words with their consonants only, as in Hebrew and Arabic, so that *Heredom*, or what came to be pronounced in this way, is in fact always written H R D M. It goes without saying that the vowels can then be variable, which explains moreover the orthographic differences that are not simply due to errors. Now H R D M can of course be read *Harodim*, the name of one of the higher grades of Masonry. These grades of *Harodim* and of *Menatzchim*, which naturally were unknown to the founders of 'Speculative' Masonry,[3] made it possible to exercise the functions of superintendent of

---

2. It is in the Adonhiramite rituals that we find, among other bizarre things, the *Shekinah* transformed into the '*Stekenna*', evidently through an error due to the ignorance of some copyist or 'adapter' of more ancient ritual manuscripts, which shows sufficiently that such documents cannot be used without some precautions.

3. The latter had only the grade of Companion as 'accepted' Masons; as for Anderson, in all likelihood he must have received the special initiation of the Chaplains in a *Lodge of Jakin* (cf. *Perspectives in Initiation*, chap. 29).

works.[4] The name *Harodim* was therefore altogether fitting for the designation of a high grade, and what seems most likely is that for this reason it must later have been applied to one of the oldest known forms (but one obviously still recent compared to Operative Masonry), the Masonic grade of Rose-Cross.

4. One could perhaps find a sort of vestige of this in the designation of the grade of 'Steward of Buildings', 8th degree of the Scottish Ancient and Accepted Rite.

13

THE MONOGRAM OF CHRIST AND THE HEART IN ANCIENT TRADE MARKS

IN A DOCUMENTARY ARTICLE ENTITLED 'Armes avec motifs astrologiques et talismaniques' which appeared in the *Revue de l'Histoire des Religions* (July–October 1924), W. Deonna of Geneva compares the signs that appear on those arms with other more or less similar symbols, and speaks especially of the 'quatre de chiffre'[1] which was

> customarily used in the sixteenth and seventeenth centuries[2] as a family and house mark for private individuals, who put them on their tombstones and on their coats of arms.

He notes that this sign 'lends itself to all sorts of combinations, with the cross, the globe, and the heart in association with the monograms of the proprietors, with added strokes,' and he reproduces a certain number of examples. We think this was essentially a 'master's mark' common to many different guilds, to which the

---

1. The idiomatic expression *quatre de chiffre* is not directly translatable. The primary sense given in all authoritative reference works is of a small animal trap or snare, known in English also under the similar designation 'figure four trap', and so called on account of the arrangement of the notched sticks from which it is formed. Since Guénon uses the term in a very different sense, the French term will be retained, or occasionally rendered as 'sign of four'. See *Symbols of Sacred Science*, chap. 50, and especially chap. 67, 'The Sign of Four'. ED.

2. The same sign was already very much in use in the fifteenth century, at least in France, and especially in printers' trademarks. We have seen the following examples: Wolf (Georges), printer-bookseller in Paris, 1489; Syber (Jehan), printer in Lyon, 1478; Rembolt (Bertholde), printer in Paris, 1489.

individuals and families who used it were doubtless linked by some bonds, often hereditary.

Deonna then speaks rather summarily of the origin and meaning of this mark, reporting that

> Jusselin derives it from the Constantinian monogram, already freely interpreted and distorted on Merovingian and Carolingian documents,[3] but this hypothesis seems altogether arbitrary, and no analogy imposes itself.

Such is not our opinion, and it must on the contrary be very natural to classify it so since this is what we, for our part, had always done, even without knowledge of any special studies that might exist on the question, and we would not even have believed it contestable, so evident does it seem to us. But let us continue, and see what other explanations are proposed:

> Would it be the Arabic number 4, substituted for Roman numerals in European manuscripts before the eleventh century? . . . Must we suppose that it represents the mystical value of the number 4, which goes back to antiquity, and which moderns have preserved?

Deonna does not reject this interpretation, but prefers another, supposing 'that it is a case of an astrological sign,' that of Jupiter.

To tell the truth, these various hypotheses do not necessarily exclude one another, for in this case as in many others there could very well have been superposition and even fusion of several symbols into a single one, to which multiple meanings are thereby attached. There is nothing surprising in this, since, as we have previously said, a multiplicity of meanings is inherent in symbolism, of which it even constitutes one of the greatest advantages as a mode of expression. Only, we must naturally be able to recognize which is the first and principal meaning of the symbol, and here we persist in thinking that that meaning is given by identification with the

---

3. 'Origine du monogramme des tapissiers', in the 'Bulletin monumental', 1922, pp 433–435.

Chrisme,[4] whereas the others are only associated with it in a secondary way.

It is certain that the astrological sign of Jupiter, the two main forms of which we give here (fig. 1), presents in its general appearance a resemblance with the figure 4; it is also certain that use of this sign may be connected with the idea of 'mastery', something we will return to later; but for us this aspect of the symbolism can only be of tertiary interest. Let us note moreover that even the origin of this sign of Jupiter is very doubtful, since some see it as a representation of the thunderbolt, whereas for others it is simply the initial of the name *Zeus*.

On the other hand, it seems to us undeniable that what Deonna calls the 'mystical value' of the number 4 has also played a role here, one that is even more important, for we would rank it second in this complex symbolism. We may note in this respect that in all the marks where it appears, the form of the numeral 4 is exactly that of a cross of which two extremities are joined by an oblique line (fig. 2). Now, in antiquity, and especially among the Pythagoreans, the cross was the symbol of the quaternary (or more exactly one of its

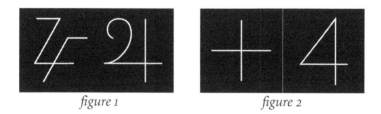

figure 1   figure 2

symbols, for the square was another); and the association of the cross with the monogram of Christ must have been established in the most natural way.

This remark brings us back to the Chrisme; and we should say first of all that it is proper to make a distinction between the so-called Constantinian Chrisme, the sign of the Labarum, and what is called the simple Chrisme. The latter (fig. 3) appears to us as the fundamental symbol from which so many others are derived more

4. The monogram of Christ. ED.

or less directly. It is considered to be formed by the union of the letters 'I' and 'X', that is, from the Greek initials of the two words *Iesous
Christos*, and that in effect is a meaning it received from the first
days of Christianity. But in itself this symbol is much earlier, being
one of those widely used everywhere and in all ages. Here then is an
example of the Christian adaptation of pre-Christian signs and legends which we have already pointed out in regard to the legend of
the Holy Grail; and for those who, like us, see in these symbols vestiges of the primordial tradition, the adaptation must appear not
only legitimate, but in a way necessary. The legend of the Grail is of
Celtic origin, and through a rather remarkable coincidence the
symbol we are speaking of now is also found particularly among the
Celts, where it is an essential element of the 'wheel' (fig. 4); the
latter, moreover, was perpetuated through the Middle Ages, and it is
not unlikely that it might even be related to the rose window of

figure 3

figure 4

cathedrals.[5] Indeed, there is a certain connection between the figure
of the wheel and floral symbols with their multiple meanings, such
as the rose and the lotus, which we mentioned in previous articles.
But this takes us too far from our subject. As for the general significance of the wheel, which the moderns ordinarily regard as an
exclusively 'solar' symbol in accordance with the kind of explanation they use and abuse in all circumstances, we say, although without being able to emphasize it as much as we should, that it is really
something else altogether, that it is first and foremost a symbol of

5. In a previous article Deonna himself recognized a relation between the
'wheel' and the Chrisme ('Quelques réflections sur le Symbolisme en particulier
dans l'art préhistorique', in the *Revue de l'Histoire des Religions*, January–February
1924). We were all the more surprised to see him later deny the relationship, even
though it is more visible, between the Chrisme and the 'quatre de chiffre'.

the World, as the study of Hindu iconography in particular suggests. And while speaking of the Celtic 'wheel',[6] let us also point out that the same origin and the same meaning should very probably be attributed to the emblem in the upper corner of the British flag (fig. 6), an emblem differing from the wheel only in that it is inscribed in a rectangle rather than a circumference, and which some Englishmen wish to see as a sign of their country's maritime supremacy.[7]

figure 5   *figure 6*

And here let us make a very important observation concerning heraldic symbolism: the form of the simple Chrisme is like a sort of general schema used to arrange the most diverse figures in the blazon. For example, when we look at an eagle or any other heraldic bird, it is not hard to realize that they follow this arrangement (the head, the tail, and the tips of the wings and the feet corresponding to the six points of figure 3), and if we look at an emblem such as the fleur-de-lis, we observe the same thing. Besides, in this last case, the real origin of the emblem in question matters little, although it has given rise to so many hypotheses: the fleur-de-lis is really a flower, bringing us back to the floral symbols we recalled just now (the natural lily, moreover, has six petals), or it may have been originally a spearhead, or a bird, or a bee, the ancient Chaldean symbol of royalty (the hieroglyphic *sār*), or even a toad,[8] or, as is more

6. There are two principal types of this 'wheel', one with six spokes (fig. 4) and one with eight (fig. 5), each of these numbers naturally having its raison d'être and its meaning. The Chrisme is related to the first; as for the second, it is interesting to note that it is clearly similar to the eight-petalled Hindu lotus.

7. The form of the 'wheel' is met with again in striking fashion when the same emblem is traced on the shield bearing the allegorical figure of Albion.

8. This opinion, bizarre as it may seem, must have been accepted in fairly ancient times, for in the tapestries of the fifteenth century in the Cathedral of Rheims,

probable, it results from the synthesis of several of these figures, but in all cases it nonetheless remains true that it conforms strictly to the schema we are speaking of.

One of the reasons for this particularity must be found in the importance of the meanings attached to the number 6, for the figure we envisage is really none other than one of the geometrical symbols corresponding to this number. If its ends are joined two by two (fig. 7) we obtain another well-known senary symbol, the

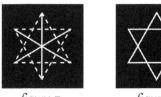

| *figure 7* | *figure 8* | *figure 9* |

double triangle (fig. 8), to which the name 'seal of Solomon' is most often given.[9] This figure is frequently used among Jews and Arabs, but it is also a Christian emblem. As Charbonneau-Lassay pointed out to us, it was even one of the ancient symbols of Christ, as was also another equivalent figure, the six branched star (fig. 9), which is basically only a variation of it, as is of course the Chrisme itself—which is another reason for establishing a close relation between these signs. Among other things, medieval Christian Hermeticism saw in the two opposing and interlinked triangles, of which one is the reflection or inverted image of the other, a representation of the union of the divine and human natures, in the person of Christ; and the number 6 includes among its meanings those of union and of mediation, which perfectly fit the Word incarnate. Moreover, according to the Hebrew Kabbalah this same number is the number of creation (the work of the six days), and in this connection the attribution of its symbol to the Word is no less well justified: it acts

---

Clovis' standard bears three toads. — It is moreover very possible that originally this toad may in fact have been a frog, ancient symbol of resurrection.

9. This figure is sometimes called 'David's shield', or again, 'Michael's shield'; the last designation could give rise to some very interesting considerations.

as a sort of graphic translation of the *per quem omnia facta sunt* of the Credo.[10]

Now what is particularly to be noted from our present point of view is that the double triangle was chosen in the sixteenth century, or perhaps even earlier, as an emblem and rallying-sign by certain guilds; especially in Germany it even became the ordinary sign of taverns or cafes where the said guilds held their meetings.[11] It was in a way a common general mark, whereas the more or less complex figures in which the 'quatre de chiffre' appeared were personal marks, particular to each master; but is it not logical to suppose that between the latter and the former there should be a certain kinship, the very same kinship we have just shown to exist between the Chrisme and the double triangle?

At first glance, the Constantinian Chrisme (Fig. 10), formed by the union of two Greek letters, 'X' and 'P', the first two letters of *Christos*, appears to be derived directly from the simple Chrisme, of which it preserves precisely the fundamental arrangement, and from which it differs only by the addition to its upper part of a loop meant to transform the 'I' into a 'P'. Now, if we consider the 'quatre de chiffre' in its simplest and most common forms, its similarity— we could even say its identity—with the Constantinian Chrisme, is

figure 10   figure 11   figure 12

altogether undeniable, and it is especially striking when the numeral 4, or the sign which assumes its form and can at the same

10. In China, six lines differently arranged similarly constitute a symbol of the Word; they also represent the middle term of the Great Triad, that is, the Mediator between Heaven and Earth, uniting in it the two natures, celestial and terrestrial.

11. In this respect, we note in passing a curious and scarcely known fact: the legend of Faust, which dates from approximately the same period, constituted the ritual of the printers' initiation.

time be seen as a distortion of the 'P', is turned to the right (Fig. 11) instead of to the left (fig. 12), for we meet with these two directions randomly.[12] Moreover, here we see the appearance of a second symbolic element that did not exist in the Constantinian Chrisme: we mean a cruciform sign introduced quite naturally by the transformation of the 'P' into a 4. Often the sign is emphasized by the addition of a supplementary line, either horizontal (fig. 13), or vertical (fig. 14), that constitutes a sort of doubling of the cross, as is seen on the two figures below taken from Deonna.[13] And note that in the second of these figures the entire lower part of the Chrisme has disappeared and been replaced by a personal monogram, just as elsewhere it is replaced by various other symbols. This is perhaps what caused doubts concerning the identity of the sign that remains constant throughout all these changes. We hold that the marks containing the complete Chrisme represent the original form, whereas the

figure 13

figure 14

others are later modifications in which the retained part was taken for the whole, probably without the meaning ever having been entirely lost from sight. However, it seems that in certain cases the cruciform element of the symbol then passed to the foreground; at least that is what seems to result from the association of the 'quatre de chiffre' with other signs, and this is the point we must now consider.

12. The figure 12 is given by Deonna with this caption: 'Marque Zachariæ Palthenii, imprimeur, Francfort, 1599.'

13. Figure 13, 'Mark with the date 1540, Geneva: doubtless Jacques Bernard, first reformed pastor of Satigny.' Figure 14: 'Marque de l'imprimeur Carolus Morellus, Paris, 1631.'

Among the signs in question, one appears in the mark on a six-teenth-century tapestry preserved in the Chartres Museum (fig. 15), and its nature leaves us no room for doubt, for it is obviously a scarcely modified form of the 'globe of the World' (fig. 16), a symbol formed from the Hermetic sign of the mineral kingdom sur-mounted by a cross. Here, the 'quatre de chiffre' has purely and sim-ply taken the place of the cross.[14] This 'globe of the World' is essentially a sign of power, power at once temporal and spiritual, for if it is one of the distinguishing marks of imperial dignity, it is also constantly found placed Christ's hand, and that not only in repre-sentations evoking more particularly the divine Majesty, like those of the Last Judgment, but even in figures of the Christ Child. Thus, when that sign replaces the Chrisme (and here we should recall the link originally uniting the Chrisme to the 'wheel', another symbol of

figure 15   *figure 16*

the World) we can say in sum that it is still one more attribute of Christ that has been substituted for another. At the same time, the idea of 'mastery' is now directly attached to this new attribute, as in the sign of Jupiter (which the upper part of the symbol calls to mind especially in such cases), but without for all that losing its cruciform value; and the comparison of the two figures above does not permit the slightest hesitation in this regard.

We finally come then to the group of marks that directly moti-vated this study. The essential difference between these marks and the one just discussed is that the globe is replaced by a heart. It is curious that these two types appear closely linked to one another,

14. We have also seen this sign of the 'Globe of the World' in several printers' marks from the beginning of the sixteenth century.

for in some (figs. 17 & 18) the heart is divided by lines disposed in precisely the same way as those that characterize the 'Globe of the World'.[15]

figure 17   *figure 18*

Does this not indicate a sort of equivalence, at least in a certain respect, and would this not already be enough to suggest that here it is a question of the 'Heart of the World'? In other examples the straight lines drawn within the heart are replaced by curved lines seeming to outline the auricles and enclose the initials (figs. 19 & 20). But these marks seem more recent than the preceding ones,[16] so that it is probably a case of a rather late modification meant perhaps to give to the figure a less geometrical and more ornamental appearance. Finally, there exist more complicated variations where the principal symbol is accompanied by secondary signs that obviously do not change the meaning; and even in the one we reproduce (fig. 21), we may be permitted to think that the stars only mark more clearly the celestial character that it is appropriate to see

figure 19   *figure 20*   *figure 21*

15. Figure 17: 'Tapestry mark of the sixteenth century, Chartres Museum.' Figure 18: 'Master's mark of Samuel de Tournes, on a pewter tankard of Pierre Royaume, Geneva, 1609.'

16. Figure 19: 'Mark of Jacques Eynard, Genoise merchant, on a stained-glass window of the seventeenth century.' Figure 20: 'Master's mark of Jacques Morel, on a pewter plate, Geneva, 1719.'

in it.[17] By this we mean that in our opinion we should see the Heart of Christ in all these figures, and we think it hardly possible to see anything else therein, since this heart is surmounted by a cross, and even in the case of those before us, by a cross doubled by the addition of a horizontal line to the number 4.

Let us digress a moment to point out another curious parallel: the schematization of these figures gives a known Hermetic symbol (fig. 22), which is none other that the reversed position of alchemical sulphur (fig. 23).

figure 22

figure 23

We find here the inverted triangle, whose equivalence with the heart and the cup we have already noted. Isolated, this triangle is the alchemical sign of water, whereas the upright triangle with point directed upward, is that of fire. Now, among the different meanings ascribed to water in the most diverse traditions, the one that is of particular interest here is that of Grace and the regeneration effected by it in the one who receives it. Let us recall in this respect baptismal water, the four fountains of fresh water of the Terrestrial Paradise, and also the water escaping from the Heart of Christ, inexhaustible source of Grace. Finally, and this also corroborates this explanation, the reversal of the symbol of sulphur signifies the descent of spiritual influence into the 'world below', that is, into the terrestrial human world; it is in other words the 'celestial dew' of which we have already spoken.[18] These are the Hermetic emblems

17. Figure 21: 'Master's mark of Pierre Royaume, on pewter plate, Geneva, 1609.'

18. Figure 24, which is the same Hermetic symbol together with initials, comes from a Genevan funerary slab (lapidary collections no. 573). Figure 25, which is a modification of it, is mentioned in these words by Deonna: 'Keystone of a house in Molard, Geneva, demolished in 1889, mark of Jean du Villard, with the date 1576.'

we alluded to, and it must be admitted that their true meaning is very far from the falsified interpretations certain contemporary sects claim to give them!

figure 24   *figure 25*

That said, let us return to our guild marks in order to formulate in a few words the conclusions that seem to us to emerge most clearly from all that we have just set forth. In the first place, we think we have sufficiently established that it is indeed the Chrisme that constitutes the fundamental type from which these marks have issued, and from which, consequently, they draw their principal meaning. In the second place, when in certain of these marks the heart takes the place of the Chrisme and of other symbols undeniably connected directly to Christ, do we not have the right to assert plainly that this heart is indeed the Heart of Christ? And then, as we have already pointed out earlier, the fact that this same heart is surmounted by a cross, or by a sign certainly equivalent to the cross, or better yet by both joined together, that fact, we say, supports this assertion as solidly as can be, for we do not see how any other hypothesis could furnish a plausible explanation for it could be furnished. Finally, is not the idea of inscribing one's name in the form of initials or a monogram in the very heart of Christ an idea worthy of the piety of Christians of bygone days?[19]

We close our study on this final thought, contenting ourselves this time with having, by clarifying some points of interest on religious

19. We should note that most of the marks reproduced here and which we borrowed from Deonna, are from Geneva, and must have belonged to Protestants; but this should not be too surprising if we remember that Cromwell's chaplain, Thomas Goodwin, dedicated a book to the devotion to the Heart of Christ. We should be pleased to see Protestants thus provide their testimony in favor of the cult of the Sacred Heart.

symbolism in general, brought to the ancient iconography of the Sacred Heart a contribution that came to us from a somewhat unexpected source, and hoping only that among our readers are some who may complete it by indicating other documents of the same kind, for quite a considerable number must certainly exist here and there, and it would suffice to gather them and bring them together to form a collection of truly impressive testimonies.[20]

20. It would be particularly interesting to ascertain whether the heart is sometimes found in the marks of master masons and stone-carvers seen on many ancient monuments, notably religious monuments. Deonna reproduces a few stone-carvers' marks taken from St Peter's Cathedral in Geneva, among which are inverted triangles, some accompanied by a cross placed below or on the inside; it is therefore not improbable that the heart may also have figured among the emblems in use in that guild.

14

CORPORATE SIGNS AND THEIR ORIGINAL MEANING

SINCE OUR ARTICLE on ancient corporate marks[1] seems to have been or particular interest to a number of readers, we now return to this too little known subject to offer further information, the reflections submitted to us from various quarters having shown us the utility thereof.

First of all, our concluding remarks regarding the marks of masons and stone-cutters, and the Hermetic symbols to which they seem directly attached have been confirmed. The particulars in question are found in an article on the Compagnonnage, which by a curious coincidence was published at exactly the same time as our article. The following passage has been extracted from it:

> Having reached its apogee, Christianity required a style epitomizing its thought, and for the dome, the plain arch, and the massive tower, substituted the slender spire and the Gothic arch, which underwent rapid development. It was at this time that the popes created the University of the Arts in Rome, where monasteries of all countries sent their students and their lay builders. These elites thus founded the universal Mastership, where stone-cutters, sculptors, carpenters, and other artistic crafts received the architectural concept they called the Great

1. This article first appeared in *Regnabit*, November 1925; it is chapter 13 in the present volume. ED.

Work. The gathering of all the foreign Masters of Works formed the symbolic association, and the trowel surmounted by a cross from the arms of which the square and compasses were suspended, the universal marks.[2]

The trowel surmounted by the cross is precisely the Hermetic symbol reproduced in figure 22 (p83); and because of its triangular shape, the trowel was taken for an emblem of the Trinity: *Sanctissima Trinitas Conditor Mundi*.[3] Moreover, it seems that the Trinitarian dogma may have been particularly emphasized by the ancient guilds, most of their documents commencing with the formula: 'In the name of the Very Holy and Indivisible Trinity.'

Since we have already pointed to the symbolic identity of the inverted triangle and the heart,[4] it is relevant to add that a Trinitarian meaning can also be attached to this latter. We find proof of this in an engraving made by Callot for a thesis submitted in 1625, of which Fr Anizan has already provided an explanation in this journal (December 1922). At the top of the composition is the heart of Christ, containing three *iods*, the first letter of the name *Jehovah* in Hebrew; moreover, these three *iods* were themselves considered as to form a divine name, which is quite naturally regarded as an expression of the Trinity.[5] 'In this connection,' wrote Fr Anizan,

> we today adore the Heart of Jesus, son of the Eternal *Father*; the Heart of Jesus unites substantially with the *Word* of God; the Heart of Jesus formed by the *Holy Spirit* in the womb of the Virgin Mary. How can we be surprised that since 1625 the noble connection of the Heart of Jesus with the Holy Trinity has been

2. Auguste Bonvous, 'La Religion de l'Art', in *Le Voile d'Isis, numéro spécial consacré au Compagnonnage*, November 1925.

3. The word *Conditor* includes an allusion to the symbolism of the 'corner stone' — The end of the same article includes a reproduction of a curious figure of the Trinity, wherein the inverse triangle holds a place of importance.

4. See *Symbols of Sacred Science*, chaps. 30, 31, and 72. ED.

5. The three *iods* placed in the Heart of Christ are arranged 2 by 1 in such a way that they correspond to the three apexes of an inverted triangle. It can be noted that this same arrangement is quite common in coats-of-arms, and more especially that of the three *fleur-de-lis* of the kings of France.

affirmed? From the twelfth century, theologians have seen this Heart as the 'Holy of the Holy' and as the 'Ark of the Testament'.[6] This truth cannot be lost: its very expression carries the support of the spirit. It is never lost. In a *Diurnal* which appeared in Anvers in 1616, one reads this beautiful prayer: 'O so sweet Heart of Jesus, where everything good is found, *organ of the ever adorable Trinity*, in you I confide, in you I recover myself completely.' The 'Organ of the Most Holy Trinity' is here right before our eyes: it is the Heart of the three *iods*. And our engraving says, in short, that this Heart of Christ, organ of the Trinity, is the 'principle of order': *Prædestinatio Christi est ordinis origo*.

No doubt we shall have occasion to return to other aspects of this symbolism, especially the mystical signification of the letter *iod*, but we are anxious to mention here forthwith the following significant comparisons.

∴

SEVERAL PEOPLE who support our intention to restore to ancient symbols their original meaning and who have genuinely wanted us to do so, have at the same time expressed a desire to see Catholicism plainly claim all the symbols that rightfully belong to it, including those such as triangles, that were appropriated by organizations such as Masonry. The idea is quite sound and corresponds well to our thinking; but an ambiguity and even a real historical error may exist in some minds and it would be well to dissipate this.

In truth, not many symbols are properly and exclusively 'Masonic', as we have already pointed out concerning the acacia (December 1925, p26). Even the more particularly 'architectural' emblems, such as the square and compasses, have been common to

---

6. These assimilations have a rather close connection with the question of 'spiritual centers', which we discussed in our study on the Holy Grail [see *Insights into Christian Esoterism*, chap. 8, and *Symbols of Sacred Science*, chap. 4]; this point will be clearer when we come to point out the symbolism of the heart in the Hebrew tradition.

a great many guilds, we could even say to nearly all of them,[7] not to mention their use in purely Hermetic symbolism.[8] Masonry employs symbols which, in appearance at least, are of rather varied character, but despite what some appear to believe, it has not appropriated them in order to divert them from their true meaning; it received them, just as did the other guilds (for originally it was one of these), at a time when they were quite different from what they have become today, and it has preserved them, although it has already been quite some time since they understood them.

'Everything indicates that common Freemasonry is a detached and perhaps corrupted branch of an ancient and respectable stem,' said Joseph de Maistre.[9] And the question should be regarded in this way, for we are too often wrong in thinking only of *modern* Masonry, forgetting that it is simply the product of a deviation. It seems that those first responsible for this deviation were the Protestant pastors Anderson and Desaguliers, who drew up the Constitution of the Grand Lodge of England, published in 1723 and disposed of all the ancient documents on which they were able to lay their hands so that their innovations might pass unnoticed, and also because these documents contained formulas which they thought troublesome, such as the obligation of 'devotion to God, *to the Holy Church,* and to the King,' an incontestable mark of the Catholic origin of Masonry.[10] The Protestants prepared this work of distortion by making the most of the fifteen years that elapsed between the death of Christopher Wren, last Grand-Master of *ancient* Masonry, and the foundation of the new Grand Lodge of England in 1717. However, they retained the symbolism, not suspecting that, for

7. The Compagnonnage forbids only cobblers and bakers to carry the compasses.

8. Thus at least from the start of the seventeenth century, the square and the compasses appear, in the hands of the Hermetic *Rebis* (see for example *Douze Clefs d'Alchemie,* by Basil Valentine).

9. *Mémoire au duc de Brunswick* (1782).

10. *Scottish* Masonry was an attempt during the course of the eighteenth century to return to the Catholic tradition, represented by the Stuart dynasty, in opposition to *English* Masonry, which had become Protestant and was dedicated to the House of Orange.

whomever understood it, the latter would bear witness against them as eloquently as would the written texts, not all of which moreover they were able to destroy. This, in brief, is what should know by everyone who wishes to effectively combat the tendencies of present-day Masonry.[11]

We have not dealt here with the whole complex and controversial question of the multiple origins of Masonry, but have confined ourselves to considering what can be called the corporate side represented by *operative* Masonry, that is to say by the ancient brotherhoods of builders. These latter, like the other guilds, had a religious symbolism, or if one prefers, a hermetico-religious symbolism, related to the conceptions of the Catholic esoterism that was so widespread in the Middle Ages, and of which traces are found everywhere on the monuments and even in the literature of that era. Despite claims by many historians, the association of Hermeticism with Masonry goes back much further than Elias Ashmole's affiliation with the latter (1646). We even think that by the seventeenth century it was a question of reconstituting a tradition of which a great part was already lost. A few, who seem well informed on the history of the guilds, even fixed 1459 as the date for this loss of the ancient tradition.[12] It seems incontestable to us that the *operative* and *speculative* aspects were always united in medieval guilds, which moreover used expressions as patently Hermetic as the 'Great Work', in ways that were different but always related by analogical correspondence.[13]

If we truly wished to get to the origins, supposing this were even possible on the basis of the necessarily fragmentary information at

11. In Latin countries another deviation occurred later on, this one anti-religious; but we should first emphasize the 'protestantization' of Anglo-Saxon Masonry that it is fitting to insist in the first place.

12. Albert Bernet, 'Des Labyrinthes sur le sol des églises', in the number already cited of *Voile d'Isis*. This article contains a minor error: it is not at Strasbourg but at Cologne that the Masonic charter of April 1459 is dated. [See chap. 22]

13. Let us also note that around the fourteenth century if not much earlier there existed a *Massenie du Saint Graal*, through which the brotherhoods of builders were connected to their Hermetic inspirers, and in which Henri Martin (*Histoire de France*) 1, III, p398) rightly saw one of the real origins of Freemasonry.

our disposal, it would doubtless be necessary to go back beyond the Middle Ages, and even beyond Christianity. This leads us to complete something we said in this same journal in an earlier article on the symbolism of Janus (December 1925),[14] for it turns out that this latter symbolism is closely connected with the question now before us.[15] In ancient Rome the *Collegia fabrorum* rendered special worship to Janus, in whose honor they celebrated the solstitial festivals corresponding to the beginning of the ascending and descending halves of the zodiacal cycle, that is, to the two points of the year which in the astronomical symbolism we have already mentioned represent the doors of the celestial and infernal ways (*Janua Cœli* and *Janua Inferni*). The solstitial festivals were retained in the builders' guilds, but in Christianity these festivals were identified with the two St Johns, of winter and of summer (whence the expression 'Lodge of St John' still retained in modern Masonry), providing another example of the adaptation of pre-Christian symbols to which we have pointed on several occasions.

Two interesting conclusions can be drawn from the above. First, among the Romans Janus was, as we have already said, the god of initiation into the mysteries; but he was at the same time the god of the artisans' guilds, and this can be no coincidence. There must necessarily be a connection between these two functions related to the same symbolic entity; in other words, it was necessary that then, as later, the guilds in question be in possession of a truly 'initiatic' tradition. We do not believe it is a question here of a special and isolated case, but that the same could be said for many peoples, and this in turn might perhaps lead to the true origin of the arts and trades, to views quite unsuspected by moderns, for whom such traditions have become a dead letter.

14. Cf. on this subject *Symbols of Sacred Science*, chaps. 37 and 58. Ed.

15. Let us note that we had not intention of making a complete study of Janus; to have done so would have required presenting analogous symbolisms encountered among various peoples, notably that of the *Ganesha* in India, which would have expanded this essay extensively. — The figure of Janus which served as a starting-point for our note has been reproduced again in an article by Charbonneau-Lassay contained in the same number of *Regnabit* (December 1925, p15).

The other consequence is this, that preservation of the ancient tradition linked to the symbolism of Janus by the builders of the Middle Ages explains among other things the importance they attributed to the figure of the zodiac, so frequently reproduced over the portal of churches and generally arranged in such a way as to make quite apparent the ascending and descending nature of these two halves. In our opinion there must have been something quite fundamental in the conception of the cathedral builders, who proposed to make of their works a sort of synthetic resumé of the Universe. If the zodiac is not always in evidence, there are nonetheless many other symbols equivalent to it, capable in a certain sense at least of evoking analogous ideas under the aspect we are considering (without prejudice to their other more particular meanings): representations of the Last Judgment are an example, and certain emblematic trees as well, as we have explained. We could go further still and say that in a way this conception is implied in the very layout of the cathedral; but we would far exceed the limits of this simple observation were we to undertake to justify this last assertion.[16]

16. We are anxious to set to rights an inaccuracy that found its way into a note to our article devoted to guild marks (November 1925, p395), and that Provençal friends have obligingly pointed out. The star that figures in the arms of Provence does not have eight rays but only seven; it is therefore attached to a series of symbols (the figures of the septenary) different from those we mentioned. But on the other hand Provence also has the star of Les Baux, which has sixteen, or two times eight, rays; and the latter even has a rather particular symbolic importance, marked by the legendary origin attributed to it, for the ancient lords of Les Baux are said to be descended from the Magi-King Balthasar.

15

THE ENIGMA OF
MARTINES DE PASQUALLY

THE HISTORY OF INITIATIC ORGANIZATIONS is often very difficult to penetrate, something easily enough understood by the very nature of what is involved, for too many elements necessarily escape the means of investigation at the disposal of ordinary historians. To see the truth of this we need not even go back very far in time, for it is sufficient to consider the eighteenth century, where we find, still coexisting with manifestations of what is most profane and most anti-traditional in the modern mentality, what really seem to be the last vestiges of various initiatic currents that formerly existed in the Western world, and characters no less enigmatic than the organizations to which they belonged or which they inspired. One such character is Martines de Pasqually, and in response to recent works concerning him and his Order of the Elect Cohens published by R. Le Forestier and P. Vulliaud, we have already remarked on how many points of his biography remain obscure in spite of all the documents now published.[1] Gérard van Rijnberk has just brought out another book on this subject,[2] which likewise contains interesting documentation largely unpublished hitherto; but in spite of this it must be said that this book perhaps raises more questions than it answers.[3]

1. *Un nouveau livre sur l'Ordre des Elect Cohens* (December 1929 issue); *A propos des 'Rose-Croix' lyonnais'* (January 1930 issue).

2. *Un thaumaturge au XVIII siècle: Martines de Pasqually, sa vie, son oeuvre, son Ordre* (Paris: Félix Alcan).

3. Let us note in passing a minor error: in speaking of his predecessors, van Rijnberk attributes to René Philipon the historical notices signed 'A Knight of the

The author begins by pointing to the uncertainty surrounding the name Martines itself, and he lists the many variants found in the relevant writings. But it is also true that too much importance should not be attached to such differences, for in the eighteenth century the spelling of proper names was hardly respected. But he adds:

> As for the man himself, who would have known better than any-one the exact spelling of his own name or of his pseudonym as chief initiator, he always signed himself Don Martines de Pas-qually (only once: de Pascally de La Tour). In the only known authentic public records—his son's baptismal certificate—his name is given as Jaques Delivon Joacin Latour de la Case, don Martinets de Pasqually.

It is not correct that the record in question, which was published by Papus,[4] is 'the only authentic public record,' for two others, which have no doubt escaped van Rijnberk's attention, have been published here in this very journal: Martines' marriage certificate[5] and the 'certificate of Catholicity' issued at the time of his departure for San Domingo. The first bears the names 'Jaque Delyoron Joachin Latour De la Case and Suzanne Dumas de Rainau',[6] and the second bears simply 'Jacques Pasqually de Latour'; as for the signature of Martines himself, on the first it is 'Don Martines Depasqually', and on the second 'Depasqually de la Tour'. The fact that on the marriage certificate gives his father simply as 'Delatour de la Case' (the

---

Rose Croissante' which serve as preface to the editions of the *Traité de la Réintegra-tion des Êtres de Martines de Pasqually* and *Des Enseignements secrets de Martines de Pasqually* of Franz von Baader published in the *Bibliothèque Rosicucienne*. Aston-ished at this assertion, we posed the question to Philipon himself; he replied that he has only translated von Baader's pamphlet, and that, as we thought, the two notices in question are in fact by Albéric Thomas.

4. *Martines de Pasqually*, pp 10–11.

5. *Le marriage de Martines de Pasqually* (January 1930 issue).

6. It will be noted that here it is Delyoron, whereas the baptismal certificate gives Delivon (or perhaps Delivron); this name, inserted between two first names, does not seem to be a family name. On the other hand, there is hardly need to recall that the separation of the particles (which do not necessarily constitute a sign of nobility) was at the time quite optional.

same moreover as his son in the baptismal certificate, although a marginal note calls him 'de Pasqually', no doubt because this name was better known) seems to support van Rijnberk's opinion that 'one is tempted to conclude that his true name was La Case, or Las Cases, and that 'Martines de Pasqually' was only a hieronym.

But this name La Case or Las Cases, which may be a gallicized form of the Spanish name Las Casas, raises yet further questions. First of all, it should be noted that the second successor to Martines as 'Grand Sovereign' of the Order of the Elect Cohens (the first having been Caignet de Lestère) was called Sébastien de Las Casas; was there some relationship between him and Martines? The thing is not impossible, for he was from San Domingo, and Martines had returned to the island to collect an inheritance, which may lead one to suppose that part of his family was established there.[7] But there is something stranger still: in his *Crocodile*, L.-Cl. de Saint Martin produces a 'Spanish Jew' named Eléazar, to whom he clearly attributes many traits of his old master Martines. Here is how this Eléazar explains what obliged him to leave Spain and take refuge in France:

I had a Christian friend in Madrid belonging to the family of Las Casas, to which, although indirectly, I am under the greatest obligation. After some prosperity in commerce he was ruined suddenly by bankruptcy. I straightaway flew to him, to sympathize with his grief and offer what few resources my meagre fortune put at my disposal; but as these resources proved insufficient to restore his business, I yielded to my friendship for him, allowing it to lead me so far astray as to make use of certain means by which I soon uncovered the fraud of his exploiters and even the place where they had hidden the riches of which they had despoiled him. Through these same means I procured for

7. It is true that his wife's parents were also at San Domingo, so that it is possible the inheritance came from this side; however, the letter published by Papus (*Martines de Pasqually*, p58), although not entirely clear, is much more in favor of the other hypothesis, for it does not appear that his two step-brothers, who were from San Domingo, had had any interest in the 'donation' that had been made to him.

him the capacity to recover all his treasures, without those who had robbed him ever suspecting who had divested them in their turn. I was no doubt wrong to make use of these means for such a purpose, since they must only be applied to the administration of things that hold no truck with the riches of this world; and I was punished for it. My friend, instructed in a timid and nervous faith, suspected witchcraft in what I had done for him, and his pious zeal took away his gratitude, just as my obliging zeal had got the upper hand on me; he denounced me to his church as both a sorcerer and a Jew. The inquisitors were immediately informed; I was condemned to the fire even before an arrest, but as they set about my pursuit, I was warned by this same particular means of the fate hanging over me, and I took refuge in your country without delay.[8]

Doubtless, the *Crocodile* includes many purely fanciful things, in which it would be difficult to see precise allusions to real events and people, but it is nonetheless most unlikely that the name Las Casas is mere coincidence. This is why we thought it interesting to reproduce the entire passage despite its length. Just what links could there have been between the Jew Eléazar, who so resembles Martines through the 'powers' and the doctrine attributed to him, and the family Las Casas, and what could have been the nature of the 'great obligations' he had to them? For the moment, we only formulate these questions, without claiming to provide any answers; we shall see whether the following allows us to envisage a more or less plausible one.[9]

Let us pass on to other points of Martines' biography no less full of surprises. Van Rijnberk says that 'the year and place of his birth are completely unknown,' but points out that Willermoz wrote to

---

8. *Le Crocodile*, canto 23.

9. Another bizarre link: Saint-Martin describes Las Casas, the friend of the Jew Eléazar, as having been deprived of his wealth. Martines, in the letter that we have already mentioned, says: 'In that region [that is to say in San Domingo] I have been given a gift of a large estate that I take back from the hands of a man who keeps it unjustly'; and it is found that this letter was written under Martines' dictation by Saint-Martin himself.

the baron of Turkheim that Martines died 'advanced in age,' adding that

> At the time Willermoz wrote this he was 91 years old himself, and as men generally tend to evaluate the age of others according to a measure that grows with their own years, one does not doubt that the advanced age attributed to Martines by the nonagenarian Willermoz could hardly be less than 70 years. Since Martines died in 1774, he must have been born in the first decade of the eighteenth century, at the earliest.

Also, he inclines to favor the hypothesis of Gustave Bord, who suggests that Martines was born between 1710 and 1715; but even the earlier date would have him dying at age 64, which is certainly not an 'advanced' age, especially in comparison with that of Willermoz... And then, unfortunately, one of the documents, which appears to have been unknown to van Rijnberk, formally precludes this hypothesis: the 'certificate of Catholicity' was issued in 1772 to 'Jacques Pasqually de Latour, squire, born at Grenoble, aged 45 years,' from which by rights it should be concluded that he was born around 1727, so that when he dies at San Domingo two years later, in 1774, he could only have reached the hardly 'advanced' age of 47 years!

This same document confirms moreover that Martines was born at Grenoble, as many had already said, contrary to van Rijnberk's opinion. And this is clearly not contrary to his being of Spanish origin, since among all the origins ascribed to him, most evidence seems to support the latter, including of course the very name Las Casas; but if so, it should be admitted that his father was already established in France before his birth, and that he may even have been married in France. This is confirmed moreover in Martines' marriage certificate, for his mother's name as shown, 'Suzanne Dumas de Rainau', can it seems hardly be anything but a French name, whereas 'Delatour de la Case' could merely be gallicized. In sum, the only serious reason we can have to doubt that Martines was born in France (for we can hardly credit the contradictory assertions of some others, all of which are no more than suppositions), are the peculiarities of language found in his writings; but this fact might be explained well enough partly by an education received from a Spanish father, and partly also by his sojourns in various countries, a point to which we shall return later.

By a curious coincidence that hardly simplifies matters, it seems that during the same period there was an established family in Grenoble whose name really was Pascalis; but judging by the names on the various certificates we have mentioned, Martines must have been completely foreign. Perhaps this was the family of the coach-builder Martin Pascalis, also known as Martin Pascal or even Pascal Martin (this not being very well settled either), that is, if the latter was truly a separate person and not simply Martines himself, who at a certain moment had to ply this trade for a living, for apparently his financial situation was never very successful. Here, yet again, is something that seems never to have been satisfactorily clarified.

Moreover, many have thought that Martines was Jewish; he certainly was not as to religion, since it is super-abundantly proved that he was Catholic; but it is true as van Rijnberk says that 'this does not prejudge in any way the question of race.' In Martines' life there are in fact clues that might lead one to suppose he was of Jewish origin, but they are inconclusive and could just as well be accounted for by affinities of a quite different kind than racial identity. Franz von Baader says that Martines was 'at the same time Jewish and Christian'. Does this not recall the relations of the Jew Eléazar with the Christian family of Las Casas? But the very fact of presenting Eléazar as a 'Spanish Jew', could very well be an allusion, not to Martines' personal origin, but to the origin of his doctrine, in which Judaic elements do indeed predominate incontestably.

Be that as it may, a certain number of inconsistencies and contradictions always remain in Martines' biography, the most striking no doubt being his age; but van Rijnberk may point to the solution without even suspecting it when he suggests that 'Martines de Pasqually' was a 'hieronym', that is to say an initiatic name. Indeed, what is to keep this same 'hieronym' from serving several different individualities, as occurs in similar cases? And it may even be that the 'great obligations' that the person whom Saint-Martin calls the Jew Eléazar owed to the family of Las Casas were, not due to what the family had in one way or another furnished as a kind of 'cover' to his initiatic activity? It would doubtless be imprudent to try to be specific on this point, but we shall see whether what can be known of the origin of Martines' knowledge might not yet be able to contribute some further solutions.

The same letter of July 1821 in which Willermoz affirms that Martines died 'advanced in age,' contains another remarkable passage, according to which initiation would have been transmitted to Martines by his father himself:

> In his Ministry he had succeeded his father, a wise and distinguished man more prudent than his son, having little wealth and living in Spain. He had placed his still young son Martines with the Walloon guards, where a quarrel led to a duel in which his adversary was killed; he had to flee promptly, and the father lost no time in consecrating his successor before his departure. After a long absence, the father, feeling his end approaching, immediately summoned his son back and gave him the final ordinations.

In truth, this story of the Walloon guards, for which by the way it has been impossible to find any confirmation, seems rather suspect, especially if as van Rijnberk says it must 'imply that Martines was born in Spain,' which, however, is not absolutely clear; moreover, it is not a question here of something Willermoz witnessed directly, for he states later that he 'had known the son only in 1767 in Paris, a long time after the death of the father.'[10] Leaving this secondary question aside, there remains the assertion that Martines received from his father not only the initiation but also the transmission of

---

10. 1767 is the year of Martines' marriage; it is therefore likely that the two brothers living in San Domingo, for whom he says he has come to Paris to solicit the cross of Saint-Louis, are indeed none other than the two 'extremely rich' step-brothers mentioned, as we have already said, in the letter of the 17th and 30th of April 1772 cited by Papus (*Martines de Pasqually*, p58). This is again confirmed by the fact that in another letter of November 1, 1771, we find this sentence: 'I am letting you know that I have finally obtained the cross of Saint-Louis from my step-brother' (ibid., p55). It had not therefore been obtained directly in 1767, at least from one of them, contrary to the statement of Willermoz, whose memory undoubtedly deceived him on this point. It is astonishing that it did not occur to van Rijnberk to draw these parallels, which seem to us to explain sufficiently this quite secondary question.

certain initiatic functions, for the word 'ministry' can hardly be interpreted otherwise; and in this connection van Rijnberk calls attention to a letter written in 1779 by the Mason Falcke, in which we read that

> Martinez Pascalis, a Spaniard, claims to possess secret knowledge as an inheritance from his family, which resides in Spain and has purportedly possessed it for three hundred years; they are said to have acquired it from the Inquisition, with which his ancestors served.

This is all very improbable, for we cannot really see what initiatic repository the Inquisition could have ever have possessed and communicated. But let us recall that in the passage cited from the *Crocodile* it is Las Casas who denounces his friend the Jew Eléazar to the Inquisition, precisely because of the latter's secret knowledge; could we not say that there is something that which has been deliberately confused?[11]

At this point we might well ask whether when Martines, or the person Willermoz knew under this name around 1767, speaks of his father, this should be understood literally or whether it is not rather more particularly a question of his 'spiritual father'. Who could the latter have been? Indeed, we can very well speak of initiatic 'filiation', and this obviously does not necessarily coincide with filiation in the ordinary sense of the word; we could perhaps again recall the duality of Las Casas and the Jew Eléazar… It should be said however that an hereditary initiatic transmission, implying in addition the exercise of a certain function, would not represent an altogether exceptional case; but in the absence of sufficient information it is very difficult to decide if this was really case with Martines. At most we could find an affirmative indication in certain particulars concerning Martines' succession: immediately after his baptism, Martine have his eldest son the first consecration in the hierarchy of the Elect Cohens, which makes one think he intended him to become

---

11. Let us again point to an oddity, from which we do not intend to draw any inference here: Falcke speaks of Martines in the present tense, although at the time he already must have been dead for five years.

his successor. This son disappeared at the time of the Revolution, and Willermoz says he could not ascertain what became of him; as for the second son, there is something still more remarkable, for we know the date of his birth, but he was never mentioned subsequently. In any case, when Martines died in 1774, the eldest son was certainly alive; however he did not succeed him as 'Grand Sovereign', for it was Caignet de Lestère who did so, and then, when the latter died in turn in 1778, Sébastien de Las Casas succeeded him. In view of this, what becomes of the idea of a hereditary transmission? The fact that the son was too young to fulfill these functions (he was only six years old) should not be put forward, for Martines could very well have designated a proxy until his majority, and this has never been suggested. On the other hand, what remains curious is that there really seems to have been some relationship between Martines and his two successors: indeed, he speaks in a letter of 'his cousin Cagnet,' who, taking into account the spelling variations customary at the time, must be the same as Caignet de Lestère;[12] and as for Sébastien Las Casas, we have already pointed out that such a relationship was suggested by his very name; but in any case, this transmission to more or less distant relatives, even when a direct heir existed, can hardly be equated with the 'dynastic succession' of which van Rijnberk speaks, and to which he even attributes 'a certain esoteric importance' that we cannot very well understand.

That Martines was initiated by his father or by someone else is not the essential question, for it does not throw much light on the real issue: from what tradition does this initiation derive? Martines' probable travels before his initiatic activity began in France might throw some light on this point, but here again we unfortunately have only quite vague and doubtful information, and even the assertion that he went to the East does not mean anything really definite, since what is often meant in such cases is only a legendary, or rather, symbolic journey. On this subject, van Rijnberk believes

---

12. 'I inform you again that I have handed over the constitutive patents to my cousin Cagnet' (letter of November 1, 1771, cited by Papus, *Martines de Pasqually*, p 56).

he is supported by a passage from the *Traité de la Réintegration des Êtres*, where Martines seems to say that he went to China, whereas nothing is said of countries much closer. But this journey, if it really took place, is perhaps of the least interest from our present point of view, for it is clear that neither in Martines' teachings nor in his ritual 'operations' is there anything that suggests the slightest direct link with the tradition of the Far East. In a letter from Martines we do however find this rather remarkable statement: 'My state and my quality of true man have always kept me in the position where I am';[13] it appears that no one has ever noticed this expression 'true man', which is specifically Taoist, but which is doubtless the only one of this kind to be found in Martines.[14]

In any event, if Martines was born around 1727, his travels could not have lasted for so many years, even if there were no reason to subtract the time of his supposed period with the Walloon guards, for his known initiatic activity begins in 1754, and by that time he would have been only 27 years old.[15] We readily admit that he must have gone to Spain, especially if his family origins were there, and perhaps also to Italy; this is very plausible in fact, and some of the most striking singularities of his language are owed to his stay in these two countries; but apart from explaining this wholly external detail, this does not get us very far, for at the time what could really remain in these countries from the initiatic point of view? We must certainly look elsewhere, and in our opinion the most accurate indication of this is that given in the following passage from a note of Prince Christian of Hesse-Darmstadt: 'Pasquali claimed that this knowledge came from the East, but it is to be presumed that he had received it from Africa,' by which must be understood in all probability the Sephardic Jews, who were established in North Africa after

---

13. Extract published by Papus, *Martines de Pasqually*, p124.

14. It should not be thought that when speaking of China, Martines should always be taken literally, for as Le Forestier has pointed out, he uses the word 'Chinese' as a kind of anagram for 'Noachites'.

15. This, of course, with the reservation that the journeys in question, instead of being wholly attributed to this one personage, should perhaps be attributed in part to his initiator.

their expulsion from Spain.[16] This would explain many things: first, the predominance of Judaic elements in Martines' doctrine; then, the relations he seemed also to have had with the Sephardic Jews of Bordeaux, as we remarked earlier in the presentation of Eléazar as a 'Spanish Jew' by Saint-Martin; and finally, the necessity, in order for an initiatic work to be accomplished in a non- Jewish milieu, to 'graft' as it were the doctrine received from this source onto an initiatic form widespread in the Western world, which in the eighteenth century could only be Masonry.

The last point raises still more questions to which we shall return, but let us first note that Martines never mentions the exact origins of his knowledge, or only links them vaguely to the 'East', is perfectly understandable: from the moment he could transmit such an initiation as he himself had received, he did not need to indicate its provenance, which would have been more or less useless. In his books he seems to have expressly alluded to his 'predecessors' only once, and that without adding any precise details and hence without asserting anything whatever of the existence of an initiatic transmission.[17] It is in any case quite certain that the form of this initiation was not that of the Order of the Elect Cohens, since it did not exist before Martines himself, and which we see gradually develop from 1754 to 1774, although he was never able to finish organizing it completely.[18]

This is the answer to the objection some have raised, that if Martines was 'commissioned' by some initiatic organization, how could it be that his Order was not fully 'preformed' from the beginning with all its rituals and its grades, and that it has in fact always remained unfixed and imperfect? Doubtless, many of the Masonic

16. The three hundred years Falck spoke of would coincide approximately with the time the Jews had been expelled from Spain; we do not wish to say however that it is necessary to attach great importance to this connection.

17. 'I have never sought to lead anyone into error, nor to deceive persons who came to me in good faith to acquire some knowledge that my predecessors transmitted to me' (cited by Papus, *Martines de Pasqually*, p122).

18. When Willermoz says that 'he had succeeded his father in his ministry,' this must not be construed—as van Rijnberk has too hastily done—as 'Sovereign Master of the Order', of which at the time there could have been no question.

systems of high grades that came to light around the same time were in the same situation, some hardly existing except 'on paper'; but there is nothing astonishing in this if these systems represented merely the particular ideas of an individual or group, whereas it seems that for the work of an authorized representative of a true initiatic organization, matters would have had to proceed quite differently. But this is to put the question rather superficially, for we must consider that Martines' 'mission' comprised precisely the work of 'adaptation' that was to result in the formation of the Order of the Elect Cohens, a task that his 'predecessors' had not had to do because for one reason or another the moment had not yet arrived; and perhaps they would not even have been able to do, as we shall see in a moment. Martines was not able to bring this work to a satisfactory conclusion, but this proves nothing against what is found at its inception. In truth, two causes seem to have contributed to his partial failure: on the one hand, it is possible that a series of unfavorable circumstances acted unremittingly as an obstacle to what he proposed, and it may also be that he himself was not up to the task despite the psychic 'powers' he evidently possessed and which would have made it easier for him, either because he possessed them in a quite natural and spontaneous way, as is sometimes the case, or more probably because he may have been specially 'prepared' to this end. Willermoz himself recognizes that 'his verbal inconsistencies and his indiscretions gave rise to reproaches and many disagreements';[19] it seems that this imprudence may have consisted particularly in making promises that he could not keep—at least not immediately—and sometimes also in too readily admitting individuals not sufficiently 'qualified'. After receiving the necessary 'preparation', he like many others doubtless had to work by himself at his own risk and peril; at least, he does not seem to have ever committed faults such that his 'mission' was withdrawn from him, since he pressed forward with his work until the very end and assured its transmission before his death.

We certainly do not think that the initiation Martines received went beyond a rather limited degree, in any case not beyond the

---

19. Letter already cited to the baron of Turkheim (July 1821).

domain of the 'lesser mysteries', or that his knowledge—though real enough—truly had the 'transcendent' character he himself seemed to have attributed to it. We dealt with this on another occasion[20] where we pointed out as characteristic traits in this respect the allure of 'ceremonial magic' that adorned his ritual 'operations' and the importance he attached to results of the purely 'phenomenal' order. This is no reason however to reduce the latter, nor with all the more reason Martines' 'powers', to the rank of mere 'metapsychical phenomena' as these are understood today; on this basis, as well as on that of modern psychological theories, van Rijnberk, who seems to be of this opinion, evidently holds very great illusions which we for out part cannot possibly share.

Moreover, we must add the particularly important observation that the very fact that the Order of the Elect Cohens was a new form prevented him from establishing a valid and regular initiation, alone and independently. For this reason he could recruit his members only from among those who already belonged to an initiatic organization, upon which latter he thus came to superpose a body of higher grades; and as we have already said above, the organization that furnished him the indispensable basis he would otherwise have lacked could only have been Masonry. Consequently, one of the conditions required by Martines' 'preparation', other than the teaching received elsewhere, must have been the acquisition of Masonic grades. This condition was quite likely lacking in his 'predecessors', which explains why the latter were unable to do what he did. From the beginning Martines presented himself as a Mason, and not otherwise, and it was 'in the interior' of the pre-existing Lodges that, as any founder of a system of high grades would have to do, he undertook with varying degrees of success to edify the 'Temples' where the most qualified members of these same Lodges would work following the rite of the Elect Cohens. On this point, at least, there can be no ambiguity: if Martines received a 'mission', it was that of founding a rite or Masonic 'regime' of high grades, in which by decking them out with the appropriate forms he could

20. *Un nouveau livre sur l'Ordre des Élus Cöens*, issue for December 1929 [see chap. 17].

introduce the teachings he had received from another initiatic source.

When we examine Martines' initiatic activity, we must never lose sight of what we have just pointed out above, that is, its double connection with Masonry and with another much more mysterious organization, the first being indispensable to the role assigned him by the second. There is furthermore something enigmatic even in his Masonic affiliation, nothing of which can be clarified (something not in the least exceptional at the time, when there was an astounding variety of rites and 'regimes'), but which in any case is before 1754, since from that time on he appears not only as a Mason, as we have just said, but also as already provided with 'Scottish' high grades.[21] This is what allowed him to undertake the constitution of his 'Temples'—with varying degrees of success depending on the case—'within' of the Lodges of various towns of the South of France until 1761, when he finally established himself at Bordeaux. We need not retrace all these documented vicissitudes, recalling only that at the time the Order of the Elect Cohens was still far from its final form; and in fact neither the list of grades, nor with greater reason the rituals, would ever be completely fixed thereafter.

From our point of view the other side of the question is the more important, and in this respect it is essential to note that Martines himself never had claimed to pose as supreme head of an initiatic hierarchy. His title of 'Grand Sovereign' does not contradict this, for the word 'Sovereign' also figures in the titles of various Masonic grades and functions without in any way implying that those who bear them are exempt from any subordination; among the Elect Cohens themselves the 'Réaux-Croix' were also qualified as 'Sovereign', and Martines was 'Grand Sovereign' or 'Sovereign of the Sovereigns' because his jurisdiction extended over all of them. The clearest proof of this is found in the following passage of a

---

21. On this subject we must however express some doubt as to the Masonic character attributed to the 'Knight of the Rose Croissante' by way of 'Squire': it is quite correct that this was the name of a Scottish grade, which has moreover survived up to our time in the Rectified Rite; but in Martines' case its mention in the official secular documents would seem rather to indicate that it was no more than a nobilary title. But it is of course true that the one does not exclude the other.

letter from Martines to Willermoz dated October 2, 1768:

> The opening of the circumferences that I performed last Septem-
> ber 12th was to open [*sic*] the operation of the prescribed equi-
> noxes so that I should not be remiss in my spiritual and temporal
> obligations. The circumferences are open until the solstices and
> are kept up by me so that I may be ready to work and pray for the
> health and peace of soul and mind of the principal chief,
> unknown to both you and your Réaux-Croix brothers, and
> regarding whom I must remain silent until he makes himself
> known. I fear no untoward event, for myself in particular or for
> any of our brothers generally, but for the Order itself in that it
> would lose a great deal if it lost such a leader. I can only speak
> allegorically to you on this subject.[22]

Thus, according to his own admission Martines was in no way the
'principal chief' of the Order of the Elect Cohens; but since in a
way we see him constitute himself as such before our eyes, it was
necessary that this leader be the one (or one of those) from the
organization to inspire this new formation; and would not the fear
Martines expressed be that the disappearance of this person might
lead to the premature interruption of certain communications?
Furthermore, it is quite clear that what he says can in any case apply
only to a living man and not to some phantasmagorical entity; the
occultists have spread so many fantastic ideas of this kind that
such a remark is not entirely superfluous.

It could perhaps still be said that here it is only a question of the
hidden leader of some Masonic organization;[23] but this hypothesis
is ruled out by another document produced by van Rijnberk, a
resumé by the baron of Turkheim of a letter Willermoz addressed to
him on March 25, 1822, of which the beginning reads:

---

22. Cited by P. Vulliaud, *Les Rose-Croix lyonnais au XVIII siècle*, p72. — We do
not know why in this connection Vulliaud speaks of 'Unknown Superiors', even saying that Martines speaks of them in this letter, whereas he has not made the least
allusion to any such designation. On the other hand, when Martines uses the word
'allegorically', it is very likely he means 'enigmatically', for there is no trace of 'alle-
gory' in all this.

As to Pasqually, he has always said that in his position as Sovereign 'Réaux' for his region, which included the whole of Europe, he could make and support successively twelve 'Réaux', who would be dependent on him and whom he would name his Equals.[24]

It follows that Martines held these 'powers', which moreover were carefully defined, from an organization that extended outside Europe (which was not the case of Masonry at this time),[25] and of which the principal seat must also have been outside, for if the latter were in Europe itself, the 'delegation' Martines received for this region would not have been able to carry any true 'sovereignty'. On the other hand, if what we said earlier of the Sephardic origin of Martines' initiation is correct, this place could very well be in North Africa, which is by far the most likely supposition. But in this case it is quite clear that it would not be a question of a Masonic organization and that it is not here that we should seek the 'power' by which Martines was instituted 'Sovereign Réaux' for a region coinciding with Masonry's entire sphere of influence, which would in other respects justify his foundation of high grades of the Order of the Elect Cohens, in the special form of a 'regime'.[26]

The demise of this Order is scarcely less obscure than is its beginning. Martines' two successors did not long exercise the functions of 'Grand Sovereign', for the first, Caignet de Lestère, died in 1778,

23. If such was the case, some would perhaps identify this person with the pretender Charles-Edward Stuart, to whom, rightly or wrongly, a similar role has been attributed. If we allude to this here, it is because it could derive some plausibility from the fact that the 'Knight of the Rose Croissante' speaks of the 'marks of esteem and recognition that the claimant Stuart seemed to show to Martines' when the latter presented himself before the Lodges of Toulouse, that is in 1760, eight years before the letter just cited; but what follows will show that something quite different must be involved.

24. These are the former, also called 'Sovereigns', as we said above. We call attention to this number twelve, which continually recurs wherever the constitution of initiatic centers is concerned, whatever traditional form may be involved.

25. It is useless to speak here of America, which from the Masonic point of view represented at that time nothing more than a dependency of Europe.

26. The terms Willermoz employs seem to indicate that the region placed under Martines' authority did not include Europe alone; it would also have included

four years after Martines, and the second, Sébastien de Las Casas, retired two years later, in 1780. What remained thereafter as far as a regularly constituted organization is concerned? It seems that very little remained, and that if a few 'Temples' did persist for a time after 1780, this hardly deferred the cessation of all activity. As for the designation of another 'Grand Sovereign' following the retirement of Sébastien de Las Casas, it is nowhere in question; there was however a letter from the Knight of Bacon, dated January 26, 1807, speaking of the 'absolute silence of the Elect Cohens, who always acted with the greatest discretion in executing the supreme orders of the Sovereign Master, G∴ Z∴ W∴ J∴'. But what can we make of such information, as bizarre as it is enigmatic, and perhaps even quite fanciful? In any case, in the letter of 1822 just cited, Willermoz states that, 'of all the Réaux he has known, none still live, just as it was impossible for him to name one after him'; and if there were no longer any 'Réaux-Croix', there will be no transmission to perpetuate the Order of the Elect Cohens.

Apart from 'direct survival', to use to van Rijnberk's expression, the latter envisages an 'indirect survival' consisting in what he calls the two 'Willermozist and Martinist metamorphoses'; but here we have an ambiguity that should be clarified. The Rectified Scottish Rite is not a metamorphosis of the Elect Cohens but a derivation from the Strict Observance, which is totally different; and if it is true that by means of the dominant role he played in the development of the rituals of its higher grades (in particular that of 'Knight Beneficent of the Holy City'), Willermoz was able to introduce some of the ideas he had taken from Martines' organization, it is no less true that the great majority of the Elect Cohens strongly reproached him for the interest he had thus shown in another rite, which in their eyes was almost a betrayal, just as they reproached Saint-Martin for a change in attitude of another kind.

America, as is shown by the importance it later assumed in San Domingo's history of his life and Order; and this again confirms that the sphere of activity attributed to him coincided with the group of countries where Masonry existed, and where it was even the sole surviving initiatic organization capable of furnishing a basis for the work with which it was charged.

This case of Saint-Martin must engage us a while longer, if only because so much has been made of it in our time; the truth is that, if Saint-Martin abandoned all the Masonic rites to which he had been linked, including that of the Elect Cohens, this was in order to adopt an exclusively mystical attitude, one therefore incompatible with the initiatic point of view, and certainly not to found a new Order himself. In fact, the name 'Martinism', commonly used only in the profane world, applies only to Saint-Martin's particular doc-trines and the adherents thereof, whether or not these latter were directly related to him. What is more, Saint-Martin himself, not without some irony, qualified those who simply read his works as 'Martinist'. It would seem however that several of his disciples did receive from him individually a certain 'deposit', which actually con-sisted of only 'two letters and some periods'; and this transmission is held to be the source of modern 'Martinism'. But even if all this is true, how could such a communication, effected without any rite, represent an initiation? The two letters in question are 'S' and 'T', which, whatever interpretation one may give them (and there are many), seem to have exercised a real fascination on some people; but in the present case what can be their provenance? Surely this was not a reminiscence of the 'Unknown Superiors' [*Supérieurs Inconnus*] of the Strict Observance; besides, there is no need to look so far, for some Elect Cohens used these letters in their signature, and van Rijnberk offers a very plausible hypothesis when he sug-gests that they could have been the distinctive mark of the members of the 'Sovereign Tribunal' charged with the administration of the Order (to which Saint-Martin himself belonged, as did Willermoz); they would therefore have indicated not a grade, but simply a func-tion. In these conditions, it could in spite of everything seem strange that Saint-Martin should have adopted these letters rather than 'R. C.', for example, if they had not had in themselves their own symbolic significance, from which when all is said and done their various usages were merely derived. Be that as it may, there is a curi-ous fact which shows that Saint-Martin really did attach a certain importance to them, which is that, in the *Crocodile*, he used these initials to form the name of an imaginary 'Society of Independents', which was not really a society or even an organization, but rather a kind of a mystical communion presided over by Madame Jof, that is to say Faith personified.[27] And another peculiar point is that toward the end of the story the Jew Eléazar is admitted into this 'Society of Independents', no doubt we should see this as an allusion, not to something concerning Martines personally, but much rather to Saint-Martin's passage from the doctrine of the Elect Cohens to this mysticism into which he withdrew during the whole of the last part of his life; and, in communicating to his nearest disciples the letters 'S. I.' as a kind of sign of recognition, may he not have wanted to say that they could consider themselves members of what he had wanted to represent by the 'Society of Independents'?

These final observations will make clear why we are far from sharing the overly 'optimistic' views of van Rijnberk, who, in wondering whether the Order of the Elect Cohens 'completely and exclusively belongs to the past,' is inclined to reply in the negative, while however recognizing the absence of all direct filiation, which is the sole is consideration in the initiatic domain. The Rectified Scottish Rite certainly still exists, contrary to what he seems to believe, but in no way originates in what we are discussing. As for modern 'Martinism', we can assure him that it has very little to do with Saint Martin, and absolutely nothing to do with Martines and the Elect Cohens.

27. For his part, Willermoz also makes use of the same initials to give the name 'Society of Initiates' to the very real group he founded for the study of certain somnambulistic phenomena.

16

ON THE
‘LYONNAIS ROSE-CROSS’

STUDIES ON Martines de Pasqually and his disciples are multiply-
ing rather curiously: following Le Forestier's book, which we mentioned here last month, Paul Vulliaud has now brought out a
volume entitled *Les Rose-Croix lyonnais au XVIII siècle.*[1] Here again
the title does not seem well justified, for apart from the introduction this book does not deal with the Rose-Cross. Could it have
been inspired by the famous term ‘Réau-Croix’, which moreover
Vulliaud does not seek to explain? This is quite possible, but the use
of this term does not imply any historical filiation between the so-
called Rose-Cross and the Elect Cohens, and in any case there is no
reason to include organizations such as the Strict Observance and
the Rectified Scottish Rite, which certainly were not Rosicrucian in
either spirit or form under the same heading. We shall go even further. The Masonic rites that include a ‘grade of Rose-Cross’ have
borrowed nothing but a symbol from the Rosicrucians, and to label
those holding the grade as ‘Rose-Cross’ without further explanation, would be an unfortunate ambiguity. The title Vulliaud has
chosen for his work is similarly unfortunate. Vulliaud regards other
terms as well, such as ‘Illumined’ for example, as having no precise
meaning; they seem a little haphazard, one being indifferently substituted for the other, which can only create confusions in the mind
of readers who already have quite enough difficulty getting their
bearings among the multiplicity of Rites and Orders that existed
at the time in question. We do not wish to believe, however, that

1. ‘Bibliothèque des Initiations modernes’. E. Nourry, editor.

Vulliaud himself failed to recognize this, preferring to regard his inaccurate use of technical vocabulary as an almost inevitable consequence of the 'profane' attitude he takes pleasure in proclaiming, and which has not failed to surprise us somewhat, for to this point we had not met people who gloried in calling themselves 'profane', other than those in university and 'official' circles, for whom we believe Vulliaud has not much more esteem than do we.

As a further consequence of this attitude Vulliaud believed he had to adopt a rather annoying ironic tone throughout the book, which risked giving an impression of partiality which an historian should guard himself against at all cost. His *Joseph de Maistre Franc-Maçon* already gave rather too much this same impression. Should it be so difficult for a non-Mason (we do not say a 'profane' person) to discuss questions of this kind without employing a polemical language best left to specifically anti-Masonic publications? To our knowledge, Le Forestier is the only exception; and we regret not finding in Vulliaud another, since his accustomed studies should have disposed him to more serenity.

All this detracts nothing of course from the value or interest of the numerous documents Vulliaud presents, though some are not as unpublished as he believes;[2] nor can we help being astonished that he devoted a chapter to the 'Sleepers' without even mentioning that a work on this subject by Emile Dermenghem already exists, and with precisely this title. But we believe the extracts from the 'initiatic notebooks' transcribed by Louis-Claude de Saint-Martin had indeed never been published. The odd character of these notebooks raises many questions that have never been explained. We have seen some of these documents, and their many bizarre and unintelligible sketches gave us the distinct impression that the 'unknown agent' who authored them must have been a somnambulist (we do not say a 'medium', which would be a serious anachronism), in which case they would quite simply represent the result of experiences of the same kind as the 'Sleepers', which greatly diminishes their 'initiatic'

---

2. Thus, the five 'Instructions' to the Elect Cohens reproduced in chapter 21 had already been published in 1914 in *France Antimaçonnique*; let us consider each according to its merits.

importance. What is certain in any case is that none of this has any-thing whatever to do with the Elect Cohens, who moreover at that time had already ceased to exist as an organization. And let us add that neither is there anything here that refers directly to the Rectified Scottish Rite, in spite of the fact that the 'Lodge of Charity' is fre-quently mentioned. For us, the truth is that Willermoz and other members of this Lodge interested in magnetism had formed them-selves into a kind of 'study group', as such things are now called, which they gave the somewhat ambitious title 'Society of Initiates'; this title, which figures in the documents, cannot be otherwise explained, and the use of the word 'society' demonstrates clearly enough that the group in question, although composed of Masons, had no Masonic character. Even today it frequently happens that for one reason or another Masons form what can be called a 'fraternal group' whose meetings lack any ritual form; and that the 'Society of Initiates' was nothing more than this seems, at least to us, the only plausible solution to this obscure question.

We think that from the initiatic point of view the documents referring to the Elect Cohens have another importance, despite gaps that have always existed in this respect in Martines' teaching, which we pointed out in our last article. Vulliaud is quite right to insist on the error of those who would make Martines a Kabbalist; that he has an incontestably Judaic inspiration does not in fact imply any knowledge of what can be properly designated by the term Kab-balah, a term so often used without rhyme or reason. But on the other hand, Martines' poor spelling the defective style, which Vul-liaud rather too complacently underlines, proves nothing against the reality of his knowledge in a certain order. Profane instruction and initiatic knowledge must not be confused; an initiate of a very high order (which Martines certainly was not) can even be quite illiterate, something witnessed often enough in the East. It seems moreover that Vulliaud may have taken some pleasure in presenting Martines' enigmatic and complex personage in its worst light; Le Forestier was certainly more impartial, but even so there still remain many points to elucidate.

Such persistent obscurities point to the difficulty of pursuing these studies of things that seem sometimes to have been intentionally confused; thus we should be grateful to Vulliaud's for his contribution, and, although he refrains from formulating any conclusion, his work nevertheless provides much new documentation that is for the most part very interesting.[3] And since this work calls for a sequel, let us hope Vulliaud will not long disappoint his readers, who in this work will certainly find many curious things well worth their attention, and perhaps even a starting-point for reflections which, in his role as historian, the author may not himself wish to express.

3. Let us note in passing an historical error too blatant not to be the effect of simple inadvertence: Vulliaud writes that along with some others, 'Albéric Thomas, in opposition to Papus, founded the Rite of Misraïm' (note from p42); now, this Rite was founded in Italy around 1805 and was introduced into France in 1814 by the Bédarride brothers.

17

A NEW BOOK ON THE
ORDER OF THE ELECT
COHENS

R. Le Forestier, who specializes in historical studies of the secret organizations of the second half of the eighteenth century, Masonic or otherwise, recently published an important volume entitled *La Franc-Maçonnerie occultiste au XVIII siècle et l'Ordre des Elect Cohens.*[1] This title calls for some reservations, however, for the word 'occultist', which seems never to have been used before Eliphas Lévi, is somewhat anachronistic here; it would perhaps have been more appropriate to choose another term, and this is no mere question of words, for what is properly called 'occultism' is really a product of the nineteenth century.

The work is divided into three parts: the first deals with the 'doctrines and practices of the Elect Cohens'; the second with 'the Elect Cohens and the occultist tradition' (here the word 'esoteric' would certainly have been more appropriate); and the third, with the 'organization and history of the Order.' The historical material, which is well presented, is based upon a very serious study of the documents the author had at his disposal, and we strongly recommend it. We regret only that there are some gaps as regards Martines de Pasqually's biography, concerning which certain points remain obscure. However, *Voile d'Isis* will soon publish new documents that may perhaps offer some clarification.

---

1. Dorbon Aîné, editor.

The first part is an excellent overview of the contents of the *Traité de la Réintegration des Êtres*, an unfinished and rather confused work, written in a faulty and at times hardly intelligible style. It was not easy to summarize it coherently, and Le Forestier is to be congratulated for having done so. There remains however a certain ambiguity as to the nature of the 'operations' of the Elect Cohens: were they really 'theurgic' or only 'magical'? The author seems not to have realized that these are two essentially different things not of the same order, and it is possible that this confusion existed among the Elect Cohens themselves, for their initiation seems always to have remained rather incomplete in many respects—but it would have been well to at least draw attention to this. What seems to be at issue is a ritual of 'ceremonial magic' with theurgic claims, which thus leaves the door open to many illusions; and the importance attributed to 'phenomenal' manifestations (for what Martines called 'passes' were nothing other than this) proves in fact that the domain of illusion had not been left behind. What is more regrettable is that the founder of the Elect Cohens may have believed himself in possession of transcendent knowledge, whereas the only knowledge involved, though real, was yet of a rather secondary order. And for the same reasons it must be said that he confused the 'initiatic' and the 'mystical' points of view, for the doctrines he expressed always take a religious form, whereas his 'operations' by no means have this characteristic. It is regrettable that Le Forestier seems to accept this confusion and does not himself have a clear notion of the distinction between the two points of view. Furthermore, it is to be noted that what Martines calls 'reintegration' does not exceed the possibilities of the individual human being. The author clearly establishes this point, but there would have been reason to draw very important consequences from this regarding to the limits of the teaching that the head of the Elect Cohens could offer his disciples, and consequently of the 'realization' to which he was capable of leading them.

The second part of the book is the least satisfying, for perhaps in spite of himself le Forestier is not always able to shake himself free from a certain 'rationalist' tendency that he probably owes to his university education. From certain resemblances between different traditional doctrines, one need not necessarily infer borrowings or direct influences, for wherever the same truths are expressed it is normal that such resemblances should exist; and this applies in particular to the science of numbers, of which the significance is in no way a human invention or a more or less arbitrary conception. We can say the same for astrology with its cosmic laws, which in no way depend on us; and we do not see why everything related to astrology need be borrowed from the Chaldeans, as if the latter had a monopoly on such knowledge. The same holds for angelology, which moreover is rather closely connected to astrology and cannot—without accepting all the prejudices of modern 'criticism'—be regarded as having been unknown to the Hebrews until the time of the Babylon captivity. And let us add that Le Forestier does not quite seem to have a true notion of the Kabbalah, which name simply means 'tradition' in the most general sense, but which he attributes to a particular written compilation of teachings, eventually maintaining that 'the Kabbalah was born in the south of France and northern Spain,' dating its origin from the thirteenth century. Here again the 'critical' spirit, which because of its bias is ignorant of the purpose of all oral transmission, has truly gone too far. And finally a last point: the word *Pardes* (which, as we have explained elsewhere, is the Sanskrit *Paradesha*, 'supreme land', and not a Persian word meaning 'animal park', which does not make sense in spite of the connection with Ezekiel's *Cherubim*) does not indicate merely 'mystical speculation' but the real achievement of a certain state, that of the restoration of the 'primordial' or 'edenic' state, which has a close similarity to the 'reintegration' Martines envisaged.[2]

---

2. On this subject we have pointed out a rather amusing error in one of Willermoz's letters to the baron of Turkheim, published by Emile Dermenghem at the end of *Sommeils*: Willermoz protests the assertion that Saint-Martin's book *Des Erreurs et de la Verité* 'came from the *Parthes*'; what he has taken for the name of this people, who in fact had nothing to do with it, is obviously the word *Pardes*, which was doubtless quite unknown to him. As the baron of Turkheim had spoken on this subject 'of *Parthes*, a classical work of the Kabbalists,' we think it must in fact be the work entitled *Pardes Rimonim*.

Given these reservations, it is quite certain that the form in which Martines presents his teaching is properly Jewish in inspiration, which moreover does not imply that he himself was of Jewish origin (this being one of those points still insufficiently clarified), nor that he was not sincerely Christian. Le Forestier is right to speak in this connection of 'esoteric Christianity', but we do not see that conceptions of this order have no right to be called authentically Christian. To confine oneself to modern ideas of an exclusively and narrowly exoteric religion is to deny to Christianity all truly profound meaning, and also to underestimate all that existed beyond this during the Middles Ages, of which we find perhaps the last, already very much weakened, reflections precisely in organizations such as that of the Elect Cohens.[3] We are well aware that this bothers our contemporaries because of their preoccupation with reducing everything to a question of 'historicism', a preoccupation shared now, it seems, by both advocates and adversaries of Christianity, although the adversaries were certainly the first to carry the argument into this territory. Let us state clearly that if Christ were considered solely as an historical personage, this would be a matter of little interest, but consideration of the Christ-principle has quite another importance; and furthermore, the one in no way excludes the other, because as we have often said historical facts themselves have a symbolic value and express principles in their own way and in their own order. We cannot dwell further on this point here, but it seems obvious enough.

The third part of the book is devoted to the history of the Elect Cohens, whose effective existence was rather brief, and to the exposition of what can be known of its rituals and grades, which seem never to have been fully established and clarified, any more than were those of its famous 'operations'. It is perhaps not quite correct to refer, as does Le Forestier, to all systems of high Masonic grades without exception as 'Scottish', or to see the Masonic character given

---

3. Instead of 'esoteric Christianity' it would be better to say 'Christian esoterism', that is, esoterism taking its basis in Christianity, in order to indicate that what is in question here does not pertain to the religious domain; and the same naturally applies to 'Islamic esoterism'.

by Martines to the Elect Cohens as a simple mask; but a thorough discussion of these questions would lead us too far afield.[4] We wish only to call particular attention to the name 'Réau-Croix' given by Martines to the highest grade of his 'regime' (as was then said), and which Le Forestier wants to see only as the imitation or even counterfeit of the 'Rose-Cross', although for us something else is involved. In the spirit of Martines, the 'Réau-Croix' must on the contrary be the true 'Rose-Cross', whereas the grade in ordinary Masonry that formerly bore the latter name was only 'apocryphal', according to the expression often used. But whence comes this bizarre name 'Réau-Croix', and what can it really mean? According to Martines, the real name of Adam was '*Roux* in the popular language and *Réau* in Hebrew,' signifying 'Man-God very strong in wisdom, virtue, and power', an interpretation which, at least at first glance, seems rather fanciful. The truth is that Adam means quite literally 'red'; *adamah* is red clay, and *adamah* is blood, which is also red. *Edom*, a name given to Esau, has the sense of 'red' also, and red is most often taken as a symbol of force or of power, which in part justifies Martines' explanation. As for the form *Réau*, there is certainly nothing Hebraic about it, and we think it should be seen as a phonetic assimilation with the word *roèh*, 'to see', which was the first designation of the prophets, and the proper meaning of which is quite comparable to that of the Sanskrit *rishi*. This sort of phonetic symbolism is nothing exceptional, as we have pointed out on various occasions,[5] and there would be nothing astonishing in Martines' using it here to allude to one of the chief characteristics of the 'edenic state', and in so doing to denote the possession of this state itself. If such is the case, the expression 'Réau-Croix', by the addition

---

4. With regard to the various systems of high grades, we were somewhat surprised to see the organization of the 'Conseil des Empereurs d'Orient et d'Occident' attributed to the aristocracy 'of birth and money', as the founder seems in fact to have been quite simply 'Master Pirlet, tailor of clothes,' according to documents of the time; as badly informed as Thory may have been on certain points, he certainly did not invent this piece of information (*Acta Latomorum*, vol. I, p79).

5. Le Forestier points out another example in the writings of Martines himself, that is, the assimilation he establishes through a kind of anagram between 'Noachites' and 'Chinese'.

of the Cross of the 'Restorer' to the first term '*Réau*', indicates 'the minor restored in its prerogatives' in the terminology of the *Traité de la Réintégration des Êtres*, that is to say the 'regenerated man' who is effectively the 'second Adam' of Saint Paul, and who is also the true 'Rose-Cross'.[6] It is a matter then not of an imitation of the term 'Rose-Cross'—which after all it would have been so much easier to appropriate, as has been done by many others—but one of the numerous interpretations or adaptations to which it can legitimately give rise, which of course is not to say that Martines' claims concerning the real effects of his 'ordination of '*Réau-Croix*' were fully justified.

In bringing this all too brief examination to a close, let us call attention to one last point. Le Forestier is quite right to see in Martines' frequently used expression 'glorious form', in which 'glorious' is as it were synonymous with 'luminous', an allusion to the *Shekinah* (which some old Masonic rituals, by a rather bizarre deformation, call the *Stekenna*);[7] but this is exactly the same thing as the 'glorious body' found in Christianity, even exoteric Christianity, ever since Saint Paul's 'Sown in corruption, it will revive in glory,' and is the same also as the designation 'light of glory', in which, according to the most orthodox theology, the 'beatific vision' takes place. This shows clearly that there is no opposition between exoterism and esoterism but only a superposition of the latter on the former, esoterism giving to the truths expressed in a more or less veiled way by exoterism, the plenitude of their higher meaning and depth.

---

6. Moreover, the cross is in itself the symbol of 'Universal Man', and one can say that it represents the very form of man restored to his original center, from which he has been separated by the 'fall', or, according to Martines' vocabulary, by the 'betrayal of trust'.

7. The word 'glory' applied to the triangle bearing the Tetragrammaton and surrounded by rays, which figures in churches as well as Lodges, is in fact one of the designations of the *Shekinah*, as we have explained in *The King of the World*.

18

A PROJECT OF
JOSEPH DE MAISTRE
FOR THE UNION OF PEOPLES

EMILE DERMENGHEM, to whom we owe the remarkable work *Joseph de Maistre mystique*, has also made available a previously unpublished manuscript by de Maistre, a memorandum of 1782 addressed to Duke Ferdinand of Brunswick (*Knight of Victoria*), Grand-Master of the Rectified Scottish Rite, on the occasion of the Wilhelmsbad Freemasons' Lodge Meeting. In September 1780, Duke Ferdinand, hoping to 'bring order and wisdom into Masonic anarchy,' had addressed to all the Lodges of his obedience the following questionnaire:

(1) Is the origin of the Order an ancient society, and if so, what is this society? (2) Are there really Unknown Superiors, and if so, who are they? (3) What is the true aim of the Order? (4) Is this aim the restoration of the Order of Templars? (5) In what way should the ceremonial and rites be organized so as to be as perfect as possible? (6) Should the Order occupy itself with secret sciences?

It was in reply to these questions that Joseph de Maistre composed a separate memorandum, distinct from the collective response of the *Perfect Sincerity* Lodge of Chambéry to which he belonged, in which, in his capacity as 'Grand Professor' or member of the highest grade of the Rectified Regime (under the name *Knight of Floribus*), he proposed to express 'the views of some Brothers more fortunate than others, who seem destined to contemplate truths of a higher order.' Dermenghem even says that this memorandum is 'the first important work to come from his pen.'

Joseph de Maistre did not accept the Templar origin of Masonry, and was unaware of the real interest of the question. He goes so far as to write: 'What does the destruction of the Order of the Templars matter to the universe?' But it matters very much, since this marks the point at which the West broke with its own initiatic tradition reaches back, a rupture that is truly the primary cause of the intellectual deviation of the modern world. This deviation in fact goes back further than the Renaissance, which marks only one of the principal stages, the fourteenth century being its actual starting-point. De Maistre, who moreover had only a rather vague understanding of the Middle Ages, knew nothing of the means of transmission of initiatic doctrine or of the representatives of true spiritual hierarchy, but he clearly maintained the existence of both, which is already a great deal, for one must realize how matters stood at the end of the eighteenth century with the many Masonic organizations, including those not confining themselves to a wholly outward formalism, but claiming to offer their members a real initiation and they all sought a connection with something the exact nature of which was unknown to them, to rediscover a tradition of which the signs still existed everywhere but of which the principle was lost. No one possessed the 'true characteristics'—as it was put during this period—and the Wilhelmsbad Lodge was an attempt to reestablish order in the besetting chaos of rites and grades. 'Certainly,' says Joseph de Maistre,

> the Order could not begin as we now see it. Everything declares that common Freemasonry is a detached and perhaps corrupted branch of an ancient and respectable line.

This is the strict truth; but how to know what this line was? He cites an extract from an English text dealing with the question of certain brotherhoods of builders, to which he adds, 'It is remarkable that these kinds of establishments coincide with the destruction of the Templars.' This remark could have opened to him wider horizons, and it is astonishing that it did not lead him to further reflection, all the more so since the sole fact of having written it hardly accords with what goes before. Let us add, moreover, that this only concerns one side of the exceedingly complex question of the origins of Masonry's.

The attempt to join Masonry to the ancient Mysteries represents another side of this same question:

> The most learned Brothers of our Regime think there are strong reasons for believing that true Masonry is merely the *Science of Man* par excellence, namely the knowledge of his origin and destiny. A few add that this Science does not differ essentially from ancient Greek or Egyptian initiation.

De Maistre objects that it is impossible to know exactly what the ancient Mysteries were and what was taught in them, and he seems to have only a rather indifferent opinion of these things, perhaps even more astonishing than the similar opinion he had adopted regarding the Templars. Since he quite rightly does not hesitate to affirm that 'remnants of the original Tradition are to be found' among all peoples, how is it that he was not led to think that the chief aim of the Mysteries would have been precisely the conservation of the deposit of this same Tradition? And yet in a certain sense he does admit that the initiation of which Masonry is heir goes back 'to the origin of things,' to the beginning of the world. 'The true religion spans far more than eighteen centuries: it was born the day that days were born.' Here again, what eludes him are the means of transmission, and one may well feel that he rather too easily accepts this ignorance—but of course he was only twenty-nine years old when he wrote this memorandum.

De Maistre's reply to another question proves again that despite the high grade he held, his initiation was far from perfect; and how many other Masons of the highest grades, past and present, are in exactly the same situation, or know even less! What we refer to are his comments regarding the 'Unknown Superiors'. Here is what he says:

> Have we Masters? No, we have not. The proof is brief, but decisive. It is that we do not know them. . . . How could we have contracted some tacit commitment to hidden Superiors, since if

they had made themselves known they would perhaps have displeased us and we would have withdrawn?

He is clearly unaware that what is really involved is the mode of action of the genuine 'Unknown Superiors'. As for the fact that the latter were not known even by the Masonic leaders, this proves only that any effective connection with the true initiatic hierarchy no longer existed; and the refusal to recognize these Superiors made the last chance that might still remain to reestablish it disappear.

The most interesting part of the memorandum is doubtless that which answers the last two questions, and we should first not the part about ceremonies. De Maistre, for whom 'form is a great thing,' nevertheless does not speak of the essentially symbolic character of the ritual and its initiatic import, and this is a regrettable omission, but he does insist on what might be called the practical value of the ritual, and what he says is a great psychological truth:

> Thirty or forty people decked out in their singular robes and speaking only with permission, ranged silently along the walls of a chamber hung in black or green tapestries, will reason sagely on any subject put to them. But take away the tapestries and robes, put out the candles, allow them to change places, and these same men will jump on one on another, no longer agreeing, or speaking of newspapers and women; and the most reasonable member of society will return home before reflecting that he acted just like the others.... Above all let us guard against the suppression of the oath, as some people have proposed, perhaps for good reasons, but which are does not understood. Theologians who have wanted to prove that our oath is illicit have reasoned poorly. It is true that the civil authority alone can prescribe and accept oaths in the various acts of society; but one cannot dispute the right of another intelligent creature the attest by oath an inner determination of his free will. The sovereign has authority only over actions. My arm is his; my will is my own!

Next comes a kind of plan of tasks for the different grades, each of which must have its particular object, and here let us dwell more particularly on this. But first it is important to dispel a confusion. Since the division De Maistre adopts consists only of three grades, Dermenghem seems to have understood this to mean that he intended to reduce Masonry to three symbolic grades. But this interpretation is irreconcilable with the constitution of the Rectified Scottish Rite itself, which is essentially a Rite of high grades. Dermenghem has not noticed that De Maistre writes 'grades or classes,' and in truth it is really a matter of three classes, each further divisible into several grades properly speaking. Here is how this apportionment seems to be established: the first class comprises the three symbolic grades; the second class corresponds to the capitulary grades, of which the most important and perhaps even the only one in fact practiced in the Rectified Rite is that of Saint Andrew of Scotland; and finally, the third class is formed by the higher grades of Novice, Squire, and Grand Professor [*Profès*] or Knight Beneficent of the Holy City. What proves again that it really must be understood in this way is that in speaking of the works of the third class, de Maistre writes: 'What a vast field open to the zeal and perseverance of the G. P.'! It is evidently a matter of the Grand Professor here, not simple Masters of the 'Blue Lodge' and not at all a question of suppressing the high grades, but on the contrary of giving them aims in keeping with their own character.

The aim assigned to the first class is the practice of charity, 'which must be the *visible* object of the whole Order.' But that is not enough, and to this a second aim must be added, which is already more intellectual:

> Not only will the heart of the Mason be formed in the first grade, but his mind will be enlightened by being applied to the study of morals and politics, which is the morality of the States. Interesting questions on these two sciences will be discussed in the Lodges, and now and then the opinion of the Brothers will be requested in writing.... But above all the great object of the Brothers will above all be to acquire a thorough knowledge of their country, of what it possesses and what it lacks, of the causes of distress and the means of regeneration.

According to the system proposed, the second class of Masonry should have as its aim, the direction of governments and the meeting of all Christian sects.

As regards the first point,

> one will be untiringly careful to exclude obstacles of all kinds interposed by the passions between truth and the ear of authority.... The limits of the State will not be able to confine the activity of this second class, and sometimes the Brothers of different nations will sometimes bring about the greatest good through zealous harmony.

And for the second object:

> Would it not be worthy of us to propose the advancement of Christianity as one of the aims of our Order? This project should have two parts, for it is necessary that each communion work by itself and work to bring others together.... We should establish committees of correspondence, composed of priests of the different communions that we will have incorporated and initiated. We shall work slowly but surely. We shall not undertake any conquest not suitable to perfect the *Great Work*.... Everything that can contribute to the advancement of religion, to the extirpation of dangerous opinion, in a word, to raising the throne of truth on the ruins of superstition and Pyrrhonism, shall be the jurisdiction of this class.

Finally, the third class shall have as its objective what De Maistre calls 'transcendent Christianity', which, for him, is 'the revelation of the revelation' and constitutes the essential of the 'secret sciences' mentioned earlier; in this way 'the solution of several troublesome difficulties shall be found in the knowledge that we possess.' And he further explains:

> The Brothers admitted to the higher class will have as the object of their studies and deepest reflections factual research and metaphysical knowledge.... All is mystery in the two Testaments, and the elect of each of the laws were merely *true initiates*. Question this venerable Antiquity and ask how it understood the

sacred allegories. Who can doubt that this kind of research equips us victoriously against modern writers who insist on seeing in Scripture the literal meaning alone? They are already refuted by the expression *Mysteries of Religion* which we use every day without penetrating its meaning. This word *mystery* in principle merely means a truth concealed beneath symbols by those who possessed it.

Is it possible to assert more clearly and more explicitly the existence of esoterism in general and of Christian esoterism in particular? In support of this, various citations are taken from ecclesiastical and Jewish authors, borrowed from *Monde Primitif* by Count de Gébelin. However, in this vast field of research everyone will find something or other with which to busy himself, according to his abilities:

> Some are courageously absorbed in erudite studies that can multiply our qualifications and explain those that we possess. The genius of others calls them to metaphysical contemplation and seeks the proofs of our doctrine from the very nature of things. And finally, others (and thanks to God there are many!) tell us what they have learned from this Spirit that blows where it wishes, as it wishes, and when it wishes.

The call to direct inspiration expressed in this last phase is not what is least remarkable here.

This project was never implemented and we do not even know whether the Duke of Brunswick was aware of it; but it was not as chimerical as some might think, and we believe it well suited to stimulate interesting reflections, as much today as when it was first conceived, which is why we have given such long extracts. In sum, the general idea that emerges can be formulated thus: without claiming in any way to deny or to suppress differences and national characteristics—of which, on the contrary, we must be as profoundly aware as possible, despite the claims of, despite the claims of internationalists today—it is a question of restoring the supranational rather than international unity of ancient Christianity, a unity destroyed by the many sects that have 'rent the seamless robe', and then of raising it to universality by realizing Catholicism in the true sense of the word, in the sense also meant by Wronski, for whom this Catholicism would have a fully effective existence only when it had succeeded in integrating the traditions contained in the sacred books of all peoples. It is essential to note that such a union as that envisaged by Joseph de Maistre must be accomplished above all in the purely intellectual realm, which is just what we ourselves have always maintained, for we think there can be no true understanding between peoples, especially belonging to different civilizations, other than one based on principles in the proper sense of this word. Without this strictly doctrinal base, nothing solid can be built: all political and economic schemes will remain powerless in this respect, no less than will sentimental considerations, whereas, if agreement on the principles is realized, understanding in all other domains must necessarily follow.

No doubt Masonry of the end of the eighteenth century no longer had the means necessary to accomplish this 'Great Work', of which certain conditions moreover would very likely have escaped De Maistre himself. Is this to say that such a plan will never again be undertaken in one or another form by some organization with a truly initiatic character and possessing an 'Ariadne's thread' to guide it through the labyrinth of innumerable forms under which the sole Tradition is hidden, in order finally to recover the 'Lost Word' and leave 'the Light of the Shadows, the order of Chaos'? We do not wish to prejudge the future in any way, but certain signs permit us to think that, in spite of the unfavorable appearances of the present time, it is perhaps not completely impossible. We shall end by citing a rather prophetic phrase, again from Joseph de Maistre, found in the second meeting of the *Soirées de Saint-Pétersbourg*:

We must be ready for a tremendous event in the divine order, toward which we are marching with an accelerated speed that must strike all observers. Terrible oracles already announce that *the time has come*.

19

THE STRICT
OBSERVANCE
AND THE UNKNOWN
SUPERIORS

OUR RESEARCH into the *Rectified Scottish Rite* has led us to undertake as its indispensable complement a study of the *Strict Observance,* a subject as profound as it is obscure, and one that has given
rise to a great deal of controversy. While awaiting the publication of
this study, it will be of interest to take note of other documents that
appear on the question, and to relate them to those with which we
are already familiar.

Let us first of all draw attention to a remarkable study by Benjamin Fabre, author of the recent article 'Franciscus, Eques a
Capite Galeato', which appeared in the *Bastille* of 6 and 13 September 1913 as 'Quelque imposteurs F∴ -M∴ : Starck et Coucoumous'.
In particular, the article deals with the *Clerks of the Late Observance,* a schism analogous to that of the *Clerks of the Strict Observance* which we mentioned in regard to the Rite founded in Malta
in 1771 by the Jutlandish merchant Kolmer.

The *Eques a Capite Galeato,* writing 'as one of the commissaries
to the Archives of *Philalethes,'*[1] describes the *Clerks of the Late*

---

1. He was Secretary-General of the Convention of Paris in 1785, and was then
charged, first alone, then with F∴ Baron de Gleichen, with establishing ties with
Cagliostro in order to sound out his intentions; but an important fact to note is

Observance[2] in these terms:

> These *Clerks* still present a problem to the impartial observer.
> Some say they were *Jesuits*(!) who wished to perpetuate them-
> selves secretly by forming the *ecclesiastical class of the inner order
> of the Rule of the Strict Observance*.[3]
> Others say they were a new *Confederation*, which, led by motives
> of pride and cupidity, wished to dominate the said *Rule* by
> means of certain forms and scientific ideas culled from manu-
> scripts and rare books of the *Rose-Cross Brotherhood of the XVI-
> Ith century*.[4]
> Still others say it was the *Clergy of the Order of Ancient Templars*
> perpetuated, and that, to the exclusion of the simple *knights*,

that he left hastily upon being instructed to write a certain letter to the *Mother Lodge of the Egyptian Rite*, and had to be replaced with F∴ de Beyerle (*Eques a Fasciā* in the *Strict Observance*). — The articles concerning this affair of Cagliostro with the Convention of Paris were published by F∴ Thory in his *Acta Latomorum*, vol. II, pp 102–127.

2. Or *of the High-Observance*(?), according to Thory (ibid., vol. I, p 103).

3. F∴ Ragon and many other Masonic authors up to F∴ Limousin, have spread this legend, as well as the one attributing the creation of the *Strict Observance* to the Jesuits; F∴ de Ribeaucourt also speaks of 'the *Unknown Superiors* of Jesuitical memory.' It has been claimed that the initials *S. I.* (or *S. J.*) came to be interpreted as *Societas Jesu*, and a sort of word-play has likewise been made, most likely intentionally, on *Clerici*, which should properly be taken in the sense of *scholars*, possessors of certain particular kinds of knowledge, rather than in the sense of *ecclesiastics*. — Some have equally seen the Jesuits at the origin of the *Grand-Orient de France*; it seems that we have here a veritable obsession.

4. Some time around 1610 the *Rose-Cross Brotherhood* in question published the *Fama Fraternitatis*, sought in vain by Descartes throughout Germany, and followed by various other manifestos. Several modern societies with initiatic claims have been founded solely on the study of the doctrines and theories contained in these writings; their *adepts*(?) thus believe they can *mystically* link themselves to the authors. The tendencies of the original group were quite clearly *protestant* and *anti-papist*, to such a degree that Kazauer interpreted the three letters *F. R. C.* (*Fratres Rosae-Crucis*) as signifying *Fratres Religionis Calvinisticae*, 'for they adorn their works with texts dear to the Reformation' (cited by Sédir, *Histoire des Rose-Croix*, p 65). This explanation, if not more literally correct, is perhaps at least more fair than that identifying the *Unknown Superiors* with the *Jesuits*, or than the opinion of F∴ Ragon, who attributes to the Jesuits the invention of the Masonic grade that carries precisely the name *Rosy-Cross*.

possessed *the doctrine and practice of the Occult Sciences, each extending the catalogue of these sciences according to the scope of his ideas and according to his own tastes.*[5]

In truth, by the ambiguity of their responses and of their constitution, and by the shrewdness of their proceedings, these *Clerks* encouraged every opinion people wished to form of them.

And Benjamin Fabre adds:

Their goal seems to have been to *superimpose themselves* upon the *Rule of the Strict Observance*[6] in order to take control of its Lodges, which were established all over Europe and even in the New World. They demanded that their adepts possess all the grades conferred by the *Strict Observance.*[7]

In 1767 this schism, 'which seemed to have been brought to life by an *occult Power*,' and which appeared first in Vienna, occurred within the *Rule of the Strict Observance.* From this period on,

5. We underline this passage, for it is particularly important in regard to the *adaptation* of initiatic teaching to the capacities, intellectual or otherwise, of those admitted into it. — Certain contemporary occultists, always driven by the same obsession, maintain that the true successors to the *Templars* in this era were the *Jesuits,* who for their part had renewed their plan of vengeance against the Royalty, the most active agents of this enterprise having been Fénelon(!) and Ramsay (cf. Papus, *Martinésisme, Willermosisme, Martinisme et Franc-Maconnerie,* pp 10–11). Under the influence of the same ideas, some have been led, contrary to plausibility, to see the Jesuits as the inspirers and secret leaders of the *Illumined Ones of Bavaria;* there are some who have moreover not hesitated to present Baron de Hundt as 'the creator of High German Masonry or *German Illuminism*' (ibid., p 67)—a singular manner of writing history!

6. Just as the latter had itself, like all other *systems of high grades, been superimposed* upon the entire *outward* order of *Symbolic Masonry.*

7. The *Clerks of the Late Observance* 'offered to communicate the true statutes and instructions of the *Order of the Templars* to the Lodges of the *Strict Observance*' (*Acta Latomorum,* vol. I, p 90). — Their *Unknown Superiors* were Baron de Raven (*Theodosius, Eques a Margaritā*) at Ranefeld in Mecklembourg, the preacher Starck (*Archidemides, Eques ab Aquila Fuiva*), doctor of theology, at Darmstadt and at Koenigsberg, and the private counselor Duffel at Lille (ibid., vol. I, p 91, and vol. II, pp 313, 369, and 383).

it seems that for one reason or another Baron de Hundt, *Eques ab Ense,* was found unworthy and lost that which had until that time given him his power, namely, communication with the *Unknown Superiors.*

When the Convention of Brunswick met in 1775, 'Baron de Hundt, representative of the Grand-Master *Eques a Penna Rubra*...was only *the shadow of a shadow.*' Perhaps the disgrace had struck higher than the leader of the *Strict Observance,* reaching this Grand-Master himself, the intermediary between Hundt and the true *Unknown Superiors.*[8]

∴

ONE OF THE LEADERS of the schism was F∴ Starck, preacher from the court of Prussia, and doctor of (Protestant) theology...and of Masonic sciences, whose masters for these latter were Gugumus and the tavern-keeper Schroepfer. The first (whose name is also written Gugomos, Gouygomos, Kukumus, Cucumur, etc., the exact spelling being quite uncertain) figures in the list of the members of the *Strict Observance* under the Masonic name *Eques a Cygno Triomphante,*[9] with the title 'lieutenant to the service of Prussia.' According to a letter of F∴ Prince de Carolath to F∴ Marquis de Savalette de Langes,[10]

8. The mysterious *Grand-Master* in question here must not be confused with the official *Superior General* of the Lodges of the *Strict Observance,* Frederic de Brunswick-Oels, *Eques a Leone Aureo,* who was elected to this position in 1772 at the Convention of Kohio near Pforten in the Basse-Lusace (*Acta Latomorum,* vol. I, p103 and vol. II, p296). — It is furthermore not a question of the *Grand-Master of the Templars,* who was officially recognized by no less than the *Strict Observance,* and then by the *Reforme de Wilhelmsbad:* from 1743 to 1788 the latter was the pretender Charles-Edward Stuart, *Eques a Sole Aureo,* whose successor from 1788 to 1792 was Duke Ferdinand de Brunswick, *Eques a Victoria,* then, from this last date on, Prince Charles de Hesse, *Eques a Leone Resugente* (ibid., vol. I, p283, and vol. II, pp295, 333, and 384).

9. Thory, op. cit., vol. II, pp136 and 328 (written *Cyano* instead of *Cygno;* this is undoubtedly an error).

10. Cited in the article by Benjamin Fabre.

Coucoumous [*sic*] or Kukumus, of a family originally from the Souabe, passed successively through nearly all the services of Germany, at times in the military, at times in the civil; he was admired for his talents but at the same time despised for his inconstancy and ill conduct He was chamberlain to the Duke of Wirtemberg [*sic*].

F∴ Clavel recounts[11] that

this Gugomos appeared in High Germany and was said to have been sent from Cyprus[12] by the *Unknown Superiors of Saint-Siege*(?). He gave himself the titles grand-priest, knight, and prince; he promised to teach the art of making gold, evoking the dead, and locating the buried treasures of the Templars. But he was soon unmasked; he tried to flee but was stopped, and was made to retract in writing all he had claimed, and to admit that he was no more than a simple imposter.[13]

What we about to see does not permit us to accept this conclusion entirely: Gugomos could indeed have been an imposter and could have acted as such under certain circumstances, but he must have been something else as well, at least for part of his career. For us, this much at least results from the rest of the previously cited letter of F∴ Prince de Carolath:

For a long time he had professed knowledge of the Occult Sciences, but it was Italy that formed him in this respect. Of this much we can be assured, that he came back from there with the most rare kinds of knowledge, which he did not fail to put into practice upon returning to his own country. By means of certain characters—which were nevertheless not true characters—and fumigations he summoned spirits. We can even be assured that a certain kind of lightning was at his command.

11. *Histoire pittoresque de la Franc-Maçonnerie*, p 187.

12. It would perhaps be a mistake to take *Cyprus* literally here, for High Masonry of the eighteenth century had its own geography, of which we shall some day speak further.

13. ∴ Clavel has taken this passage almost word for word from Thory's *Acta Latomorum* (vol. I, pp 117–118, 1775).

Now, according to witnesses we have no reason to doubt, even today certain Rabbis in North Africa[14] still have precisely 'a special kind of lightning at their command,' and by means of 'characters' or kabbalistic figures produce a veritable storm in miniature, with cloud formations, lightning, thunder, etc., in the room where they accomplish this operation.[15] It is probably this, or something similar, that Gugomos did; and this connection, significant from the point of view of certain Jewish influences, also leads us to recall the 'mysterious hidden adept named Valmont who often came from Africa to Italy and France and who initiated F∴ Baron de Waechter.'[16]

It would have been interesting to have more precise information on the subject of the 'characters' used by Gugomos in his 'operations'. Besides, who among the *Philalethes*—or for that matter, among so many other various and rival FF∴ of *Regimes* that attempted with such zeal and such little success to bring 'Light from the Darkness' and 'Order from Chaos—who among them especially at this time[17] could boast of possessing the *true characters*, which is in short to ask who could link them to an emanation of what in the eyes of the *true Unknown Superiors* would constitute a *legitimate Power*? The destruction or disappearance of archives sometimes occurred in all too opportune a manner not to raise suspicion. Had not the *Grand Lodge of England* under the inspiration of the Rev∴ Anderson (ex-Chaplain of an *Operative Lodge*) been the first to provide an example of such a procedure from its beginnings (1717–1721)?[18]

14. The Jews of North Africa are of the *Sephardim,* that is, the descendents of Spanish and Portuguese Jews, who claim to possess a much purer 'tradition' (*Kabbalah*) than those of the *Ashkenazim,* or German Jews.

15. Let us recall here the existence of 'rain-makers' among a great number of peoples, and particularly among the blacks of Africa, where they can be counted among the most influential members of various secret societies.

16. 'Baron de Waechter, Danish ambassador to Ratisbonne, ardent zealot of the *System of the Strict Observance,* in which he was known under the characteristic name *Eques a Ceraso*' (Thory, op. cit., t. II, p 392). — Benjamin Fabre has devoted other articles to this figure.

17. The letter from Prince de Carolath is from 1781, the year preceding the Convent [*sic*] of Wilhelmsbad.

18. We could add that on occasion their example has been followed, even in our own times, by many Masonic Obediences.

But let us continue with our quotation:

> The rumor of so many marvelous things attracted the attention of the whole world, which is to say the Masonic world, for in fairness it must be acknowledged that he [Gugomos] never displayed such things to the profane.

This discretion on the part of Gugomos was in conformity with the most elementary rules of prudence; but even in Masonic circles he ought to have shown himself more circumspect out of interest for himself as well as for his 'mission'; and the display he made of his 'knowledge' and powers was perhaps one of the causes of his subsequent disgrace, as we shall see from what immediately followed.

> Soon, full of confidence, he had the boldness to convene a General Congress, where he intended to display his rare knowledge. But, O wonder!, his power left him. He could not produce the things of which he had boasted. What is more, he was subsequently debarred from the Order on account of his ill conduct. Now he continually wanders, though we are assured he has regained a portion of his knowledge. His present whereabouts are unknown.

Thus Gugomos, manifestly abandoned by the *Unknown Superiors,* for whom he was obviously only an instrument, lost all his powers just at the moment when he had greatest need of them. It is quite possible that he had had recourse to various hoaxes in order to try to justify his claims, claims which were no longer backed by the possession of real powers, of which he had only been the momentary depository; and these claims were not of a nature to be proven by any written document, which the FF∴ , even those of the High Grades, would have been unable to decipher.[19] Under these circumstances,

---

19. Baron de Hundt himself could not explain the figures on his own coded certificate. — Later, members of the *Grand Orient of France* gave up hope of reading the two columns of conventional signs figuring above the 'constitutional title' of the *Primitive Rite* (see chap. 5 of the first part of Benjamin Fabre's work). Let us recall what the *Eques a Capite Galeato* has said on this subject: 'that these columns allow certain *Grand Officers*(?) to recognize one another when they meet at the entrance to one of our Lodges, *since they carry no certificate or sign of their position*' (p 63).

Gugomos, hard pressed by indiscreet questions, had no other route of escape than to confess himself an imposter, and he was 'debarred from the Order,' that is, from the *known* High Grades, the *interior* organization of *Symbolic Masonry,* which is still *exterior* in relation to others, those to which Gugomos had earlier been able to attach himself, but as a simple auxiliary rather than as a true initiate.

His misfortune should be all the less surprising in that the history of High Masonry during this period provides a number of similar examples: it is more or less what happened to Baron de Hundt himself, to Starck, to Schroepfer, etc., not to mention Cagliostro. Moreover, we know that even in our day a similar fate has met the envoys or agents of certain *Unknown Superiors,* truly *unknown* and truly *superior*: if they compromise themselves, or even if without otherwise erring they fail in their mission, all their powers are immediately withdrawn from them.[20] This disgrace can only be temporary, however, and such was perhaps the case with Gugomos; but F∴ Savalette de Langes's correspondent is mistaken, or expresses it poorly, when he writes that, consequently, 'he would have regained a part of his knowledge,' for, if *powers* can always be taken away or granted at the will of the *Unknown Superiors,* the case is obviously different as far as *knowledge* is concerned, since such knowledge is acquired once and for all through initiation, however imperfect this initiation may be.

Prince de Carolath, who is rather severe toward Gugomos, nonetheless hesitates to accuse him of imposture; while not reaching a verdict about him, he appears to suspect the quality of his 'knowledge' rather than its very reality:

In this Masonic Congress [of 1775] Waechter managed to confound Kukumus.[21] It seems that Kukumus did not have the *true*

---

20. All of this will no doubt seem fabulous to certain anti-Masons, those historians scrupulously faithful to the 'positivist method' for whom the existence of *Unknown Superiors* is only a 'false Masonic claim'; but we have our reasons for not subscribing to this too... definitive judgement, and we are not aware of having put forth here anything that is not rigorously exact; those who wish are free to refer to written documents alone and thereby guard all their negative 'convictions'!

21. After having spoken of Gugomos (who, let us recall, had received at least part of his initiation in Italy), Thory adds that on this date 'Baron de Waechter

light, and that by continuing the relationship he had perhaps established with *impure spirits* he thereby contributed to the increase of his own and others' perversity, and to the forging of new chains instead of freeing himself from the old.

It does indeed seem that Gugomos, seduced above all by the possession of certain powers of a quite inferior order, was attached almost exclusively to their practice; here again is perhaps one of the causes of his disgrace, for such might not have been in accord with the views of his *Unknown Superiors.*[22]

In another letter also addressed to F∴ Savalette de Langes on the subject of Gugomos or Kukumus, F∴ Baron of Gleichen clearly declares him 'an imposter', although he is quick to add: 'But I know nothing of his *doctrine,* concerning which I have been assured that there was real evil.' Thus, independently of his *powers,* Gugomos possessed at least the rudiments of *doctrine,* something perhaps less interesting in his own eyes but which nevertheless constituted a more real 'knowledge', as he must indeed have seen at his own expense. This *doctrine*—from whom had he received it? This question, far more important than that of Gugomos' eminently suspect moral value, amounts precisely to this: who were his *Unknown Superiors?* And we cannot of course accept the solution offered by Baron de Gleichen, who, haunted by an obsession we have already seen manifest in other cases, declares: 'Most believe he was an emissary of the *Jesuits*[!], who have indeed made various attempts to attach themselves to Masonry.' Others than the Jesuits could have made attempts of this sort; the Jews, for example, were excluded from one part of Masonry, and what is more they still are in Sweden

---

(*Eques a Ceraso*) was sent as a representative to Italy by the former *Scottish Grand Lodge of Franconie.* The hidden motive for his trip was to reunite Italian Masons with those of Franconie; the apparent motive was to rediscover the secret of the Order, which was said to be known in these countries. There he instituted a few Chapters' (op. cit., vol. I, p 118).

22. Let us cite a sentence from a second letter of Prince de Carolath, which again reveals Judaic inspiration: 'At the Convention of Wiesbaden, Kukumus claimed to be able to perform a sacrifice that would be consumed by the fire of heaven through the ardor of his prayer.' In this order of ideas, one could find curious information by studying the *Elect Cohens,* as well as Cagliostro's *Egyptian Rite.*

and in several Grand Lodges in Germany. Now Germany is precisely the country that saw the birth of most of the *Regimes* for which the *Strict Observance* served as prototype. This is certainly not to say that they all had the same origin *in fact*, which we believe rather unlikely, but it is easily conceivable how in taking hold of the High Grades by means of emissaries without official mandate, it would have been possible to direct all of Masonry *invisibly*, and that suffices to explain the multitude of attempts made to achieve such an end.[23]

∴

LET US OPEN a parenthesis here. Certain people are sometimes reproached with seeing a Jewish influence everywhere. Although it is perhaps not necessary to see this influence in an exclusive manner, there are others who, falling into a contrary excess, do not wish to see it at all. This is what happens in particular with the mysterious Falc (F∴ Salvette de Langes writes it thus) whom some 'believe to be *the chief of the Jews*':[24] there are those who wish to identify him, not with Falk-Scheck, Grand-Rabbi of England, but with F∴ Ernest Falcke (*Epimenides, Eques a Rostro*), burgomaster of Hanover, which in no way explain the rumors in circulation about him at the time. Whoever this enigmatic figure was, his role, like that of many others, remains to be made clear, and it seems even more difficult with him than with Gugomos.

23. To finish with Gugomos, let us note further that according to the *Eques a Capite Galeato* he demanded *trials* of all his disciples. 'These *trials* consisted principally in *severe fasting and the solving of extremely subtle problems*.' The use of these two initiatic procedures should be kept in mind, for it allows us to establish certain instructive analogies to which we shall later have occasion to return. — It seems that, like Baron de Hundt, 'Kukumus displayed an extraordinary certificate,' but as we saw above, this proves nothing either for or against the reality of his 'mission'. In the same way, the refusal of the FF∴ of the High Grades to recognize the *Unknown Superiors* and to commit themselves to their service (without knowing them) by no means inevitably implies the negation of their existence, whatever 'positivist' historians may say.

24. See page 84 of the work by Benjamin Fabre.

As for Falk-Scheck, we learn something in *Notice historique sur le Martinesisme et le Martinisme*—of which we shall speak again—that merits citing:

> Mme De la Croix, exorcist of the possessed and too often possessed herself, boasted above all of having destroyed a lapis-lazuli talisman that the Duke of Chartres (Phillipe-Egalite, later Duke of Orleans, and Grand-Master of French Masonry) had received in England from the famed Falk-Scheck, Grand-Rabbi of the Jews, a talisman that would have led the prince to the throne and that, she claimed, was broken against her chest by virtue of her prayers.

Whether or not this claim is justified, this story does throw a singular light on certain of the occultist influences that contributed to preparing the Revolution.

∴

BENJAMIN FABRE devotes the rest of his article[25] to F∴ Schroepfer, 'who also had an eventful career' terminating in suicide,[26] a career 'that is presented to us in a very curious light in the correspondence of Savalette de Langes.'

F∴ Bauer describes one of his evocations, which he had himself witnessed, as follows:

> At one assembly of the FF∴, who hailed from Leipzig to Frankfurt, all of them men of letters, the sciences, etc., after dining at an ordinary Lodge, [F∴ Schroepfer] made us divest ourselves of all metals and prepared a little table apart for himself on which

---

25. *La Bastille,* September 13, 1913 issue.

26. Here is what Thory says: 'October 29, 1768 — Schroefer set himself up as café owner, opening his place in Leipzig. In a Lodge in the city he instituted his system, founded on evocation and magic. He was subsequently pursued and denounced as an imposter and swindler; six year later (October 8, 1774), he shot himself in the head at the *Rosenthal* near Leipzig, at the age of thirty-five (op. cit., vol. I, p94).

lay a card painted with all manner of figures and characters of which I knew nothing. He had us say a rather long and *very efficacious* prayer, and we formed ourselves into a circle. At the first hour of the morning we heard a noise as of chains and shortly thereafter three great, astonishing knocks in the same room where we lay on the floor. Afterward, he began a kind of prayer with his second in command, *in a language I did not understand,* upon which there entered through the door that had previously been closed and locked a black phantom he called *the evil spirit,* whom he addressed in the same language. The spirit in turn responded to him and left upon his command. At the hour of two there came another, with the same ceremonies, called *the good spirit,* and he was likewise sent away. Upon which we departed to our homes, our heads full of chimeras. . . .

The *Eques a Capite Galeato* says he had been told by another witness 'that all of these occurrences, however renowned, were merely physical illusions, assisted by the presumption or credulity of the spectators.' However, Dr Koerner admits to 'having thus far failed to reconcile the contradictory perspectives on this man'; and F∴ Massenet assures us that

it was this same man who showed the Marshal of Saxony[27] to Prince Charles of Courlande[28] in the presence of six witnesses, each of whom testified to the same circumstances and affirmed the fact, although they had previously had no inclination to believe such a thing.

And what should we make of all this? Certainly, it is much more difficult for us than for his contemporaries to form a precise and final opinion on the nature of these 'pneumatological phenomena' of Schroepfer, whose students themselves, like the Baron of Beust,

27. This must have taken place between 1768 and 1774; the Marshal of Saxony, dead in 1750, was also a Mason during his lifetime, and 'he [like the Prince of Conti] had several votes for the Grand-Mastery [of French Masonry] at the electoral assembly of Count de Clermont in 1743' (ibid., vol. II, p378).

28. 'Charles, Duke de Courlande, member of the *Strict Observance* under the title *Eques a Coronis*' (ibid., vol. II, p304).

Chamberlain to the Elector of Saxony, if we rely on Savalette de Langes, were still 'at the same point' as the *Philalethes* in their search for the '*true light*'. After having 'seen many doctors, Theosophists, Hermeticists, Cabbalists, and Pneumatologues,' this is quite a mediocre result![29]

All that can be said with certainty is that if Schroepfer ever did possess certain real powers, they were of an order inferior even to those of Gugomos. In short, persons of this kind were manifestly only imperfectly initiated, and in one fashion or another they disappear without leaving a trace after playing an ephemeral role as subordinate, and perhaps indirect, agents of the *Unknown Superiors*.[30]

As Benjamin Fabre has quite rightly said, 'Judaizing Kabbalists and magicians, *as well as* imposters and rogues, such were Starck's masters.' And he adds, 'At so good a school, this intelligent disciple knew how to profit greatly, as we shall see.'

∴

THE ARTICLE THAT FOLLOWED[31] was again devoted to F∴ Starck (*Archidemides, Eques ab Aquila Fulva*), whom we find at the Convention of Brunswick (May 22, 1775) grappling with Baron de Hundt (*Eques ab Ense*), founder of the *Strict Observance*, 'contributing to his removal from the presidency of the Order,' but without succeeding in establishing his own claims. As we shall elsewhere return to this point, we shall not dwell on it here, but let us point

29. This can be judged by the questions (*Proponenda*) submitted to the Convention of Paris, which was convened by the *Philalethes* in 1785 (see Thory, op. cit., t. II, pp98–99). In our day, certain occultists have treated these same questions in too fantastical a manner, which proves that they too are always 'at the same point,.

30. It seems, indeed, that this might apply equally to Kolmer, whom we have already mentioned, and even to Schroeder, master of the *Rose-Cross* of Wetzlar, who is sometimes wrongly confused with Schroepfer, and whom Thory simply sets forth in these terms: '*Schroeder*, surnamed *the Cagliostro of Germany*, introduced in 1779 a new system of magic, theosophy, and alchemy' within a Lodge of Sarrebourg, (op. cit., vol. I, p141 and vol. II, p379).

31. *La Bastille*, September 1913 issue.

out that in 1779[32] Starck made an equally unsuccessful attempt recounted by Thory as follows: 'Doctor *Stark* [*sic*] brought together the *Brothers* and *Clerks of the Strict Observance* at Mittau; he sought to resolve their disputes, but failed in this project.'[33]

Here is how the *Eques a Capite Galeato* recounts the real or supposed end of the *Clerks of the Late Observance*:

> At one of the *Provincial Conventions* of the *Rule of the Strict Observance* in Germany, [the *Clerks*] were pressed with questions to which they did not know how, or did not wish, to respond. As to what is claimed, two among them [Starck and the Baron of Raven], who were said to be the last [of these *Clerks* or *Clerici*], exchanged their resignations with one another and renounced all propagation of their secret Order.
>
> Some believe this resignation was only feigned and that, not having found in the *Strict Observance* propagators after their hearts, they made pretense of renouncing it in order that their traces might not be followed, and that they might be forgotten.
>
> Be that as it may, F∴ Starck, learned Mason and learned minister of the Holy Gospel, who, as I have been assured, was one of the *Clerici*, left to the public a great number of works from which it is not impossible to judge to a certain degree the doctrines and goal of his secret Order.
>
> Those of his works that have come to my knowledge are: *L' Apologie des F∴ -M∴* ; *Ephestion, le But de l'Ordre des F∴ -M∴* ;[34] *Sur les Anciens et les Nouveaux Mystères*. The first two are translations.[35]

---

32. Precisely the year when Schroeder, or at least his *system*, appeared; perhaps this is only a coincidence, but there might also be a link between all of these figures, and that even without their knowing it.

33. Op. cit., vol. I, p141.

34. *Über den Zweck des Freymaurer Ordens*, 1781 (Thory, op. cit., vol. I, p368).

35. Thory further cites the following works: *Saint-Nicaise, ou Lettres remarquables sur la Franc-Maçonnerie*, Leipsic, 1785–1786 (ibid., p373); *Sur le Catholicisme caché des Jésuites, et leurs machinations pour faire des proselytes* (*über Kripto-Katholicismus*, etc.), Frankfurt-on-the-Main, 1787–1789 (ibid., p376).

We should add that in 1780 in a brochure entitled 'La Pierre d'achoppement et le Rocher de scandale', 'he publicly attacked the *system of the Templars* as seditious and contrary to government.'[36]

It is possible that the *Clerici* were perpetuated in secret; at any rate, Starck did not disappear from the Masonic scene, since he appears again at the Convention of Paris in 1785.[37] Despite his misfortune, he had retained a great deal of authority; should we then be astonished to see, on the death of Baron of Hundt, a medallion being struck in honor of this other 'learned Mason'[38] who was also at least suspect of imposture and hoax?

As for the exclusive information the *Clerici* claimed to possess, we quote from F∴ Meyer[39] writing (in 1780) to Savalette de Langes:

> You know there were *Clerici* in the Chapter of a certain Order that I do not name,[40] and it is claimed that they alone were entrusted with the science or the secret. This does not suit modern Masons, whose curiosity is piqued. After being named *Knights,* they demand the censer as well the sword. The ease with which this grade is communicated does not testify in its favor; thus, those who have it know at most only a few enigmatic words.

Thus the FF∴, who were already provided with High Grades that penetrated into this supposedly more 'inward' *system,* did not find the *secret of Masonry* therein either, nor did they become *true initiates.*

This observation calls to mind these words of F∴ Ragon:

---

36. *Der Stein des Antosses,* etc. (Thory, op. cit., vol. I, pp146 and 367).

37. See the list given by Thory (op. cit., vol. II, p96).

38. Thory (op. cit., vol. I, p123) adds that this medallion 'offers a quite life-like portrait of this famous Mason.'

39. This F∴ Meyer was present at the Convention of Paris of 1785, and Thory designates him thus: 'de Meyer, Russian Major, at Strasbourg' (op. cit., vol. II, p95). The same author identifies him, perhaps incorrectly, with the writer who translated from English to German a work entitled *La Franc-Maçonnerie n'est que le chemin de l'Enfer* (ibid., vol. I, p361 and vol. II, p354).

40. It is obviously a question of the Templars.

No known grade either teaches or unveils the *truth*; they only make the veil more transparent. . . . . The grades practiced up to this day have made Masons and not *initiates*.[41]

Is it not then behind the various *systems*, and not in such and such a particular one of them, that the *Unknown Superiors* can truly be discovered? But as for proofs of their existence and of their more or less unmediated activity, these are only hard to find when one does not wish to see them. It is this that we especially wished to bring out, and, at least for the moment, we shall abstain from formulating any other conclusions.

41. *Rituel du Grade de Maître,* p34. — Ragon continues, quoting the well-known words of F.'. J.-J. Casanova on *the secret of Masonry,* which only serve to confirm this declaration.

20

CONCERNING THE
UNKNOWN SUPERIORS
AND THE ASTRAL

WHEN WRITING our article 'The Strict Observance and the Unknown Superiors', in which we pointed out the singular obsession that led certain Masonic and occultist writers to see everywhere the action of the Jesuits in eighteenth-century High Masonry and Illuminism, we certainly did not think a similar obsession among anti-Masons themselves would be brought to our attention. But this is just what has turned up in an article that appeared in the *Revue Internationale des Sociétes Secrètes* in the section 'Antimaçonnique de l'Index Documentaire'[1] under the signature A. Martigue, an article in which we read this truly astonishing sentence:

> In studying the Illuminati we must not forget that Weishaupt had been a pupil and then a teacher of the Jesuits, and that he was greatly inspired—of course bending them to the service of evil—*by the methods that the Reverend Fathers of Ingolstadt formerly used for good with so much success . . . except when they used them to form Weishaupt and his first disciples!*

Despite the care with which they are phrased, these insinuations take on a particularly serious character from the pen of an antimason; would Martigue then be able to justify them? Could he explain in what way the Reverend Fathers of the eighteenth century can be made even indirectly responsible for the revolutionary doctrines of

---

1. Oct. 20, 1913 issue, pp3, 725–3, 737.

Brother Weishaupt and his adepts? Until this is demonstrated it seems to us that the Reverend Fathers of the nineteenth century are being held responsible for anarchist theories developed in our time by their ex-pupil and novice, Brother Sebastian Faure! One could certainly go far in that direction, but that would be neither serious nor worthy of a writer who claims to employ 'exact and rigorous methods.'

Here is what Martigue writes shortly before the sentence just cited regarding a study entitled 'Les Pièges de la Secte: le Génie des Conspirations', published in the *Cahiers Romains* of the *Agence Internationale Roma*:

> The author seems familiar only with the works of Father Deschamps, Barruel, Claudio Janet, and Créatineau-Joly. This is a great deal, but not enough. And if these excellent works, which will certainly always be consulted with profit by students of antimasonry, were written by respectable masters whose efforts everyone must praise and recognize, we cannot fail to note that *they date from an age when science and historical criticism had not been carried to the point at which we find them today. Our methods, further perfected each day, are rigorous and correct. From the point of view of scientific exactitude, this is why it is dangerous to neglect more modern works; it is even more regrettable to look down on them prejudicially.*

One must be very sure of oneself and of all one is putting forward to accuse four authors who are among the undisputed masters of antimasonry of a lack of 'scientific exactitude'. Assuredly, Martigues has confidence in the 'progress of science and criticism,' but since this same 'progress' is used to justify such things as modernist exegesis and the so-called 'science of religions', we find it difficult to consider it a convincing argument. We did not expect to see Martigues make a declaration so… evolutionist, and wonder whether the methods he advocates, and which he opposes to 'the methods and defective habits of some' (to whom is he alluding?) do not rather closely approximate the 'positivist method' about which we have already spoken. Finally, if he is acquainted with 'the papers of Weishaupt himself,' as he gives us to understand, we hope he will not be long in communicating to us the discoveries he must have made in them, notably as concerns the relations of Weishaupt with 'the Reverend Fathers of Ingolstadt'; nothing could better prove the value of his methods.

However, would it not be preferable to confine ourselves to the role the Jews could have played at the beginning of Bavarian Illuminism, as well as behind certain 'systems' of High Masonry? Let us quote this sentence from the study in *Cahiers Romains*:

> The schemes of this genius [Weishaupt] were doubtless abetted by Jews, heirs to the implacable hatreds of the old Synagogue, for the famous Bernard Lazare did not shrink from making this avowal: '*There were Jews around Weishaupt*' ('L'Antisémitisme, son histoire, et ses causes', pp339–340).

We mention this because we have already had occasion to speak of this Jewish influence, but there would be many other interesting things to point out in this work, against which the editor of the *Revue Internationale des Sociétés Secrètes* shows a bias bordering on partiality. After criticizing him for 'absence of variety in the documentation,' while nonetheless recognizing his 'real value', he adds: 'there is another very regrettable gap, if one wishes to study Illuminism; *it is ignorance of mysticism and occultism.*' We will come back to this point a little later, but for the moment wish only to point out that mysticism, which arises from theology, is one thing, and occultism is something altogether different: occultists are in general profoundly ignorant of mysticism, which has nothing to do with their pseudo-mysticism.

Unfortunately, something makes us fear that Martigues' criticisms are due above all to an outburst of ill humor brought on by the article in *Cahiers Romains,* which contains a criticism, a very fair one in our opinion, of the summary of Benjamin Fabre's book *Un Initié des Sociétés Secrètes supérieurs: Franciscus, Eques a Capite Galeato* given by Gustave Bord in the same *Revue Internationale des Sociétés Secrètes.*[2]

---

2. September 5,1913 issue, pp3, 71 and following.

Speaking of some Masonic adventurers who tried to foist themselves on the 'fools' of the Lodges, flaunting themselves as authorized representatives of the mysterious 'S. I.' [*Unknown
Superiors*], a restricted center of the whole Sect, Bord notes that
these adventurers were merely boasting, *from which he deduces
that the 'S. I.' did not exist. This deduction is very risky.* If the
adventurers in question misrepresented themselves as *missi
dominici* of the 'S. I.', not only is there nothing to prove that these
latter did not exist, but rather it testifies to a general belief in
their existence, for it would be very strange if these impostors
had invented the mandates from start to finish. Their calculation
of success must clearly have been based on this conviction, and
the latter obviously does not testify against the existence of the
Superiores Incogniti.

But this constitutes the very evidence for anyone unblinded by the
preoccupation of upholding the opposed thesis at any price, for

> is it not Bord himself who, in opposition to the masters of anti-
> masonry, denies the *evidence,* and absolutely ignores [according
> to his own expressions] 'the location, the tactics, and the
> strength of the adversary'?.. there are some very strange anti-
> masons.

Let us add that when we alluded to the 'positivist method' of certain
historians, we were thinking precisely of this summary by Gustave
Bord, no less impartial than is the estimation of Martigue. And now
here is Martigue in turn accusing Benjamin Fabre and Copin-
Albancelli of 'the desire to introduce an argument on a preconceived thesis as to the existence of the unknown directors of the
Sect'; is it not rather Bord whom we could reproach for having a
'preconceived thesis' about the non-existence of the *Unknown Superiors*?

Let us see what Martigue has to say on this subject:

> As for the thesis opposed to Bord regarding the *Unknown Supe-
> riors,* we must be clear that *if the director of the Cahiers Romains
> means by the latter men of flesh and bone, we think he is in error
> and that Bord is right.*

And after enumerating some of the eighteenth-century chiefs of High Masonry he continues:

> If they presented themselves as authorized representatives of living men, one could with reason treat them as impostors, as one can rightfully to do in our time, for example, with Madame Blavatsky, Annie Besant, and the other leaders of Theosophy when they refer to *Mahātmās* residing in a lodge in Tibet.

To this we might very well object that the so-called *Mahātmās* were invented precisely on the more or less distorted model of the true *Unknown Superiors*, for there are few impostures that do not rely on mimicking some reality, and besides, it is the clever mixture of the true and the false that makes them the more dangerous and difficult to unmask. On the other hand, as we said, nothing prevents us from considering as impostors, in certain circumstances, men who could nevertheless really have been subordinate agents of an occult Power. We have offered reasons for this, and do not see any purpose in defending such persons from that accusation, even supposing the *Unknown Superiors* were not 'men of flesh and bone.' In that case, what were they then, according to Martigue? The rest of the citation will inform us, and this will not be the least cause of astonishment to be found in his article.

'But that is not what is in question [*sic*]; this is an altogether exoteric interpretation for the profane and non-initiated adepts.' Until now we had thought that the 'adeptat' was a higher stage of 'initiation'; but let us continue.

> The esoteric meaning has always been different. *The famous Unknown Superiors, the true initiates, certainly exist, but they live . . . in the astral.* And it is from there, through theurgy, occultism, spiritualism, clairvoyance, etc., that they direct the heads of the Sects, *at least according to what they say.*

Is it, then, to conceptions as fantastic as these that knowledge of occultism, or at least a certain occultism, must lead, despite all the 'rigor' and 'exactness' of the scientific and critical methods and the 'indisputable historical proofs required today[!] from serious and erudite historians?'

Either Martigue admits the existence of the 'Astral' and of its inhabitants, *Unknown Superiors* or others, so that we are entitled to conclude that 'there are some very strange anti-masons' other than Gustave Bord; or he does not admit it, as we claim to believe according to the last restriction, in which case he cannot say that those who admit it are 'true initiates'. We think, on the contrary, that they are only very imperfect initiates, and even that it is only too obvious that the spiritists, for example, cant in no way be considered initiates. Nor should we forget that spiritism dates only from the manifestations of Hydesville, which began in 1847, and that it was unknown in France before Brother Rivail, better known as Allan Kardec.[3] It is claimed that the latter 'founded his doctrine with the help of communications that he obtained and that were collected, supervised, reviewed, and corrected by *superior spirits*.'[4] Without a doubt, this would be a remarkable intervention of the *Unknown Superiors*, according to Martigue's definition, if unfortunately we did not know that the 'superior spirits' taking part in that work were not all 'disembodied', and that some are still not so: although Eugène Nus and Victorien Sardou have since then 'passed onto another plane of evolution,' to use spiritualist language, Camille Flammarion continues to celebrate the festival of the Sun at each summer solstice.

And so, for the chiefs of High Masonry in the eighteenth century there could be no question of spiritism, which did not yet exist any more than did occultism; for even if 'occult sciences' existed at that time, there was no doctrine called 'occultism'. It seems that Eliphas Lévi was the first to use that term, which was monopolized after his death (1875) by a certain school of which, from the initiatic point of view, it is better not to say anything. It is these same 'occultists' who currently speak of the 'astral world', which they invoke to help explain all things, especially those of which they are ignorant. It was Eliphas Lévi again who gave currency to the term 'astral', and although this word goes back to Paracelsus, it seems to have been

3. For extensive documentation on spiritism and Allan Kardec, see *The Spiritist Fallacy*. ED.

4. Dr Gibier, *Le Spiritisme*, pp136–137.

virtually unknown to the High Masons of the eighteenth century, who in any case would never have understood it as do present-day occultists. Is it because Martigue, whose knowledge of occultism we do not contest, is quite sure that this same knowledge does not precisely lead him to an 'altogether exoteric interpretation' not only of Swedenborg for example, but of all the others whom he quotes in comparing it, or almost so, to spiritist 'mediums'? Let us quote the text:

> The *Unknown Superiors* are the *Angels* who dictate to Swedenborg his works, the *Sophia* of Gichtel, of Boehme, the *Thing* of Martinez Pasqualis [*sic*], the *Unknown Philosopher* of Saint-Martin, the manifestations of the École du Nord, the *Guru* of the Theosophists, the spirit incarnated in the medium who raises the foot of the turning table or dictates the wild imaginings of the planchette, etc., etc.

We for our part do not think that all this is the same, even with 'variations and nuances'; it is perhaps looking for the *Unknown Superiors* where there could be no reason to do so. We have just said what the spirits are, and as for the 'Theosophers' or 'Theosophists', we know what to make of their claims. Regarding these last let us note in addition that they announce the incarnation of their 'Great Teacher' (*Mahāguru*), which goes to prove that they do not expect to receive his teachings on the 'astral plane'. Moreover, we do not think *Sophia* (who represents a principle) ever manifested herself perceptibly to Boehme or Gichtel. As for Swedenborg, he has described symbolically some 'spiritual hierarchies' all of whose levels could very well be occupied by living initiates, in a way similar to what we find, in particular, in Islamic esoterism.

As regards Martinès de Pasqually, it is assuredly rather difficult to know exactly what he mysteriously called '*the Thing*', but it seems that he employed this word whenever he did not wish to designate anything other than his 'operations', or what is ordinarily meant by *Art*. It is the modern occultists who have tried to see the latter as simple 'apparitions', in conformity with their own ideas; but Brother Franz von Baader warns us that 'we would be wrong to think his physics [that of Martinès] is confined to spectres and spirits.'[5] In all this, as in the basis of the High Masonry of this period, there was something much more profound and more truly 'esoteric' than the knowledge present-day occultism ever suffices to penetrate.

But what is perhaps most singular is that Martigue speaks of the '*Unknown Philosopher of Saint-Martin*,' when we know perfectly well that Saint-Martin and the *Unknown Philosopher* were one and the same, the second being only the pseudonym of the first. We are of course acquainted with the legends current on this subject in certain circles, but here is something that settles the matter admirably:

> The *Superiors Incogniti* or 'S. I.', have been attributed by a fanciful author to the Theosopher Saint-Martin, perhaps because the latter signed his works *an Unknown Philosopher*, which was the name of a grade of the *Philalèthes* (an order to which, moreover, he never belonged). It is true that the same fantasist attributed the book *Des Erreurs et de la Vérité*, by the *Unknown Philosopher* to an *Unknown Agent*; and that he gives himself the title 'S. I.' When one takes from the *unknown*, one cannot take too much of it![6]

From this we see how dangerous it can be to accept without verification the assertions of certain occultists; in such a case it is especially important to exercise prudence and, according to the advice of Martigue himself, 'not exaggerate anything.'

Thus, we would be very wrong to take these occultists seriously when they present themselves as the descendants and successors of ancient Masonry; and yet we find an echo of such 'fanciful' assertions in the following sentence of Martigue:

> This question [of the *Unknown Superiors*] raises problems that we study in occultism, problems that Freemasons of the eighteenth century tried ardently to solve.

Not to mention that, if too literally interpreted, this sentence could cause the editor of the *Revue Internationale des Sociétes Secrètes* to

---

5. *Les enseignements secrets de Martines de Pasqually*, p18.
6. *Notice historique sur le Martinésisme et le Martinisme*, pp35–36, in a note.

be taken for an 'occultist' in the eyes 'of superficial readers not having the time to go deeply into things.'

But, he continues, 'we can only see clearly into this question if we are thoroughly acquainted with the occult sciences and mysticism.' This is what he wanted to prove against the contributor to the *Agence Internationale Roma*; but has he not actually proved, against himself, that this knowledge ought to extend even further than he had supposed? 'This is why so few antimasons succeed in penetrating these mysteries, mysteries which those who claim to stay on positivist terrain will never know.' In our opinion this is much more justifiable than all that goes before; but does this not somewhat contradict what Martigue has said about his 'methods'? And then, if he does not adhere to the 'positivist' conception of history, why does he defend Gustave Bord against all comers, even when he is least defensible?

> If one does not take the trouble to study both the language they speak and the subject they treat of in their letters and their works, it is impossible to understand the writings of men who live in the supernatural and let themselves be directed by it, such as the Swedenborgian Theosophists or Martinists of the eighteenth century. And even less so if, with one's mind is already made up, one denies the existence of the supernatural atmosphere into which they were plunged and which they daily breathed.

Yes, but apart from the fact that this rebounds on Bord and his conclusions, it is no reason for passing from one extreme to the other and to attribute more importance than one should to the 'wild imaginings' of spiritist planchettes or those of pseudo-initiates, to the point of reducing everything 'supernatural', whatever its quality, to a narrow astral interpretation'.

Another comment: Martigue speaks of 'Swedenborgian Theosophists or Martinists' as if these two were nearly equivalent. Would he therefore be tempted to credit the authenticity of a certain filiation that is however very far from any 'scientific fact' and from any 'positive basis'?

On this subject, we feel obliged to say that when Papus maintains that Martinès de Pasqually received initiation from Swedenborg in the course of a visit to London, and that the system he propagated under the name of rite of the *Elect Cohens* was only an *adapted Swedenborgianism*, the author is deluding himself or is seeking to delude his readers in the interest of a very personal thesis. To lend oneself to such assertions it is not enough to have read in Ragon (who himself had read it in Reghelini) that Martinès took the rite of the *Elect Cohens* from the Swedish Swedenborg. Papus could have refrained from reproducing and amplifying a valuation based on nothing serious. He could have researched the sources of his document and ascertained that there are very few connections between the doctrine and rite of Swedenborg, and the doctrine and rite of the *Elect Cohens*. . . . As for the alleged trip to London, it took place only in Papus' imagination.[7]

It is regrettable that an historian should let himself be carried away by his imagination... 'in the astral'; and unfortunately the same could be said of many other writers who try to establish most unlikely links 'in the interest of a very personal thesis,' often all too personal!

But let us return to Martigue, who informs us once again that

without the help of these sciences, known as occult, it is completely impossible to understand the Masonry of the eighteenth century and even—and this will astonish the uninitiated—that of today.

Here, one or two examples would have helped us better grasp his meaning, but let us see what comes next:

It is from that ignorance [of occultism], shared not only by the profane but also by Masons, even those of high grades, that such errors as the one under consideration derive. This error has set antimasonry in search of *Unknown Superiors who, according to*

---

7. *Notice historique sur le Martinésisme et le Martinisme*, p17, in a note.

the pen of true initiates, are merely extra-natural manifestations of beings living in the Astral World.

As we have said, we for our part do not believe that those who can uphold such a thesis are 'true initiates', but if Martigue, who affirms it, really does believe it, we do not see why he should hasten to add: 'Which does not prejudge anything regarding their existence [of those *Unknown Superiors*], any more moreover than about the said *Astral World*,' without seeming to notice that he thereby calls everything into question again. While 'only claiming to indicate what the High Masons of the eighteenth century thought,' is he quite sure he is faithfully interpreting their thought and not simply introducing a new complication into one of the problems the solution of which these FF∴ 'passionately pursued,' because that solution could help them become the 'true initiates' they obviously were not so long as they had not found it? This is because 'true initiates' are still rarer than one thinks; but that does not mean none exist, or that they exist only 'in the Astral'; and why, although living on earth, would such 'adepts' in the true and complete sense of the word not be the true *Unknown Superiors*?

> Accordingly, by writing the words *Unknown Superiors*, 'S. I.', the Illuminati, the Martinists, the members of the Strict Observance, and all the Masons of the eighteenth century indeed speak *of beings considered as having a real higher existence, under the direction of which each Lodge and each initiated adept* [*sic*] *is placed.*

To make the *Unknown Superiors* 'astral beings' and then to assign them such a role as 'invisible helpers', as the Theosophists say—is that not to wish to connect them rather too closely with 'spiritual guides' who from a 'higher plane' similarly direct mediums and spiritist groups? It is therefore perhaps not altogether 'in this sense that the *Knight of Capite Galeato* and his correspondents write,' unless one wishes to speak of a 'higher existence' able to be 'realized' by certain categories of initiates who are 'invisible' and 'astral' only to the profane and the pseudo-initiates already mentioned. Whatever Martigue may say, all contemporary occultism, including even spiritism, Theosophy, as well as the other 'neo-spiritualist' movements, can still only lead to an 'altogether exoteric interpretation.' But if it so difficult to know exactly what the High Masons of the eighteenth century thought, and consequently to 'interpret their letters as they themselves understood them,' is it not indispensable that these conditions be integrally fulfilled in order not to 'be completely mistaken in pursuing these studies, which are already so difficult even when one is on the right track'? And is there anyone among the antimasons who can say of himself 'on the right track' to the exclusion of everyone else? The questions they have to study are much too complex for that, even without having the 'Astral' intervening where it has no right to. That is why it is always 'regrettable to look down on them prejudicially' even in the name of 'science' and of 'criticism', activities which, as the editor of the *Cahiers Romains* so well puts it, '[while] not definitive, does not prevent their being very important, such as they are.' Gustave Bord does claim impartiality, but does he really possess that quality to the degree required to realize the ideal of Martigue, 'the mature historian who knows how to find what he wants everywhere, and whose sound criticism allows to judge the value of documents'? Again, there can be several ways of being 'on the right track', and it is enough to be on it in one way or another, not to 'be completely deceived,' even without it being 'indispensable to light the right path in the murky lights[?!] of occultism,' which is hardly clear!

Martigue concludes in these terms:

While waiting, we will gladly acknowledge that, if he understands occult power in the sense we just indicated, the editor of the *Cahiers Romains* is correct in writing: 'We note that no convincing argument has until now been presented against the occult central power of the Sect.' But if, contrary to the initiated Freemasons of the eighteenth century, he means by this a committee of men of flesh and blood, we are obliged to turn back the argument and say: 'We know that no convincing document has until now been presented in favor of that unknown directing Committee.' And it is up to those who assert that existence to bring forth the decisive proof. We are still waiting. The question remains open.

Indeed, it is always open, and it is certain that 'it is one of the most important'; but who has ever claimed that the *Unknown Superiors*, even in 'flesh and blood', constituted a 'committee', or even a 'society' in the ordinary sense of the word? On the contrary, that solution seems very unsatisfactory when it is known that there exist certain truly secret organizations which are much closer to the 'central power' than outward Masonry, and that their members have neither meetings, insignia, diplomas, nor exterior means of recognition. It is good to respect 'documents', but we know it may be rather difficult to discover 'convincing' ones precisely when, as we wrote previously, the things concerned 'are not of a nature to be proved by any written document whatever.' Here again, therefore, we must not 'exaggerate anything,' and must above all avoid being absorbed exclusively by 'documentary preoccupation' to the point of losing sight, for example, of the fact that ancient Masonry recognized several sorts of Lodges working 'on different planes,' as an occultist would say, and that in the thought of the High Masons of that time this in no way meant that the 'meetings' of certain of those Lodges took place 'in the Astral', the 'archives' of which moreover are scarcely accessible, except to the 'students' of Leadbeater's school. If there are today any of these 'fanciful S. I.' who claim to meet 'in the astral', they do so very simply in order not to admit that they do not meet at all; and if their 'study groups' were indeed transported 'to another plane', it was only in the manner common to all beings 'in sleep' or 'disembodied', whether individualities or collectivities, profane 'committees' or so-called 'initiatic societies'. In these last there are many people who would like to pass themselves off as 'mystics' whereas they are only common 'mystifiers' who do not hesitate to join charlatanism to occultism, without possessing even the few inferior and accidental 'powers' that a Gugomos or Schöpfer was sometimes able to exhibit. Also, would it perhaps not be better still to study more closely the 'operations' and the 'doctrine' of these latter, however imperfectly initiated they may have been, than those of so-called contemporary 'Magi', who are not initiated at all or at least not initiated into anything serious, which amounts to exactly the same thing.

None of this means, of course, that it may not be good to study and even to be familiar with current and 'popular' occultism, although giving it only the very relative importance it deserves, and much less to seek in it a profound 'esoterism' that is simply not there, if only to show on occasion all its inanity, and to alert those who would be tempted to be seduced by the deceptive appearances of an 'initiatic science' that is altogether superficial and second or third hand. We must have no illusions: if in spite of everything the actions of the true *Unknown Superiors* do exist to some degree, in the 'neo-spiritualist' movements in question, whatever their titles and their claims, it is only in a quite indirect and distant fashion as in the most exterior and most modern Masonry. What we have just said already proves it, and we will have occasion in forthcoming studies to bring to this subject other no less significant examples.

21

SOME UNPUBLISHED DOCUMENTS ON THE ORDER OF THE ELECT COHENS

WE HAVE ALLUDED on various occasions to the *Order of the Elect Cohens,* founded by Martines de Pasqually. In a preface to the *Traité de la Réintegration des Êtres,* the 'Knight of the Rose Cross', whom we have already frequently quoted, writes:

> This man [Martines], with a disinterest and sincerity beyond all suspicion, sought to bring certain Lodges back to the essential principles of Freemasonry, from which they had considerably departed during this period [the second half of the eighteenth century], through a series of events that need not be related here.
>
> Martines' task was a difficult one: traveling successively from 1760 to 1772 through the major towns of France, he selected from among the Masonic crafthalls those he judged capable of serving as a nucleus, a center for his subsequent operations. In the name of his *Sovereign Tribunal,* established in Paris in 1767, he delivered constitutional patents to the clandestine Lodges of the provinces, not hesitating to recruit from abroad men he deemed worthy of the ministry they would be called upon to exercise.[1]

---

1. In the mind of its founder, it was a question of a truly *sacerdotal* ministry, for the Hebrew word *Cohen* means *priest;* his efforts therefore represent to a certain degree an attempt to restore the Judaic priesthood within *interior* Masonry.

Thus was formed what M. Matter has aptly termed *Martinisme*,[2] which, under the name *Rite of the Elect Cohens,* is none other than a perfectly orthodox branch of true Freemasonry, grafted onto the ancient trunk, and based on an ensemble of very precise traditional teachings transmitted in rigorous accordance with the receptive power acquired by each of its members through an entirely personal effort. Theory and practice were closely joined together.

We quote this extract in order to establish the true character of the *Elect Cohens.* Let us now turn to a few details concerning the role played in this Order by Louis-Claude de Saint-Martin, details useful to keep in mind in the light of certain confusions:

A few years after Martines de Pasqually's departure for the Antilles (1772), a schism arose within the order he had labored so hard to establish, certain disciples remaining strongly attached to all that the Master had taught, while others, led by the example of Saint-Martin, abandoned active practice for the incomplete, passive path of mysticism.[3] This change of direction in the life of Saint-Martin might surprise us were it not known to what degree the disciple had remained aloof, during the five years he spent at the Lodge of Bordeaux, from the outward operations of the Master. . . .

The teaching of Rodolphe de Salzmann played a large part in endowing France with a remarkable mysticism, but for Saint-Martin this teaching was unable to unlock the doctrine of the eminent theurge of Bordeaux [Martines]. . . .

We dwell on these particular points in the life of Saint-Martin only to show how incorrect it is for certain misinformed historians to have attributed the succession of the theurge of Bordeaux

2. As for us, we cannot find this term *apt;* it would be so only if the system of the *Elect Cohens* merely translated the personal ideas of Martines, which it does not, according to the rest of the very same passage quoted; but the author had particular reasons for showing proof of his goodwill in regard to Matter.

3. This clearly characterizes the opposition, which we have already noted, between the path of 'mystics' and that of 'initiates'.

to the theosophist of Amboise, and for certain others, even less well-researched, have made him the founder of an *Order of Martinism*. Saint-Martin never founded any Order; he never had this aim, and the term *Martinists* simply designates those who had adopted a perspective that conformed to his own, with the tendency to free themselves from the ritualistic dogmatism of the Lodges, and to reject it as useless.[4]

Thus, everything concerning the *Elect Cohens* must be related exclusively to Martines,[5] and it is nonsense to attribute the name *Martinism* either to this Order or to the doctrine it professes. We wished to make this clear, above all.

∴

THERE ARE VERY FEW published documents on the *Order of the Elect Cohens*, the most important being those we have already mentioned, which form two volumes of the *Bibliotheque Rosicrucienne*, published under the auspices of the *Rite of Misraïm*. The first is the work of Martines himself, entitled *Traité de la Reintegration des Êtres dans leurs premieres proprietes, vertus et puissance spirituelles et divines*. The second contains the *Enseignements Secret de Martines de Pasqually*, as they were received and explicated by Franz von Baader.

Then there is Papus' work on *Martines de Pasqually*, which contains letters of various provenance, some of which are interesting, although they are not always presented intelligibly. To this same work the *Catechisms* of the following grades are also appended:

4. We point to this passage in particular in response to those who claim, for example, that 'the introduction of Martinist Lodges in Russia dates from St. Martin [*sic*] himself.' We shall refer these people to the same author's *Notice historique sur le Martinésisme et le Martinisme*, pp175–192. There were never any 'Martinist Lodges', save in the imagination of contemporary occultists.

5. Which is not to say, let us emphasize this, that it is a question of a *personal* work, since it was on the contrary 'based on an ensemble of very precise traditional teachings'

(1) *Apprentice Elect Cohen*; (2) *Companion Elect Cohen*; (3) *Master Particular Elect Cohen*; (4) *Master Elect Cohen*; (5) *Grand Master Cohen, surnamed Grand Architect*; (6) *Grand Elect of Zorabel, so-called Knight of the Orient*.[6]

We believe that nothing of importance has been omitted from this list, which as can be seen is rather short; the least authentic fragments relating to the *Elect Cohens* are therefore of interest by very reason of their rarity.

∴

THE DOCUMENTS we intend to publish here consist of a series of *Instructions* given to the *Elect Cohens* of Lyon early in 1774. These initiates belonged to the Lodge *La Bienfaisance,* presided over by Willermoz; but as a whole this Lodge never practiced the *Rite of the Elect Cohens,* as some have wrongly claimed. On this subject, the 'Knight of the Rose Cross' writes:

> We shall point out to Papus, who speaks of a Lodge of *Elect Cohens* that has been situated in Lyon since 1765 under the presidency of Willermoz, that at the beginning of 1770 there were still only six barely initiated *Elect Cohens,* including Willermoz, in Lyon.[7]

During this period they petitioned Martines that they might obtain the foundation of a regular establishment, but it seems these steps never met with success.

It is therefore quite probable that there never was a complete organization of the *Elect Cohens* in Lyon, all the more so since Saint-Martin, who passed through the town in 1774, and there wrote his book *Des Erreurs et de la Verite,* speaks simply 'of a circle he instructed

---

6. This collection lacks the *Catechism* of the seventh and last grade, that of *Rose-Cross,* which was in reality the tenth grade, counting the 'grades of the porch', that is, the three ordinary, symbolic grades that necessarily precede all others.

7. *Notice Historique sur le Martinésisme et le Martinisme,* p33, n 2.

at the residence of Villermas [*sic*],'[8] an expression that would not be applied to a regular 'correct and complete' Lodge. Moreover, following the *Convention of Lyon* in 1778 the Lodge *La Bienfaisance* definitively adopted the *Rectified Scottish Rite*, which Papus 'deemed useful to baptize as *Willermozisme*,'[9] but which never had anything to do with the *Order of the Elect Cohens*. The greater part of the archives of Lyon, today dispersed, naturally relate to this *Rectified Rite;* the ignorance of certain authors in this regard has led to some singular confusions.[10]

To return to our *Instructions*, we do not think they were written by Martines himself, who, departed for Port-au-Prince on May 5, 1772, and died there on September 20, 1774. It is certain, however, that they are directly inspired by his teachings, for in various places they present striking analogies with certain passages from the *Traité de la Reintegration des Êtres*, written in Bordeaux in the course of the year 1770.

The six *Instructions*[11] in our possession are here reproduced in their entirety, with scrupulous respect to all particularities of language, style, and even orthography in the original manuscript. We shall limit ourselves to adding a few brief notes when called for, reserving our comments on the more interesting points for the end.

---

8. Ibid., pp 41–42.
9. Ibid., pp 175–176.
10. Ibid., pp 177–178, note.
11. Editor's note: The 6th Instruction was never published, owing to the discontinuation of *La France antimaçonnique*.

INSTRUCTIONS ON UNIVERSAL, MATERIAL, TEMPORAL
CREATION AND THE SENARY NUMBER THAT PRODUCES
IT AND ITS RELATIONS WITH MAN

FIRST INSTRUCTION[12]

Wishing to form this physical universe from visible matter for the manifestation of his Power, his Justice, and his Glory, the plan the Creator conceived presented itself to his imagination in a triangular form, rather as the plan or design for a picture presents itself to the imagination of a painter before he begins to execute it. This plan being triangular, the work derived from it must bear its imprint, must, like it, be triangular or ternary, and such is indeed the case.[13]

I say that universal material Creation was enacted by the Creator for the manifestation of his Power, his Justice, and his Glory; his Power is indeed manifested by the very act of Creation, which has been produced from nothing by his will alone; his Justice has been manifested by the punishment of the first disobedient spirits, whom he drove from his presence. The Creator, being immutable in his decrees, could not deprive them of the virtues and powers that were innate to them on account of their principle of divine emanation, but he did change their Laws of spiritual action; he formed this material Universe, to which he relegated them, to be a place of privation, in order that they might exercise their action, Power, and bad Will within the Bounds that he has fixed for them; from this manifestation of the Creator's Power and Justice results without contradiction the manifestation of his Glory; this Universe must further serve to manifest his infinite Goodness and mercy, as will be explained in its place.

---

12. This first instruction is the only one without a date in the manuscript; as will later be seen, it is from January 7, 1774.

13. In these instructions it is essentially a question of the 'plan of the Great Architect of the Universe' realized by Creation. — However, as we will see in what follows, the two expressions 'Creator' and 'Great Architect' are not synonyms.

It is through the senary number that Universal Creation was enacted, as Moses gives us to understand through the six days he speaks of in Genesis, which is only a veil he has employed to express what he wished to say. The Creator is a pure spirit, the eternal simple that cannot be subject to time; moreover, since time began only at the universal Creation of which we are speaking, nothing preceding it could have been temporal. Therefore Moses could not have wished to speak of six days, nor of any Lapse of determined time, but rather of six divine thoughts that in reality enacted the Creation; we learn to know them through the mysterious addition of the three divine faculties the Order teaches: thought, will, and action, or in another sense that we shall explain at the proper time, intention, Word, and operation.

Thought is one, simple, and indivisible, like the Mind that produces it; it is the principle of all free spiritual action, and it consequently holds the first rank among the three spiritual faculties in question; for this reason we reckon it ONE, in engendering Will, without which it would be null and would produce nothing; in virtue of its binary rank we reckon it TWO, and, joining to it thought from which it is derived, we reckon it THREE, which completes[14] the first spiritual ternary. But thought and Will would be nothing and would produce no effect were they not put into act. It is this faculty productive of effect that we term action; this action, on account of its ternary rank, we reckon THREE, and adding to it the preceding ternary of the thought and Will whence it proceeds, it completes the senary number that has enacted universal Creation.

This table of the three potent, innate faculties within the Creator gives us at the same time an idea of the incomprehensible mystery of the Trinity, Thought given to the Father 1, Word or intention attributed to the Son 2, and operation attributed to the Spirit 3. As will follows thought, and as action is the result of thought and will, the Word likewise proceeds from thought, and operation proceeds from thought and Word, the mysterious addition

---

14. The manuscript has the word 'forms' added above 'completes'.

of these three numbers also yielding the principial senary number of all temporal Creation. In this example you will recognize three faculties that really are distinct, that proceed from one another and that produce different results, but that are brought together in the same single being, unique and indivisible.

You have been taught that man was created in the image and likeness of God. As the Creator is pure spirit, it cannot be in his bodily form that man is his image and likeness, but only in his spiritual faculties, since the lesser spiritual being, or man, is an emanation of the divinity and must participate in the very essence of this divinity and its faculties. We have a quite feeble but sensible image of this in the day-to-day reproduction of temporal beings; but for all that, the being produced, though similar to the being that produced it, and though participating in its nature, is not the producing being itself; in the same way, man comes from God and participates in his essence and faculties without being God himself; without destroying the image and likeness that link the two, the immense difference that must exist between Creator and Creature will always remain. Thus, as man senses within himself the Power or the distinct faculties of Thought, Will, and action, we can say with truth that by these three faculties, which are united in him, he really is the true image of the Creator, just as he bears his likeness through the three potent faculties that are likewise innate to him, namely Thought, Word or intention, and operation, of which we shall speak at another time, and which must not be confused with thought, will, and action.

Having explained the senary number by virtue of which Creation is enacted, I shall now speak of the ternary number, the producer of forms, and of the novenary number we attribute to matter, for this visible and palpable matter that strikes our senses must no longer be confused with the impalpable principles that constitute it; it is the union of these principles put into action that composes bodies.

NOTES ON MATTERS TREATED IN THE FIRST
INSTRUCTION AT THE GENERAL ASSEMBLY[15]
OF JANUARY 7, 1774

On the material temporal Universal Creation enacted by virtue
of the senary number of divine thoughts, veiled in Genesis by the
six days of Moses.

Mysterious addition of the three divine faculties, Thought, Will,
and Action.

Plan of Creation present in the mind of the Creator in a ∇ [tri-
angular] form.

Imprint of this triangle in all the products of Creation.

Ternary number of spiritual essences, the producers of the forms
mysteriously called sulfur, salt, and mercury.

Principial essences of the elements, principial elements of bodies.

Produced by the spirits of the axis, central fire or uncreated fire.

Spiritual essences in respect to one another.

In their state of indifferentiation, having their vitriol innate
without action, produced Chaos.

Envelope of Chaos formed by the spirits of the axis.

Elders in infancy, their spiritual being sometimes occupied elsewhere.

Sensible terrestrial circle to the West, visual to the North, rational to the South, sensible at the mother's breast, visible during
life, rational during Reintegration, sensible from the earth to the

---

15. These notes contain, by way of summary, the rest of the first instruction,
which appears not to have been written down entirely. — The expression 'general
assembly' must, we believe, be understood to refer to a meeting common to all the
grades.

moon, visual from the moon to the Sun, rational from the Sun to Saturn.

Lesser spiritual beings led and driven by the greater beings in these three circles.

Free will destroyed through the function of the greater, *felix culpa.*

Lesser ternary spirits are bodily without intelligence.

The ordinary axis is the horizontal line that supports and runs through Creation.

The uncreated fire axis is at once the envelope, the support, and the center of Creation, and is uncreated because the ternary spirits that produce it are emanated and not created.

Man destined for persecution by the wicked spirits.

He disrupts the work of the Creator in taking his own life, in falling into excess. His body is a temple. Fasts enfeeble the attacks of the enemy. The five senses are the gates of the enemy and of the watchman.

The bodily soul or vehicle resides in the blood; the spiritual soul likewise acts on the blood or the adherent vehicle.[16]

SECOND INSTRUCTION[17]
FROM MONDAY, JANUARY 20, 1774

Quaternary emanation of man deriving from the fourfold divine essence represented by thought 1, will 2, action 3, and operation

---

16. We draw attention to the role here attributed to the blood; it is the mark of a theory that is essentially Judaic in origin.

17. The date indicated in the manuscript is certainly erroneous; comparing it to the others, it is easy to see that the true date is January 10. — There were two meetings each week, on Mondays and Fridays.

4, the mysterious addition of which completes the denary number 10 or ⊕, that is, the circumference, which is the emblem of eternal power and of universal creation, and its center, which represents the indivisible unit from which all is derived and within which all will be reintegrated.

∴

Quaternary emanation and power privileges of man, represented by the 4 signs or characters applied to him in the reception of the first grades of the order: the 1st, to the heart, recalls his spiritual existence; the 2nd, to the right side, the good companion given to him to direct him; the 3rd, to the top of the head, the greater spirit of double power that drives and rule over[18] the 2 others; finally, the 4th, perpendicularly drawn from the top of the head to the stomach, represents the divinity that presides, directs, and governs, and whence all power derives.

The first three, forming a triangle, represent the power of man over universal creation through his principle of quaternary emanation, whereby he receives the laws, precepts, and commandments which he lost through his disobedience, and which he can only regain by placing himself once again in direct correspondence with his quaternary number, represented by the perpendicular crossing the center of the triangle; this triangle in turn represents the ternary power granted him after his reconciliation with the three terrestrial horizons, West, North, and South, and with the three parts of universal creation, terrestrial, celestial, and supercelestial; but this power is useless and without action if he does not obtain the divine quaternary power represented by the perpendicular.

∴

18. The manuscript has the word 'directs' added above 'rules over'.

Quaternary correspondence of man, to wit:
Man or the lesser spiritual being 1,
The good companion spirit 2,
The greater spirit of double power 3,
The Creator 4 — 10 —

∴

Man was emanated and placed at the center of six circles or divine thoughts in order that he might command, direct, preserve, and defend universal creation; he possessed a power proportional to these acts, but after the fall the Creator had to replace him with a being invested with a double power that was much more considerable, since he had to execute all of the same acts for which man had been destined, as well as to direct, either directly or through his agents, the lesser spiritual being and its form in preserving, supporting, and defending the lesser spiritual being and its form against the snares and daily attacks of the wicked spirits, to whom man had been subjugated through the fall.

∴

Triangular figure of man formed from the extremity of the hands, with arms outstretched, to the feet, dominated by the head, or the celestial perpendicular that crosses the center.

∴

Ternary division: the bones of …,[19] the Pelvis or the stomach 1, the sides or the breadth of the chest 2, the head 3, form three parts that cannot be separated without their being destroyed; the 4 members belong to the vegetative part; they form a receptacle of which the Chest is the center; their Reunion repeats the septenary number that directs creation.

---

19. A word has been left blank here in the manuscript.

THIRD INSTRUCTION[20]
FROM FRIDAY, JANUARY 14, 1774

Opening of the 4 gates of the Temple and of the 3 gates of the Porch.

The 3 circles, sensible visual, rational, and their 3 relationships.

The septenary of Creation and its duration.

The binary number opposition of two powers.

The quinary number division of the denary.

The quaternary Good opposed to evil thought and intellect.

The lesser becomes an evil intellect and perverts its fellows.

The novenary, 3 essences, three elements, three bodily principles.

The novenary by the multiplication of the three mixtures.

The novenary by the senary number of manufacture, creation, and the three created essences.

Higher spirits 10, greater 8, lower 7, lesser terrestrial 3, or d° higher 10, greater 8, lower 3, lesser man 4, or all was made by the senary and is directed by the 7th.

The joining with the greater spirit is accomplished at the age of seven.

Men and Religion do punish before the age of seven.

Producers.

Vehicle inserted into Chaos develops what redounds through the descent of the higher agent Spirit; there is no action without reaction.

Explosion of Chaos through retreat of the greater Divine agent.

---

20. Here again, we have only a sort of summary, the all too brief notes of which are not always perfectly comprehensible.

Extension of Chaos, Limits of Creation fixed by the Spirits of the axis; they maintain the limits of Creation.

It [Creation] serves as a barrier to the evil will of the first perverse spirits.

They exercise their malice against it and relentlessly seek its deterioration.

Ternary of the three fires of the axis, the earth, and the Sun.

Effects of these three fires acting upon one another.

Passive and active mercury, vegetative and active sulfur, sensitive salt.[21]

FOURTH INSTRUCTION
FROM MONDAY, JANUARY 17, 1774

All beings derived from the Creator are temples. One must distinguish between the different gates of the temple.

$$\therefore$$

Material temple, the smallest atom of matter is one of these since it has its vehicle that animates it.

$$\therefore$$

Spiritual temple of beings who drive and direct temporal Creation without themselves being subject to time, such was Adam in his first principle.

---

21. As one may have noticed, alchemical language is employed here from time to time, but not in a constant manner, as in the properly Hermetic Rites; first place is reserved for the symbolism of numbers and their Kabbalistic interpretation.

∴

Spiritual, temporal temples raised visibly on this surface for the duration of time for the Resurrection.

∴

The 7 principal days, those of Adam, of Enoch, of Melchizedek, of Moses, of Solomon, of Zorobabel, and of Christ, types of deliverance and of resurrection.

∴

The others, like Noah, Abraham, etc., days of different types.

∴

The body of man is a lodge or a temple, which is a repetition of the general, particular, and universal Temple.

∴

Masonry consists in raising up edifices on their foundations. We are thus spiritual Masons.

∴

Apocryphal Masonry derived from the order calls its assemblies lodges and we temples. They give themselves the name of Masons, and we today, to distinguish ourselves, call ourselves Elect Cohen Philosophers.

∴

The Temple of Solomon, on which all Masonry is founded, holds a remarkable rank among the seven principal spiritual, temporal temples, through its infinite allusions within universal Creation.

∴

Relations within the ternary division: the porch wherein the multitude of Levites assembled in order to assist with the sacrifices, the Temple wherein assembled the Priests who aided the High Priest in his functions, the Holy of Holies wherein the High Priest alone entered to perform his particular tasks. — Relationships with the terrestrial, celestial, and super-celestial parts of Creation, and with man's stomach, his chest—or the seat of his soul through the blood—and his head.

∴

The Vestments of the G.P. were allegorical with respect to his functions or particular tasks. He ran the risk of death if he presented himself impure or ill-prepared within the Holy of Holies; he wore bells at the base of his robe, in order that it might be noticed if he were inactive for too long; he entered therein with long cords trailing behind him, the ends of which remained in the temple; they allowed the priests who were unable to enter the Holy of Holies to retrieve his body were he to die therein.

∴

The Priests of our day have preserved these cords, the stoll or receptacle, the alb, the miter, etc.

∴

All spiritual temples have been founded on seven Columns, which allegorically represent the seven gifts of the Spirit originally accorded man; of these gifts, the faculty of action can only develop within him through the junction and direct correspondence with his quaternary of divine emanation.

∴

The seven Columns were represented in the Temple of Solomon by the 7-branched candlestick, which held seven stars or lit lamps, and which represented the 7 planets, the 7 columns of universal Creation. The G. P. moved this candlestick according to the different parts on which he wished to work.

∴

Man was created at the third hour, the number of the spiritual essences that cooperated with the formation of bodies; he fell at the fifth hour, the number of the joining of his divine quaternary with the false, evil unity, and was embodied at the sixth hour, the number of the manufacture of the Universe over which he should have ruled, and was driven out at the ninth, the number of the matter in which he had been clothed.

∴

Three powerful words, Mor. Ya. In., [22] by which he was to execute his power, represented by these words, laws, precepts, and commandments, in virtue of which, directed by the Creator, he executes the three acts of power that were innate to him over the general, the particular, and the Universal, or terrestrial, celestial, and supercelestial; but, contrary to the will of the Creator, he also wished to execute power over the divine, and lost use of his three powers. They were restored to him through the Reconciliation; but these three faculties in him remain without action and without life if they are not reactivated through the Divine quaternary power that each must work to obtain.

These three powers, words, or faculties are represented to the Candidate in his first grades by the three ∧ signs placed on him: on the heart, the right side, and on the head; the perpendicular line drawn from the forehead to the stomach represents the

---

22. The first of these three words is *Moriah* (see more later); the second is in all probability *Jehovah*, though with what spelling we do not know; the third must be *Inri*.

Divine, quaternary power that marks the center of the three others and without which they are nothing.

The Temple of Solomon was constructed (on) the Mountain of Mount Mor,[23] ground elevated above all senses, which corresponds to the Garden of Eden, or the terrestrial paradise, in which the first man was created;[24] it was raised without any metal tool in order to symbolize the fact that universal Creation proceeded from the sole will and power of the Creator, and that matter supplies only the surface appearance, or again to symbolize the fact that the material body of the first man as well as that of Christ was formed without the aid of any physical, material operation. It was built in six years and dedicated on the 7th, to symbolize the six days or six divine thoughts that enacted the manufacture of the Universe, together with the 7th, which is the Creator's blessing of his work, the presentation made of it to him by the G. A., and the temporal embodiment of the greater emanated agents to maintain and guide it under the direction of the greater Spirit or G. A.[25]

∴

Origins of the Sabbath, necessity of its observance, manner of doing so, all the days and at each hour thus meriting the protection of the 7 principal agents[26] and of their chief 8th. The 8th directs the 7th, the 7th directs and governs the work of senary creation; likewise, the senary will be destroyed by the retreat of the 7th, after which the 8th will reintegrate all that it formed.

23. *Moriah,* which Martines, in his *Traité de la Reintegration des Êtres,* writes *Morija:* 'This word,' he says (p216), 'is divided into two parts: the first, *mor,* signifies *destruction of visible, bodily forms,* and *ija* signifies *vision of the Creator.'*

24. The symbolic significance here accorded to Mount *Moriah* strikingly recalls that of the Hindu *Meru.*

25. A distinction is being made here between the 'Creator' and the 'Great Architect', but the way it is expressed is rather obscure; this point would therefore necessitate a deeper study.

26. It is rather curious to note that the word 'agents' [*agens*] can, by anagram, be read as 'angels' [*anges*].

∴

The seven seals of the Book of the Apocalypse, on which lies the Lamb or the 8th who alone possesses the key to it.

∴

In the Temple of Solomon, there were four hieroglyphs for each number.

FIFTH INSTRUCTION
FROM FRIDAY, JANUARY 21, 1774

At the entrance to the Temple of Solomon there were two equal columns of 18 cubits in height. The right column was named *Jak.*,[27] which means 'he will establish'; the left column was named *Bo.*, which means 'confusion'; the first alluded to man's incorporation within his natural body, the second to woman's. The columns were equal because, the lesser spiritual being of man and of woman having the same origin, the same emanation, they are equal and have the same act to fulfill. They were divided into three parts, to wit: 10–4–4. Which represents through the 10 the correspondence of the lesser with the Divinity, the circumference to the center; through the 4, the correspondence of the terrestrial surface with the celestial region; and through the other 4, that of the celestial region to the super-celestial.

The work *Jak.*, 'he will establish', proclaims the power of command that was reserved for man in his original state. The word *Bo.*, 'confusion', expresses what has resulted from the disobedience of the first man, which repeated that of the first Spirits, whom he should have contained, harassed, and who alone could have served them with a good intellect, and by communication

27. Jakin.

with them inspired them to repent, and thenceforth to cease from evil; but leading man astray, they are deprived of this unique resource.

In spite of his fall, man always has the same task to fulfill, that for which he was destined, and he must therefore work towards Reconciliation, the sole means of reacquiring his three powers over the West, North, and South, which represent the terrestrial, celestial, and supercelestial, and conform himself once again to his quaternary, to harass without cease the wicked spirits, refusing to fall into their traps, ceaselessly destroying their wicked projects, and finally to reclaim the authority over them that was reserved for them, because if the divine mercy ever wishes to work some Good in their favor, it will be solely through man's communication with them that they might be brought to desire such a thing, since man was established for this end and since the immutable decrees of God must be fulfilled. The man who yields his will to them frustrates the designs of the Creator and, as long as he is in them, forsakes his original purpose; by joining his will and action to their chief, he becomes one with him and becomes inferior to him and his subject; he is equipped with a demonic intellect to seduce and pervert his fellow man through his example, and he renders himself more at fault than they themselves and must therefore expect a worse fate than theirs, since he strengthens the part he was charged to destroy.

The number of confusion of the second column is designated by the binary rank held by the first letter of the word Boaz in the Hebrew alphabet.

These two columns have yet another application: that of the South designated the soul of man or the lesser, that of the North the Good spirit given to him to direct him; if within universal Creation the South is the region to which the wicked spirits were more especially relegated, the Northern region must be inhabited by beings with the ability and charge to contain them, which Holy Scripture often gives us to understand in speaking either of the Demon of Noonday,[28] or of the Holy Spirit, who is always made to come with the North Wind.[29]

These things were likewise symbolized by the two columns, the one of stone or brick, which had been raised in the Northern part, the posterity of Seth, the other, the one made of earth, which had been raised in the Southern part, that of Cain. The first announced the strength and subtlety of spiritual works. Good, it resisted the inundations of the Flood and was preserved long after. The other offspring announced the weakness and corruption of works of matter, which was again designated by the number of confusion and its proportions. They were thus totally destroyed by the waters of the flood.

It was forbidden the children of God to couple with the children of men.[30] This prohibition must not be understood materially. Men of this time only being able to multiply in accordance with the physical laws of nature to which they, like all other animals, were subject, they should have been free to couple indiscriminately with women of the two races; but it was forbidden to the children of God, that is, to those who observed the laws, precepts, and commandments of God, to couple with women who had forgotten or scorned them, for fear of letting themselves be perverted or led into the same forgetfulness through their example.

From Adam until the flood, only two nations were reckoned: that of the Children of Seth, established in the North and called Children of God, since his law was preserved with them, and that of Cain, called the Children of Men and relegated to the South. The two nations, by the places in which they abode, represented the wicked spirits relegated to the South of Creation, and the

28. Cf. Ps. 96:1. Note that the French 'midy' or 'midi' means both 'South' and 'midday'. ED.

29. The correspondence made here is ordinarily reversed in Masonic symbolism, the North being designated as the tenebrous region, and the South as the luminous region.

30. Across from the start of this paragraph there is a cross in the margin of the manuscript.

good spirit in the region of the North. Only two nations were considered to have come from Adam, because Abel, his second son, left no *material* posterity. He came only to enact through his death the reconciliation of Adam his father, and to be the type of universal Regeneration. Cain and his posterity stand as the type of the evil spirits first emanated from their chiefs; Seth and his posterity stand as the type of the lesser, or of man, second emanated, but become elder in the spiritual order. We should observe that all the spiritual types occurring among men until Noah were transmitted for man's instruction in the posterity of Seth and of Enos his son.

In the beginning Adam, temporal father of all his descendents, is seen as the type of the Creator, Abel as that of the Regenerator, and Seth as that of the Spirit who instructs and directs.

Although all men have the same task of persecution [of wicked spirits], it does not follow as an absolute necessity for the fulfillment of the Creator's decrees and the good of Creation that all must fulfill it; a small number or even one can suffice, as is proven in several places in Scripture, where, to save a considerable number, it is enough to find ten Righteous, or even one.

Man's posterity is saved through Noah, alone found righteous in the eyes of the Creator. Noah, at the time of the flood, of 600 years old, stands as the type of the Creator, floating on the waters and preserving in the ark the seed of all animal reproductions. The dimensions of the ark further have a sensible relationship with universal Creation, which recalls the three spiritual essences from which all bodily forms are derived. In its dimensions of length (300 cubits), of width (50 cubits), of height (30 cubits), one recognizes the number of Creation, and in its total product, that of confusion deriving from two powers in opposition, to sustain on the one hand, and to liberate on the other.

In the number 5, which caused its construction.

The Temple of Solomon was 60 cubits long, 20 wide, and 30 high.

The ark was 20 cubits in length, width, and height.[31]

The Temple was 40 cubits long[32] and 20 wide.

In front of the Temple, a vestibule of 20 cubits long by 20 wide.

Same relationships in the dimensions of the Temple of Solomon, 20 wide, 60 long, 30 high, divided into three stages or distinct parts, the porch, the Temple, the Sanctuary in which was the Holy of Holies; which announces the correspondence between the divine immensity and the earth, represented by the porch by means of the celestial and...[33]

Since Noah, there have been 3 nations, to wit, Ham, Shem, and Japheth. Ham, the eldest, relegated to the region of the South, represents the type of Cain and the corrupt first emanated spirits. Shem, father of the descendents of the Israelites through Abraham, stands as the type of Seth. Japheth is the father of the third nation, that of the Gentiles, to whom the light was carried on account of the contempt the Hebrew descendants of Shem had for it, in punishment of their abandonment of the divine law; and through the pure mercy of the Creator, Christians today, or the Gentiles derived from Japheth, have become the eldest in the order of Grace of the descendents of Shem; but as these descendants of Shem were the people chosen by the Creator to manifest his marvels and his glory, and that his decrees might always be fulfilled, they will recover their rights at the end of time, and, through a complete reconciliation, become again the elders of the Gentiles, who, through the abuse of their light, knowledge, and aid, deserve to be deprived of them in their turn, which already begins to be manifest in the present Century.

In all that is recounted concerning them in the Holy Scriptures, the wicked, demonic Spirits and their chief are represented by the Egyptians descended from Ham, along with their King. The

---

31. These dimensions are obviously incorrect, and moreover in contradiction with those already given.

32. Without the porch or vestibule.

33. Doubtless 'supercelestial'; the sentence is left unfinished in the manuscript.

land of Egypt represents the part of Creation where they were relegated to work their evil wills, which helps to explain many passages.

Deprived of all celestial light, their vision obscured by the dark cloud that hid from them the column of fire illuminating the righteous, in blindness they followed the path cleared before them, they were swallowed up beneath the waters, and the same passage that led the Israelites in surety hurled their enemies into the abyss. The various camps they formed in the wilderness after this passage seem to announce the painful travails of the lesser in the sensible circle. Does not the law they received at the base of Sinai announce their return to their first power in the visual circle? Finally, the entry of the Israelites into the Promised Land announces the entry of the lesser into the place of spiritual Reintegration, or the full exercise of his power within the rational circle.[34]

34. The manuscript here has '*etc.*' three times, followed by the words: 'Notes to review.'

22

COLOGNE
OR STRASBOURG?

THE question raised in the October 1926 issue of *Voile d'Isis* should be divided into two parts, one historical and the other symbolic, and the divergence noted there concerns primarily only the first of these points of view. Moreover, the contradiction is perhaps only apparent, for if the Strasbourg cathedral is really the official center of a certain guild rite, would not the Cologne cathedral likewise be the center of another rite? And for this reason would there not be two distinct Masonic charters, one dating back to Strasbourg and the other to Cologne, which could well have given rise to confusion? This would need verifying and we would also need to know whether these two charters bear the same or different dates. The question is interesting above all from the historical point of view, and although for us the latter is not the most important, neither is it without value, for it is connected in a certain way with the symbolic point of view itself. Indeed, there is nothing arbitrary in the place chosen as a center by organizations such as those in question.

Be that as it may, we fully agree with Albert Bernet when he says that there must be a 'sensitive point' in all cathedrals built according to the true rules of the art, and also when he states that 'they should be dealt with from the symbolic point of view above all.' On this subject there is a curious parallel to point out: Wronski asserted that in every body there is a point which, if once touched, the body thereby at once completely disintegrates, is volatilized as it were, all its molecules being disassociated; and he claimed to have found the means to calculate the position of this cohesive center. Is not this, especially if taken symbolically—as we think one must do—exactly the same thing as the 'sensitive point' of cathedrals?

In its most general form, what is in question here could be called the 'vital knot' that exists in all matter as the point of juncture of its constitutive elements. A cathedral built in accordance with the rules forms a true organic whole, which is why it too has a 'vital knot'. The point here is the same as that expressed in antiquity by the famous symbol of the 'Gordian knot', although modern Masons would no doubt be quite surprised if told that in this respect their sword can play the same role ritually as that of Alexander...

In addition, we can note that the effective solution to the problem in question is related to the 'power of the keys' (*potestas ligandi et solvendi*)[1] understood in its Hermetic significance, or, what amounts to the same thing, that it corresponds to the second phase of the *coagula, solve* of the alchemists. As we observed in the article in *Regnabit* to which Paul Redonnel refers, it must not be forgotten that *Janus*, Roman god of initiation into the Mysteries, was at the same time patron of the *Collegia fabrorum*, the guilds of workers that persisted throughout the Middle Ages, and, through the Compagnonnage, right up to modern times; but in our day there are doubtless very few who still understand something of the profound symbolism of the 'Lodge of Saint John'.

---

1. The power of binding and loosing; according to Catholic tradition, the power bestowed on St Peter, represented by the keys. ED.

23

REVIEW OF
BY-WAYS OF FREEMASONRY

As the author himself states in his Foreword, the series of essays collected under this title[1] were intended to show that, at least in England, there are other subjects worthy of interest beyond the purely historical and archaeological studies that currently seem the almost exclusive focus of Masonic literature, and we believe he has succeeded. In this volume he proposes to address various questions raised almost daily concerning what could be called the 'periphery' of Freemasonry; and he begins with the question of the number of its degrees, a subject we have ourself dealt with in a previous issue of this journal.[2]

According to the Book of Constitutions, 'there are only three degrees, including the Holy Royal Arch,'[3] and this is indeed the only answer that conforms to the strictest orthodoxy.[4] From this it follows that 'Arch Masonry' is not really or originally distinct from

---

1. By The Rev. John T. Lawrence (P.A.G.C., Eng.)[This review was published in *La Gnose,* January 1912, under the initial 'P'] published by A. Lewis, 13, Paternoster Row, London, E.C.; and the author's residence, St Peter's Vicarage, Accrington. — The same author (former editor of *The Indian Masonic Review*) has already published various other works on Masonic subjects: *Masonic Jurisprudence and Symbolism, Sidelights on Freemasonry,* etc.

2. 'La Gnose et la Franc-Maçonnerie', 1st year, no. 5 [See 'Gnosis and Freemasonry', chap. 7 in present text].

3. The degree of 'Holy Royal Arch Mason', as it is practiced in the English and American chapters of 'Arch Masonry', must not be confused with the 13th degree of the Scottish hierarchy, which also carries the title 'Royal Arch'.

4. It should be noted that the three 'degrees' in question here are exactly the same as what are elsewhere called the 'initiatic grades', which are then distinguished

'Craft Masonry'. Within the latter, 'Arch Masonry' merely came to be superimposed upon 'Square Masonry' in order to serve as a complement to Mastery,[5] without in any way constituting a special degree. Another consequence of there being only three degrees is that the various orders, rites, and systems known as high grades cannot be considered essentially Masonic, or even having any effective part in Masonry. In reality they are only 'peripheral' organizations that have been grafted over the course of more or less distant—but always relatively recent—periods of time onto the primitive Fraternity of 'Ancient Free and Accepted Masons',[6] and more often than not have hardly any connection either with this Fraternity or with each other apart from the fact that they recruit their members exclusively from the possessors of such and such Masonic grade.[7] 'Mark Masonry', which could in a certain sense be

from 'degrees of initiation' properly speaking, 'the multiplicity of which is necessarily indefinite' (cf. *L'Initiation Maçonnique*, by F∴ Oswald Wirth).

5. By 'Square Masonry' is meant Masonry of a purely rectilinear symbolism, while 'Arch Masonry' refers to Masonry of a curvilinear symbolism (having the circle as its mother-form, as is particularly evident in the shape of the ogive), the geometric figures borrowed from ancient operative Masonry naturally having no more than a symbolic character for speculative Masonry, as they (like the tools of construction) had already for the ancient Hermeticists (see *La Hierarchie Operative et le Grade de Royale Arche*, by F∴ Oswald Wirth, and also *Le Livre de l'Apprenti*, pp 24 –29). — In ancient French Masonry the expression 'to pass from the triangle to the circle' was used to describe passage from the 'symbolic grades' to the 'grades of perfection', as can be seen, notably, in the Catechism of the *Elect Cohens* (on this subject, see further 'A Propos du Grand Architecte de l'Univers', 2nd year, no.8, p215, n1 [see 'The Great Architect of the Universe', chap. 2 in present text]; and on the solution to the Hermetic problem of 'squaring the circle', see 'Remarques sur la production des Nombres', 1st year, no.8, p156 [pt. 1, chap. 7 of Guénon's *Miscellanea*].

6. In American Masonry, the 'Grand Lodge of Ancient Free and Accepted Masons' is still the distinctive title of every order rigorously bound to the practice of the three symbolic grades and officially recognizing no other; although it is true that for its part the Scottish Rite also declares itself 'Ancient and Accepted', and that there are other systems of multiple degrees of an even more recent origin that proclaim themselves 'Ancient and Primitive', or even 'Primitive and Original', in spite of all historical evidence.

7. Often, too, their rituals are hardly anything other than more or less successful developments of those of symbolic Masonry (see 'Les Hauts Grades Maçonniques', 1st year, no.7 ['The Masonic High Grades', chap. 8 in present text]).

regarded as a continuation of the grade of companion (Fellow Craft),[8] and which in turn serves as the basis for the organization of 'Royal Ark Mariners',[9] is an example of such an organization. So also are the various orders of knighthood, most of which admit only 'Royal Arch Masons' as members; among which we could cite chiefly the 'United Orders of the Temple and of Malta' and the 'Order of the Red Cross of Rome and Constantinople'.[10] Among the other systems of high grades practiced in England (aside from the 'Ancient and Accepted Scottish Rite') we shall mention only the 'Royal Order of Scotland' (comprising the two grades of H. R. D. M. and R. S. Y. C. S.),[11] the Rite of 'Royal and Select Masters' (or 'Cryptic Masonry'), and that of the 'Allied Masonic Degrees', to say nothing of the Order of the 'Secret Monitor',[12] the 'Rosicrucians',[13] etc.

We shall not speak here of the chapters that pertain only to specific aspects of English Masonry; of a much more general interest are those in which the author (who, let it be said in passing, shows himself somewhat severe with regard to the Grand Orient of France[14]) considers various subjects of a symbolic and more properly specula-

---

8. The 'Mark Degree', which is subdivided into 'Mark Man' and 'Mark Master', is founded on this verse of Scripture: 'The very stone which the builders refused is become the head of the corner.' (Ps. 118:22), cited in the Gospel (Luke 20:17). — Among the emblems characteristic of this degree, the keystone plays a role analogous to that of the T-square in 'Craft Masonry'.

9. This additional degree, rather unimportant in itself, is connected with the Biblical Flood, as its name indicates.

10. The cross in one or another of its diverse forms is the principal emblem of all of these orders of chivalry, the rituals of which are essentially 'Christian and Trinitarian.'

11. Abbreviations of *Heredom* (or *Harodim*, the derivation of which is highly disputed) and *Rose-Cross*.

12. The rituals of this order (which appears to have originated in Holland) rest upon the history of the friendship of David and Jonathan (1 Samuel 20:18 ff.). — Onto the order of the 'Secret Monitor' is superimposed that of the 'Scarlet Cord', which is founded on Josh. 2:18.

13. The object of the Rosicrucian Order, which comprises nine degrees, is entirely literary and archaeological, and despite its title it has nothing in common with the 'Rose-Cross', the 18th degree of the Scottish hierarchy.

14. In this regard, see 'L'Orthodoxie Maçonnique, 1st year, no. 6 [chap. 6 in present text]; 'A propos du Grand Architecte de l'Univers', 2nd year, nos. 7–8 [chap. 2 in

tive order, yielding reflections that might contribute, notably, to the elucidation of various questions relating to the explication of the symbolic grades and their value from the historical point of view. Unfortunately, lack of space constrains us to do little more than translate here the titles of the most important of these chapters: 'King Solomon, The Bible, and Ritual';[15] 'The Two Saint Johns';[16] 'The Tetragrammaton';[17] 'The Perfect Ashlar';[18] 'Jacob's Ladder';[19] 'The Holy Land'; and 'The Branch of Acacia'. We recommend this intriguing work to all who take an interest in Masonic studies.

present text]; and 'Conceptions scientifiques et Idéal maçonnique', 2nd year, no. 10 [chap. 1 in present text]. — But, at least for the time being, we do not wish to treat the question of the 'Landmarks' of Freemasonry.

15. Let us make just one remark on this subject: for us, the Hebrew Bible constitutes in reality only a portion of the 'Volume of Sacred Law', which, in its universality, must necessarily embrace the Sacred Scriptures of every people.

16. The author's strictly 'evangelical' point of view differs markedly from that of F∴ Ragon, who dealt with this question in *La Messe et ses Mystères*, chap. 21 (see *L'Archéomètre*, 1st year, no. 11, pp 244–245).

17. At the beginning of this chapter there seems to be some confusion between the two divine names אֶהְיֶה (signifying 'I am') and יְהֹוָה, which are both four-letter words, and which are both derived from the root הָיָה, 'to be'.

18. It is regrettable, from our point of view, that the author should have restricted himself to an exclusively moral interpretation of this and several other symbols.

19. In regard to this symbol, see *L'Archéomètre*, 2nd year, no. 12, pp 311–313. — The author remarks, with reason, that the Ladder (of seven rungs, formed respectively from the metals corresponding to the different planets) figures equally in the Mysteries of Mithra (8th grade); on these Mysteries and their connection to Masonry, see *Discours sur l'Origine des Initiations*, by F∴ Jules Doinel (1st year, no. 6).

REVIEWS

BOOKS

PAUL CHACORNAC, *Le Comte de Saint-Germain* (Paris: Chacornac Frères). This new book from our Director is the result of many years of long and patient research. We are astonished at the prodigious quantity of works and documents of all kinds that were consulted in order to confirm each piece of information carefully, and we cannot adequately to pay tribute to the scrupulous integrity of such a work. If all points are not entirely clarified, which was doubtless impossible, there are at least a good number that are, and in a way which seems quite definitive. To have done so would have required above all dispelling the confusions that have been perpetrated regarding various other individuals, especially Lieutenant-General Claude-Louis de Saint-Germain. The confusion regarding this latter is one of the most frequent, but, despite the similarity of name and title which explains it, it is no less astonishing, for it is a question of a man who played a perfectly known historical role having nothing either obscure or mysterious about it. There is also Prince Rakoczi, of whom certain people in our time have inferred a large part, but whose alleged history is only a web of improbabilities. What is most likely is that in certain circumstances this name has simply served to conceal the true origin of the Count of Saint-Germain. There are also a certain number of real or supposed individuals, some of whom must have a semblance of existence only in the imaginative fancies resulting from the names taken by the Count of Saint-Germain himself at various periods and in different countries. The ground being thus prepared, it becomes much easier to follow the hero from his first known appearance in London in 1745 to his 'official' death at the home of the Prince of Hesse in 1784. When he was able to refute the rumors of Casanova, and other untrustworthy 'memorialists', the hoaxes of the illusionist Gauve and of yet other stories which were falsely imputed to the Count of Saint-Germain, like the role that some attributed to him in the Russian revolution of 1762, which certainly bears little resemblance to the 'adventurer' and 'charlatan' that so many have depicted, we see in reality a man endowed with remarkable talents of various kinds, possessing little-known knowledge on many things from whatever source, and who, if he had friends and admirers wherever he went, also had, as so often happens in such cases, bitter enemies to ruin his enterprises, be it his diplomatic mission in Holland or the industry he later wished to set up in Flanders under the name of de Surmount... However, next to this strictly 'historical' life, or its sequel, there is also the 'legend', which has continued to grow up to our day, especially concerning the 'survival' of the Count of Saint-Germain and the appearances which have been attributed to him after the date of what, for precisely this reason, we just now called his 'official' death. There are surely many exaggerations in all of this, those which the Theosophists, taking responsibility for the identification with Prince Rakoczi, spread on the subject of their 'Master R', not being the least. But it also seems more difficult to reject purely and simply other things which, even if they have been misrepresented or wrongly interpreted, make one wonder if at the very least they do not contain a certain measure of truth. There remains an enigma here, and to tell the truth there is yet another of the purely historic order, for up to now the mystery of the birth of the Count of Saint-Germain has not been solved. On this latter point, the author envisages a solution that he presents only as a hypothesis, but which is in any case rendered very likely by a whole host of rather striking parallels. According to this hypothesis the Count of Saint-Germain would have been the natural son of Marie-Anne de Neubourg, widow of King Charles II of Spain, and the Count of Melgar, Amirante of Castille, whose immense fortune had earned him the name of 'the banker of Madrid', which could have caused the confusion that has made some people claim that he was the son of a Jewish banker. If this supposition is correct, many things are easily explained, especially the considerable resources which the Count of Saint-Germain evidently had at his disposal, the precious stones and paintings by masters which he owned, and also, what is still more important, the trust placed in him by sovereigns and illustrious people who, from Louis XVth to the Prince of Hesse, must have been aware of the origins that allied him to them, but which, constituting in a way a 'state secret' had to be carefully concealed from everyone else. As for the other enigma, that of the 'legend', it is explained as far as possible and interpreted in the light of traditional doctrines in the final chapter. As this chapter first appeared in this publication (issue of December 1945), we shall content ourself with recalling the great interest shown it without

dwelling further on it. We think that, at least if one does not want to continue hold on to the daydreams which until now have been used to excess
in certain circles, it will henceforth no longer be possible to speak of the
Count of Saint-Germain without referring to this work, for which we
offer its author our hearty congratulations.

JOHN CHARPENTIER, *L'Ordre des Templiers* [*The Order of the Templars*]
(Paris: 'La Colombe'). The author of this book has previously published
novels in which he assigns to the Templars, or to their real or supposed
successors, a role that seems to attest to rather remarkable ideas on this
subject. We were rather afraid we would find further digressions of the
kind here, but fortunately there are none, for this is a serious historical
study, which is certainly much more valuable. We regret, however, especially as this is the most interesting aspect of the question, that it is nearly
impossible to ascertain precisely what the author really thinks concerning the esoterism of the Templars. It seems that originally they possessed
no 'esoterism' (but did not knighthood itself generally have a certain initiatic character?), so that esoterism would have had to have been introduced much later. But from where? No doubt from the East. Yet, from
their contacts with the Ismailis, they would scarcely have inherited more
than the idea of a certain hierarchy of grades (grades here appearing to be
confused with functions) and that of a 'pacifist universalism' [*sic*] which
in fact is possibly the idea of the Empire presented by Dante. In discussing the question of the alleged Templar 'heresy', Charpentier draws primarily on the articles of Probst-Biraben and Maitrot of the Motte-
Capron. Since we have already examined the articles in detail (issue of
October–November 1945), we shall not revisit them here. The author
does not believe the Templars were really heretics, but admits that they
could have been 'gnostics', and rightly observes in this connection that
'under this label one meets many unusual ideas, ideas that are unrelated
and sometimes even irreconcilable'; and that in addition, 'the only particulars we possess on gnosticism are those furnished by its adversaries.'
At this point matters become strangely complicated: on the one hand,
'the Templars were distantly connected' to Valentinian gnosticism; on the
other hand, 'in order to speak of the Templars' gnosticism, there must
have been an active Gnosis at the time they lived,' which is not the case.
In addition, it was not a question of a doctrine, for 'no convincing proof
has been gathered,' and the Templars 'did not present themselves as pro-
pagandists(?) except for social and political ideas based on solidarity.'

However, they would have had among themselves an oral transmission (but founded on what?). And finally, it appears that they possessed an esoterism of Pythagorean origin, although we have no clue how they had received it. It is really very difficult to get one's bearings in all this! Nor do we understand how one can think that 'Johannism' proceeds, not from Saint John the Evangelist, but from Saint John the Baptist. As for what from Pythagorism comes from, the key to the enigma may perhaps be found in the relations of the Templars with the constructors' guilds (which are mentioned here only incidentally) In the final chapter the question of 'Templar' Masonry is 'settled' in rather a summary way (and in passing let us note the curious lapse that led the author to write 'Magnus Grecus' for 'Naymus Grecus', and then of the Neo-Templars of Fabré-Palaprat. And here we were greatly astonished to find ourself named among those who 'substantiated the thesis according to which Larmenius was actually Molay's legitimate successor'! Now, as far as we can remember, we have never written a word anywhere on this question, and in any case we were the less likely to remember any such thesis, as we are not even sure the said Larmenius actually existed, for we hold as extremely suspect anything that comes from a neo-Templar source (including the 'secret alphabet'). We hope that when the occasion arises, this correction can be made known.

G. DE CHATEAURHIN, *Bibliographie du Martinisme* (Lyon: Derain et Racle). This bibliography (the author of which seems to have a very close relationship with Gerard van Rijnberk, whose own work on Martines de Pasqually we have also examined), in accordance with the usage established above all by contemporary occultists and their ignorance of eighteenth-century Masonic history, includes under the general term 'Martinism' several things that are in reality quite different: Martines de Pasqually's Order of the Elect-Cohens, with J.-B. Willermoz's Rectified Scottish Rite, L.-Cl. Saint-Martin's mysticism, and finally Martinism properly speaking, that is to say the recent organization founded by Papus. We think it would have been preferable to divide it into sections corresponding to these different subjects rather than into 'works particularly devoted to Martinism' and 'works in which Martinism is treated incidentally,' which would have been a simple subdivision of each of these sections. As to the 'doctrinal sources' mentioned separately, these are solely the writings of Martines de Pasqually and L. Cl. de Saint-Martin, and he could in fact hardly have cited others. It would also have been advisable, above all for the recent works, to have made some kind of distinction between writings of a Martinist and those of a Masonic character, those which are on the contrary hostile (above all the anti-Masonic works), and those written from a 'neutral' and purely historic point of view, which would have helped the reader order things more easily. All in all, the list seems fairly complete, although Stanislas de Guaita's *Discours d'Initiation*, which deserves a place, is absent. But we do not really see the justification for including the improbable mystification called *Le Diable au XIXe siècle* [*The Devil to the 19th Century*] (not to mention the brochure *Le Diable et l'Occultisme* [*The Devil and Occultism*] that Papus wrote in response), seeing that he neglected to cite Jean Kostka's (Jules Doinel) *Lucifer démasqué* [*Lucifer Unmasked*], where Martinism is however much more directly endorsed.

W.-R. CHETTÉOUI, *Cagliostro et Catherine II* (Paris: Éditions des Champs-Elysées). — Among the numerous plays written by Catherine II are three that are directed against what she called the 'visionaries', the term under which she included the Masons and members of various other initiatic organizations, as well as more or less independent 'visionaries' and 'mystics', Cagliostro in particular seeming to have attracted her hostility. These plays are translated here for the first time into French. The first, 'Le Trompeur' [The Deceiver], introduces a character who is obviously a caricature of Cagliostro; the second, 'Le Trompé' [The Deceived], is a violent attack against Masonic and similar organizations; as for the third, 'Le Chaman de Sibérie' [The Siberian Shaman], it contains no direct allusion to these latter, whatever the translator seems to think, but again obviously refers to Cagliostro. The volume also includes a short pamphlet entitled 'Le Secret de la Société Anti-Absurde dévoilé par quelqu'un qui n'en est pas' [The Secret of the Anti-Absurd Society revealed by someone who is not one of them], which parodies the Masonic rituals and catechisms while at the same time taking the counter view in the name of common sense. The whole thing testifies to incomprehension and is marked with the narrowest rationalist outlook, as might be expected on the part of a disciple of the 'philosophers'. We need not turn to these plays, therefore, for credible information on the subject, nor are these masterpieces from the literary point of view, but the book is incontestably a true historical curiosity.

The translation is preceded by a lengthy introduction providing interesting information on Masonry in Russia in the eighteenth century.

Unfortunately, Chettéoui's knowledge of Masonic history does not seem perfectly sure, for he makes certain mistakes of the kind commonly made in the profane world: thus, contrary to what he claims, even if it recruited its members from among the Masons, the Golden Rose-Cross was not itself Masonic. As for the mixture of very different things brought together under the common appellation 'Martinism', this is certainly not his doing, although he does not seem to have known how to unravel the matter. And does he not really believe that there were initiates of St Martin? He makes a more surprising and quite inexplicable error when he says that the Strict Observance is a 'form derived from the Templar Order destroyed forty years before'! Let us add that after the Freemasons' Wilhelmsbad Lodge Meeting the Strict Observance no longer existed but was replaced by the Rectified Scottish Rite. It is rather curious that this rather important distinction is almost never made.... There follows an account of Cagliostro's career, which takes its inspiration above all from Marc Haven, and tends to present Cagliostro as a true 'Master'. We have somewhat the impression that under the cloak of Cagliostro the author perhaps had in view other individuals, as did Marc Haven himself did when he wrote his *Unknown Master*. We shall not dwell on various other details, such as the accounts of healers who are far from having the 'spiritual' importance attributed to them, or again the quite unjustified belief in the authenticity of certain pseudo-Gospels recently spread about by the Theosophists and their 'Liberal-Catholic Church'. But we must take up a point that concerns us directly, one which recent events have rendered rather amusing for us, if not for everyone.

Chettéoui felt the need to slip the following note into his book: 'Whether it pleases or displeases the negative intellectualism of a René Guénon, France has the distinguished privilege of having the highest Initiatic School of the Western world. This School, with its well-tested methods, is destined to wield an immense influence throughout the world.' And, in order that no one be in any doubt as to what he is referring, the passage is immediately followed by a long quote from the founder of a so-called 'Divine School', which, unfortunately(!), has subsequently experienced misfortunes on which it is better not to dwell, so that rather than an 'immense influence', the said School has left behind it only the most unfortunate memories. It must be noted that there was no plausible motive for involving us, for we have never had occasion to say, publicly at least, anything at all on the pseudo-initiation in question. But we acknowledge quite willingly that our attitude toward him could not have been anything other than that he imputes to us, and will have to be admitted that events would only have borne us out in a most telling and complete way. Will Chettéoui believe us if we tell him that precisely when we spoke of his book we were only waiting for such an ending, already anticipated by us some time ago! Moreover, from what we have heard from various sources, we think that he himself must now have abandoned the illusions he entertained on this subject, while waiting (at least we wish it for him) for him to likewise cast aside those he retains on some other things! *Sic transit gloria mundi* [so passes away the glory of the world]....

DR R. SWINBURNE CLYMER, *The Rosicrucian Fraternity in America*, Vol. I (Quakertown, Pennsylvania: The Rosicrucian Foundation) — This thick volume comprises several sections that seem initially to have been published separately, some relating to the history of 'Rosicrucian' organizations, or supposedly such, in America, others providing a typical example of the quarrels that sometimes occur between these organizations, and to which we referred in a recent article. Moreover, we may wonder why the author restricts himself to denouncing only a single organization that rivals his own—the one known as *A.M.O.R.C.*— when there are certainly more than a dozen others that he should logically consider as equally 'illegitimate' since they also use a title whose monopoly he claims. Is this because in this case the 'competition' is more complicated from the fact that the two rivals both claim to constitute under their auspices a 'Universal Federation of Initiatic Orders and Societies', which obviously means there is one too many? Whatever the case may be, it is hard to understand how associations that claim to be initiatic can be *registered* or *incorporated*, and bring their differences before profane tribunals, or how certificates issued by the State can establish anything other than the mere 'priority' in the public exercise of a denomination, which definitely has nothing to do with the proof of its legitimacy. All this attests to a rather strange mentality, and one that is wholly 'modern'... That said, it in no way justifies Dr Clymer's own claims to recognize that he furnishes highly edifying documentation on the 'plagiarism' of his adversary, especially by showing that his so-called 'secret teachings' are taken word for word from published and known books like those of Franz Hartmann and Eckartshausen. Concerning the latter, here is something rather amusing: the author says that he 'carried out careful research, but he was unable to find any writer, recognized as an authority or not, who quotes or classifies Eckartshausen as a Rosicrucian.' We gladly provide him the 'source' that eluded him: in the *Histoire des Rose-Croix* by Sédir, among biographical notes on various alleged 'Rosicrucian' characters, we come across a note—the last of the series—dedicated to Eckartshausen (First edition, pp 159–160; 2nd edition, p 359). Here again, the *Imperator* of *A.M.O.R.C.* cannot even take credit for invention! Moreover, being in the know regarding certain things, we could point out yet other 'plagiarisms' of a slightly different kind. Thus, we see the reproduction of a diploma certificate under the heading of a so-called 'Grand College of Rites', whereas this title has in fact always belonged to the Grand-Orient de France alone. Knowing exactly under what circumstances the *Imperator* discovered its existence, and noticing that the diploma in question is dated later, we have no doubt that it is 'borrowed', not to speak of certain very significant details in this respect concerning a more or less cleverly modified seal. . . . There are things of a more fanciful nature also, like the diploma of a non-existent 'Rose-Cross of Egypt', although in truth, the 'Libyan chain' he wears seems to be inspired by some pre-existing model. In this connection, why would Dr Clymer, in an inscription written in French (which moreover is approximate), prefer that one say *Rose-Cross*[1] and not *Rose-Croix*? It is true that one cannot expect much linguistic knowledge from someone who writes the titles of his own organization in a Latin which we believe it more charitable not to reproduce!

Let us pass on to something more important, the quite apparent fact that the *Imperator* fabricated his *A.M.O.R.C.* from start to finish, despite the fantastic story of a charter he is supposed to have received in Toulouse in 1915 and whose alleged signatory has never been found. Later on he came in contact with the many organizations run by the famous Aleister Crowley one of whose lieutenants he in some way became, which shows clearly that the passage from 'pseudo-initiation' to 'counter-initiation' is often only too easy... Calling Crowley a 'black magician' certainly does not amount to 'defamation', since he was in fact 'officially' recognized as such in a judgment delivered against him in London a few years ago. Nonetheless, from a completely impartial standpoint let us say that this charge would only be supported by more solid arguments than those put forth by Dr Clymer, who even displays a rather surprising ignorance of symbolism. We have often explained that the same symbols can be taken in an opposite sense; what matters in such cases is the intention

---

1. In English in the original text. ED.

behind their use and the interpretation given them, but obviously that could not be recognized from their external aspect, which does not change; it is even an elementary skill on the part of a 'black magician' to make the most he can from such ambiguity. The downright 'plagiarisms' abundant in Crowley's writings, as, for example, his emblem of the dove of the Grail, which comes directly from Péladan, must also be taken into account. What is especially curious about Dr Clymer is what could be called an obsession with the inverted triangle. He does not seem to suspect that in the most orthodox symbolism this image has important meanings, which we may perhaps explain one day; and how is it that he does not at least know that this triangle figures in the high ranks of Scottish Masonry, where there is most certainly no trace of 'black magic'? One problem we admit we are unable to resolve is that of knowing how a sash worn 'around the neck' could possibly not be pointing downward; but we do not think that anyone before Dr Clymer had ever thought of seeing the figure of an inverted triangle in the form of such a sash (or of a canon's vestment, if one prefers). Neither need one draw much of an inference, except as an example of 'forgery', from the fact that the leaders of pseudo-Masonic organizations draw a triple cross before their signature solely to imitate the members of authentic Supreme Councils; this has nothing to do with a 'symbol of the Antichrist'! Crowley, and later the *Imperator*, use a cross overloaded with various signs, but a closer examination reveals on the whole only Hebrew letters, alchemical and astrological symbols, all things that are neither original nor characteristic; and since the signs of the four elements appear among them, how could one not find inverted triangles? There is also a so-called 'black cock', the appearance of which may seem more 'sinister' at first sight, but this too is quite simply... the rather faithful reproduction of one of those strange composite figures that archeologists call 'gryllus', of which the origin is rightly or wrongly attributed to the Basilidian Gnostics. Let us point out that the 'gryllus' in question was published in the collection of Rossi and Maffai, *Gemme antiche*, vol. 1, no. 21, and reproduced in Matter's *Histoire critique du Gnosticisme*, plate 1f, figure 2b. All this proves only one thing: that one should always make sure of knowing exactly what one is talking about, and that it is imprudent to let oneself be led by the imagination. But enough on these 'curiosities'.... As for certain more or less bogus methods of 'advertising' denounced by Dr Clymer, it goes without saying that we fully agree with him on that point; but does he himself remember—although this was around a quarter of a century ago—a little journal entitled *The Egyptian*, containing announcements of which the style hardly differed from this?

We shall dwell more briefly on the 'historical' aspect of the book, at least for the time being. Let us note first of all that the *Militia Crucifera Evangelica,* which is one of the 'origins' Dr Clymer relies on, was a specifically Lutheran, and not a Rosicrucian or initiatic organization. Furthermore, it is doubtful that its recent American 'reconstitution' could claim a genuine filiation, for between 1598 and 1901 there is a break which seems rather difficult to fill... Georges Lippard, a little-known author of certain works of fiction with almost solely political and social themes, is included among the authorities cited, some chapters of whose works are reproduced here, and in which he presents would-be members of the Rose-Cross, concerning whom all one can say is that they appear much less as initiates than as simple conspirators. Yet this is the basis for the entire history of an introduction of the Order in America in the eighteenth century. Without meaning to appear too difficult, one could certainly hope for something better! As a more certain 'connection', what finally remains after all this are the ties binding Dr Clymer and his organization to P. B. Randolph and his successors. Can this be considered as constituting a sufficient and truly valid guarantee, especially from the Rosicrucian point of view, which is what it is supposed to be? We shall not answer this question now, although our readers can easily guess what we really think. To end, we shall simply mention a chapter dedicated to Randolph's relationships with some of his contemporaries (and incidentally let us note a rather remarkable error: the work on Eliphas Lévi by our director Paul Chacornac is attributed here to... Paul Redonnel), and as this story is not without a certain interest, we shall perhaps come back to it on another occasion.

DR R. SWINBURNE CLYMER, *The Rosicrucian Fraternity in America,* Vol. II, (Quakertown, PA: 'The Rosicrucian Foundation'). We previously reviewed (April 1937) the first volume of this work, but until now circumstances have prevented us from reviewing the second volume, which is truly enormous (almost a thousand pages!). Dr Clymer's main adversary, the *Imperator* of *A.M.O.R.C.*, has died meanwhile, but clearly this in no way decreases the interest this work presents from a particular point of view, since it is a question of a typical case of pseudo-initiatic charlatanism, to which also have been added influences of a still more suspect character, as we have already explained. As others before us have noted, Dr

Clymer does great harm to his cause by too often using an 'argotic' and abusive language, of which the least one can say is that it lacks dignity, but this is no concern of ours, for we are not at all inclined to take part in such a quarrel. Whatever one may think of the merits of its claims, Dr Clymer's account is in any case 'instructive' in many respects. We see for example how, among other things, a lawyer can reach an agreement with his opponent for the purpose of settling a matter unknown to his client, and to the detriment of the latter's interests. Unfortunately, it is likely that such morals are not peculiar to America! Let us repeat that it is really difficult to understand how organizations claiming to be initiatic can carry their disputes before a secular jurisdiction in this way. Even if they are not really initiatic, the case does not change, for in all logic they should at least behave as if they indeed were what they wish to appear. One of two things necessarily happens: either the judge is himself secular and so incompetent by definition, or he is a Mason, and, since Masonic questions are themselves implicated, he finds himself in a rather false and singularly embarrassing position between his obligations of initiatic discretion and the duties of his public charge. . . . Concerning the questions just mentioned, we should say that Dr Clymer has quite peculiar ideas regarding Masonic regularity. Of two equally irregular organizations, both of the same origin, he has only praise for one, while heaping abuse and denunciations on the other, his reason quite simply being that the first has adhered to his own 'Federation' and the second to the rival 'Federation'. But such contemptible motives do not prevent the documentation concerning the latter, the *F.U.D.O.S.I.* (or *Federation Universalis Dirigens Ordines Societatesque Initiatis* [what Latin!]), from being one of the most interesting parts of the book—always from the same point of view. The intrigues of these so-called 'fraternal' circles are most edifying! The book also contains old knowledge, including some survivals from the old French occultist movement, that seems bent on not disappearing altogether... Naturally, we again find Theodore Reuss, *alias* 'Frater Peregrinus', Aleister Crowley, and their *O.T.O*, not to mention many other no less strange individuals (real and imaginary), and groups that are no less strange. We cannot summarize everything found here, but taken in its entirety it constitutes an important collection of documents that should be consulted by anyone who proposes to detail the fantastic history of modern pseudo-initiations.

Emile Dermenghem, *Joseph de Maistre mystique* [*Joseph de Maistre Mystic*] (Paris: 'La Colombe'). A new revised edition of this book has just come out, to which have been added numerous notes clarifying certain points and indicating works devoted to related questions that have appeared since its first publication. For those of our readers who still do not know this work, we would say that it summarizes as completely as possible Joseph de Maistre's Masonic career, his links with initiatic organizations connected to the Masonry of his time and with various individuals belonging to these organizations, and the considerable influence that the doctrines exercised on his thought. The whole is very interesting, and all the more so given that de Maistre's religious and social ideas have most often been very poorly understood, indeed sometimes even entirely misrepresented and interpreted in a sense in that in no way corresponds to his true intentions. Knowledge of the influences in question could alone set the record straight. Our main criticism is in short that which bears on the title itself, for in truth we see nothing 'mystical' in all this, and even when de Maistre held himself aloof from all activity of the initiatic order, it does not appear that he ever turned to mysticism as others sometimes did. It does not even appear that he had a real change of orientation, but a simple attitude of reserve that he considered, rightly or wrongly, to be imposed on him by his diplomatic functions. But dare we hope that the confusion between the initiatic and mystic domains may ever be entirely dispelled in some minds?

Pierre de Dienval, *La Clé des Songes* [The Key to Dreams] (Paris: Imprimerie Centrale de la Bourse). — 'The world we live in is much more deceptive than a stage set.' Indeed, nothing is more true, but is it so in precisely the way the author contends? According to his theory there exists a certain 'monetary secret', which in his opinion is the true 'philosopher's stone' held simultaneously by two groups of 'initiates', one English and the other Jewish, who contest for occult domination of the world, although they occasionally enter into alliance against a third party. This secret is supposed to be that of Masonry, taken to be nothing essentially but an instrument created by the English group to ensure its influence in all countries. Oddly enough, tat first glance these ideas remind us of those expressed earlier in the works of the Hiéron of Paray-le-Monial and Francis André (Mme Bessonnet-Favre). This similarity extends to more particular points, including many historical or so-called historical considerations: the role attributed to the Templars and to Joan of Arc, the self-styled 'Celtism' represented by the 'French'(?) race, and so on. There is an essential difference however, for this book, far from being Catholic in spirit, is quite explicitly irreligious. Carried away by his anti-Judaism, not only does the author furiously deny the divine inspiration of the Bible (which, he says, 'is not in the least a religious book in the sense that the French attach to this word'... as though there could be a specifically 'French' conception of religion!), but it is also quite obvious that for him all religion is wholly human... and political. Furthermore, he coolly considers the hypothesis that the role which until now has been played by Masonry is to be imparted to the Catholic Church, thanks to the 'domestication of the Pope' [*sic*]. Moreover, judging from what he says, this is already supposed to have partially realized. Thus he denounces the canonization of Joan of Arc (which, according to him, wrongly deprives her of 'her character as a national heroine), as 'a maneuver carried out with the hateful assistance of the official leaders of the Catholic Church, who have progressively defected to serve the occult masters of England.' But let us leave this aside and rather than waste time pointing out the all too numerous pseudo-historical fantasies the book contains, instead focus on the essential. First, it is obvious that the author has not the slightest notion of what initiation is. If the 'high initiates' (whom he imagines as forming a 'superior committee', probably on the pattern of the administrators of a financial firm) had no concerns other than those he ascribes to them, they would simply be completely profane. Furthermore, the so-called 'secret', as he describes it, is of childish simplicity, as he himself recognizes. If this were indeed the case, how could this 'secret' have been so well kept and how is it that many others through the ages did not discover it just as he did? For in fact it is only a matter of an elementary law concerning modifications. The author even gives a graphic picture of it in which, amusingly enough, he tries to find the explanation of the 'equilateral triangle intertwined with a compass'(?) which he believes to be 'the emblem of Masonry' (which, by the way, was not 'founded by Ashmole in 1646')—here is something which is hardly ordinary as symbolism, to say the least! We are far from contesting that there is, or was, a traditional 'monetary science' and that this science has its secrets, but these secrets have nothing to do with the 'philosopher's stone' and are of an entirely different nature than what we see here. Moreover, by endlessly repeating that money is a purely 'material' and 'quantitative' thing, one adopts precisely the same outlook as those one imagines one has targeted, and who in reality destroy both this traditional science as well as any other kind of knowledge having the same character, since it is these very people who have deprived the modern mentality of any notion going beyond the field of 'matter' and 'quantity'. Even though they are not 'initiates' (for they in fact belong to the domain of 'counter-initiation'), these people are in no way fooled by the 'materialism' which they have imposed upon the modern world for ends having nothing to do with 'economics'. Whatever instruments they may use according to the circumstances, they are slightly more difficult to detect than any 'committee' or a 'group' composed of Englishmen or Jews... As for the real 'monetary science', we shall simply say that if it were of a 'material' order it would be perfectly incomprehensible that for as long as it had a real existence the questions pertaining thereto were not left to the discretion of the temporal power—how could it ever have been accused of 'altering the currencies' if it had been sovereign in this respect?—but, on the contrary, subject to the control of a spiritual authority (we have addressed this point in *Spiritual Authority and Temporal Power*). This control was manifest in the mark of which one can find a last misunderstood vestige in the inscriptions that figured not so long ago on the rim of coins. But how to explain this to someone who pushes 'nationalism' (yet another of those suggestions aimed at the systematic destruction of all traditional spirit) to the point of indulging in a pompous eulogy of Philip the Fair? Furthermore, it is a mistake to say that the 'monetary' metals do not have an intrinsic value in themselves; and if their value is essentially symbolic (gold and silver, Sun and Moon), it is only so much the more real, for it is only through symbolism that things in this world are connected to the higher realities. To these fundamental objections we must add some rather odd observations: the chapter dedicated to the 'Intelligence Service' is extremely disappointing, not to say disturbing, for although it contains some clever but nonetheless hypothetical constructions, especially as regards the Dreyfus affair, there is no mention of one single precise and certain fact, even those of public notoriety, although there is no dearth thereof, and despite a vast array of choices... On the other hand, the author refers us to an earlier study that he devoted to related questions. How is it that this fierce anti-Mason brought out this study in a publication of which the Masonic connections are perfectly well-known to us? We do not mean to impugn anyone's sincerity here, because we only know too well how many people are 'led' without their knowledge. But we must consider this book as yet another of those more likely to mislead than enlighten. From our entirely impartial point of view we cannot but acknowledge the fact that books of this sort are on the increase these days, and in abnormal and rather disturbing proportions... Whatever the case may be, the best proof that the author never really laid his hands on the 'great arcanum' that he believes he is revealing, is the simple fact that his book could appear without hindrance!

ALFRED DODD, *Shakespeare, Creator of Freemasonry* (London: Rider and Co.) — A few years ago the author of this book published an edition of Shakespeare's sonnets with the aim of restoring their initial order and proving that they are in fact the 'personal' poems of Francis Bacon, who, according to the author, was Queen Elizabeth's son. Furthermore, Lord Saint-Alban, that is to say this same Bacon, was said to have been the author of modern Masonic ritual and the first Grand-Master of Masonry. This book, on the other hand, no longer deals with the question of Shakespeare's identity, which has and still does provoke so much controversy; rather, it concentrates on showing that, whoever he may have been, Shakespeare introduced numerous references to Masonry into his works in a more or less hidden manner that is sometimes completely cryptographic. In truth, this is not surprising to those who do not accept the very 'simplistic' opinion according to which Masonry is supposed to have been wholly created at the beginning of the eighteenth century, but the author's 'decipherings' are not equally convincing, particularly the initials, except when they are clearly presented in groups forming abbreviations whose Masonic usage is well-known and which can of course be understood according to more or less plausible multiple interpretations. Yet even when the dubious cases are discarded a sufficient number still seem to remain to prove that the author is right concerning this specific part of his thesis. Unfortunately, the case is entirely different when it comes to the excessive consequences he wishes to draw in believing that he has thereby discovered the 'founder of modern Masonry'. If Shakespeare, or the character known under this name, was a Mason, he must necessarily have been an operative Mason (which in no way means a worker), for the foundation of the Grand Lodge of England really marks the beginning, not of Masonry without epithet, but of the 'lessening'—if one may put it so—that is modern or speculative Masonry. However, in order to understand this we should not set out with the peculiar preconceived idea that operative Masonry was something quite similar to our present-day 'trade unions' and that the sole preoccupation of its members was 'matters of wages and working-hours'! Obviously, the author has not the least idea of the mentality and knowledge of the Middle Ages, and what is more, he goes against all the historical facts when he declares that operative Masonry ceased to exist as early as the fifteenth century and accordingly could not have maintained any continuity with speculative Masonry, even if according to his hypothesis the latter dates back to the end of the sixteenth century. We fail to see why certain edicts would have been more effective against Masonry in England than similar edicts were in France against the Guilds, and whether one likes it or not the fact remains that operative Lodges have existed before and even after 1717. This way of looking at things leads to many other improbabilities. Thus, the manuscripts of the *Old Charges* are said to be fakes fabricated by the same persons who are supposed to have composed the ritual so as to mislead investigations and lead us to a belief in a nonexistent filiation, so as to conceal their real aim of reviving the ancient mysteries under a modernized form. The author does not realize that this opinion, which amounts to denying the existence of a regular transmission and admitting in its place only an 'ideal' reconstitution, would thereby deprive Masonry of all true initiatic value! We pass over his remarks regarding the 'illiterate workers' who would have exclusively made up the membership of the old operative Masonry, whereas in reality the latter always 'accepted' members who were neither laborers nor illiterates (in each of the Lodges, it was in any event obligatory to have at least an ecclesiastic and a doctor). Moreover, how could the fact of not knowing how to read or write (understood literally and not symbolically, which is of absolutely no importance from the initiatic point of view) possibly keep someone from learning and practicing a ritual which clearly was never meant to be committed to writing? If we are to believe the author, it would seem that the medieval English builders did not even possess any kind of language through which they could communicate! Even if it is true that the terms and the phrases of the ritual in its present form carry the mark of the Elizabethan period, this in no way proves that it is not simply a new version made at the time from a much more ancient ritual, and subsequently preserved just as it was, because the language has not undergone any notable changes since that time. To claim that the ritual does not go back any further is a little like trying to uphold that the Bible also dates from the same period by citing as a support the style of the 'authorized version' which, by a curious coincidence, is also attributed by some to Bacon, who, let it be said in passing, would have had to live a very long time to write everything attributed to him. The author is perfectly right in thinking that 'Masonic questions ought to be looked into masonically', but it is precisely for this very reason that he himself should above all have avoided the prejudice about 'great men', which is essentially profane. If Masonry is really an initiatic organization, it cannot have been 'invented' at a given moment and its ritual could not possibly be the work of one particular individual (or for that matter of a 'committee' or any group whatsoever); that this individual is a renowned writer and even a 'genius' makes absolutely no difference. As for saying that Shakespeare would not have dared insert Masonic references into his plays had he not as founder been above the obligation of secrecy, this is a very poor reason, especially if one reflects that many others besides Shakespeare have done the same thing and even more openly: the Masonic character of Mozart's *Magic Flute*, for example, is certainly much more obvious than that of the *Tempest*... Another point on which the author seems to entertain a number of illusions is the value of the knowledge the founders of the Grand Lodge of England could have possessed. It is true that Anderson took care to conceal many things, and perhaps 'by order' rather than on his own initiative, and for ends that were assuredly not initiatic; and if the Grand Lodge really kept certain secrets concerning the origin of Masonry, how can we explain that numerous historians, who were its distinguished members, showed such complete ignorance in this regard? Moreover, two or three remarks on details will succeed in showing how wrong it is not to be sufficiently wary of the imagination (and perhaps also of certain 'psychic' revelations to which the former work of the same author discreetly seemed to refer). Thus regarding a passage by Anderson there is no need to wonder 'what is the degree that makes an *Expert Brother*' as though some mystery were involved (the author's ideas about the high grades are quite fanciful moreover), for at the time the expression *Expert Brother* was simply used as a synonym for *Fellow Craft*; the Companion was an 'expert' in the Latin sense of the word, whereas the Apprentice was not yet. The 'extraordinarily talented young man' Thomas de Quincey refers to is not Shakespeare or Bacon, but quite clearly Valentin Andreae, and the letters *A.L.* and *A.D.*, followed by dates, figuring on a *Royal Arch* jewel, were surely not put there to form the words *a lad*, which would apply to the 'young man' in question. How, especially when one makes a 'specialty' of interpreting initials, can one not be aware that these letters mean nothing other than *Anno Lucis* and *Anno Domini*? We could point out many other things of the same kind, but we believe it is of little use to dwell on them. Let us just add that it is rather difficult to know exactly what the author means by *Rosicrosse Masons*; he speaks of them as of a 'literary society', which, even were it secret, is something hardly initiatic. It is true that for him Masonry itself is only an 'ethical system' which scarcely goes any further and is not of a much more profound order. Can an organization whose biggest secret is nothing other than its founder's identity be taken seriously? Surely it is not by the name of any individuality whatsoever, even that of a 'great man', that any valid answer will ever be given to the question raised by a 'word' that has been distorted in so many different ways—a question which, curiously, reads even more clearly in Arabic than in Hebrew: *Mā al-Banna*?

MARK HAVEN (annotated by), *Rituel de la Maçonnerie Egyptienne de Cagliostro* [*Ritual of Cagliostro's Egyptian Masonry*], including an introduction of Daniel Nazir (Nice: Éditions des Cahiers Astrologiques). Dr Marc Haven long intended to publish a complete edition of this Ritual, which constitutes an interesting document for the history of Masonry. Circumstances never allowed him to realize this project, nor to write the commentaries that should accompany it. His notes, which amount to very little indeed and hardly provide clarification, are in fact only pointers that he noted down for himself in planning this work. As to the introduction, it contains nothing new for those who know Marc Haven's works, consisting as it does entirely of extracts drawn from them, so that in the final analysis it is the text of the Ritual itself which provides all the interest of this volume. In sum, it is a matter of a whole 'system' of high grades insofar as they existed in the second half of the eighteenth century, and its division into three degrees, introducing a kind of parallelism with those of symbolic Masonry, arising from a conception of which one could find other examples. We need hardly add that in actual fact there is nothing 'Egyptian' there that could justify its name, unless we consider as such the pyramid figuring in certain paintings, without the least explanation being given as to its symbolism. We do not even come across a few of these pseudo-Egyptian fantasies found in other Rites, and which, around this time, were especially made fashionable, if one may say so, by Abbé Terrasson's *Séthos*.[2] Basically, the invocations contained in this Ritual, and

---

2. Jean Terrasson (1670–1750) was a Philosopher and Professor of Greek and Latin at the Collège Royal, as well as a Member of the Académie des Inscriptions. He published a philosophical novel *Séthos*. ED.

especially the use made of the Psalms as well as the Hebraic names found there, give it a clearly Judeo-Christian character. What naturally presents itself in particular are the 'operations' which it would be interesting to compare with those of the Elect Cohens. The objective at which they aim is apparently quite similar, but the processes used are in many respects different. Here is something which above all seems to be derived from 'ceremonial magic', and which, through the role that 'subjects' play therein (the children were designated 'Doves'), is also related to magnetism. From the strictly initiatic point of view, all this could certainly occasion serious objections. Another point calling for some comment is the character of the feminine grades: for the most part they retain the customary symbolism of the Masonry of adoption, but in truth this latter represents a mere pretence of initiation meant to give a semblance of satisfaction to the women who reproached Masonry for neglecting them, and in general it was hardly taken seriously, its role being limited to things of the wholly outward order, such as the organization of 'semi-profane' holidays and charitable work. It seems clear that, on the contrary, Cagliostro may have intended to confer a proper initiation on women, or at least what he considered to be such, for he had them participate in 'operations' quite similar to those of the masculine Lodges. This is not only an exception, but also, insofar as it concerns a Masonic Rite, a real 'irregularity'. If we wished to go into detail, other strange facts could be found, even in the masculine grades, for example the peculiar way in which the legend of Hiram is modified and explained, all of which would quite naturally lead to a question: like many others, Cagliostro obviously wanted to establish a particular system, whatever its proper value, basing himself on Masonry, but did he ever really have a sufficiently deep knowledge of Masonry to adapt it correctly? Perhaps Cagliostro's enthusiastic admirers would be indignant at such a doubt being raised, whereas his detractors would probably seek to infer excessive consequences against him. In our opinion, no one would have more grounds than the others, and there are many probabilities that the truth about this enigmatic character is not to be found in any of these extreme opinions.

ALICE JOLY, *Un Mystique lyonnais et les secrets de la Franc-Maçonnerie* (1730–1824) [A Mystic from Lyons and the Secrets of Freemasonry (1730–1824)] (Mâcon: Protat Frères) — This thick volume is a comprehensive biography of Jean-Baptiste Willermoz, very conscientiously done and seriously documented. However, it is not devoid of certain shortcomings that are probably inevitable when one attempts to study matters of this kind from a purely profane point of view, as is the case here. To achieve true understanding in this order of things, it is certainly not enough to have a kind of outer sympathy, or a curiosity extending as far as the search for minute anecdotal details. We admire the patience involved in thus treating a subject for which one does not feel a deeper interest, but we admit that in place of an accumulation of pure and simple facts we would prefer a more 'synthetic' view enabling the meaning to be brought out, and also avoiding many errors and confusions. One such confusion is present in the title itself, which defines Willermoz as a 'mystic' whereas nothing of the sort emerges from what has been expounded in the book, and in any case the truth is that he was no 'mystic'. If one can blame him for seemingly abandoning the Elect Cohens, it is not at all because he turned toward mysticism like Saint-Martin, but only because he developed a more active interest in other initiatic organizations. Moreover, the author shows an obvious lack of 'technical' knowledge concerning the things of which she speaks, whence some peculiar errors. Thus, for example, she mistakes the different Masonic rites for so many 'societies'. She is unaware of the difference between a 'Grand Lodge and a Grand-Orient'. She designates 'rectification' as the connection of a Lodge to the Strict Observance, whereas this term on the contrary designates the change undergone by the Lodge of the Strict Observance itself, when the latter ceased to exist as such and was replaced by the one which, precisely for this reason, was called (and is still being called) the Rectified Scottish Rite, in the development of which Willermoz played a leading role. That said, we readily admit that this work contains a mine of information that will always come in handy when one wants to study the organizations in which Willermoz played a role. However, in our opinion the most important part concerns his interest in magnetism and the rather unfortunate consequences that resulted therefrom, for this was surely not the happiest episode of his career. Moreover, there is something remarkable in this story which calls for deeper reflection. Whatever one might think of Mesmer's character, on which the most contrasting opinions have been expressed, there is no doubt that he appears to have been deliberately 'instigated' to provoke a deviation among the Masonic organizations which, in spite of all they lacked in terms of effective knowledge, were still continuing their work seriously and doing their best to renew the link with the true tradition. Instead of that, the greatest part of their activity then came to be taken up by rather childish experiments which in any case had nothing initiatic about them, not to mention the discords and dissensions that followed. The 'Society of Initiates' organized by Willer-moz had no Masonic character as such, but due to the quality of its mem-bers, it nevertheless exercised a kind of guiding influence on the Lodges of Lyons, which influence was finally nothing but that of sleepwalkers who were consulted on everything. Under these circumstances it should come as no surprise that the results were so deplorable! It has always been our belief that the famous 'Unknown Agent' who dictated so many con-fused and often quite unintelligible lucubrations, was simply one of these sleepwalkers, and we recall having written this about Vulliaud's book in this same publication quite a few years ago. Mrs Joly brings further con-firmation of this which can leave no room for any doubt, for she has suc-ceeded in uncovering the identity of the person involved, Mrs de Vallière, sister of Commander de Monspey, through whom these messages were transmitted to Willermoz. The author's research will certainly not have been in vain even if it serves only to bring to light the final solution to this mystery and thereby puts a halt to certain 'occultist' legends. — Let us also add in passing that certain proper names are distorted in a rather curious way. We do not mean to speak of certain eighteenth-century characters, for we know the difficulties involved in establishing their exact spelling. But why are Vulliaud and Dermenghem constantly called 'Vulliand' and 'Dermenghen' in the references? Doubtless this is of no fundamental importance, but in the work of an 'archivist' it is neverthe-less somewhat embarrassing...

ALBERT LANTOINE, *Les Sociétés secrètes actuelles en Europe et en Amérique* [*Contemporary Secret Societies in Europe and America*] (Paris: Presses Universitaires de France). This little volume, ready for publication in 1940 but delayed by circumstances for five years, belongs to a collection obviously intend for the 'general public', which explains its somewhat superficial character. It does have the merit of drawing an important dis-tinction between 'initiatic secret societies' and 'political secret societies', whence its division into two parts that 'have nothing in common between them but the similarity of their names.' As for saying that the first are distinguished from the others in that 'the solidarity is not of the sentimental, but of the spiritual order,' this is certainly correct, although inadequate, seeing that here 'spiritual' seems to be conceived as a simple matter of 'thought', which is far from being the true initiatic point of view. In any case, the question is actually far more complex, and we take the liberty of referring the reader to what we have said in our *Perspectives on Initiation* (chap. 12). On the other hand, it is quite impossible for us to share certain views on an alleged opposition between religion and anything that has a secret character in general, or an initiatic character in particular. A clear distinction between exoterism and esoterism suffices to put each thing in its place and does away with all opposition, for the truth is that two entirely different domains are involved. — The first part opens with a short chapter on 'minor initiatic societies', which the book could have done without, for the few particulars it contains are taken from very secular sources, and moreover it includes a rather unfortunate statement that seems to accept the claims of pseudo-initiatic organizations of all kinds. It is certainly not because a group enacts a sham or parody of initiation that it has 'the right to call itself initiatic'! Let us immediately add that the chapter on the Compagnonnage, although containing nothing incorrect, is regrettably insufficient. Is it because it is looked upon rather as a 'thing of the past', and therefore 'not current', that it is not granted more space in the book? What is more interesting and better done is the summary of Masonry in Europe and especially in France, no doubt because it is the author's 'speciality' as it were; but as regards the origins, it is terribly simplified. And why always the fear of going back beyond 1717? As for American Masonry, the author clearly has inadequate knowledge: concerning the high grades, in particular, he seems ignorant of the very existence of everything that is not the Ancient and Accepted Scottish Rite, which however is very far from being the most widespread in the Anglo-Saxon countries. . . . Concerning America, we also find also some historical information on the *Odd Fellows* and the *Knights of Pythias*, as well as of certain Negro associations of which the character is poorly defined. Here again we encounter the regrettable tendency to believe that it is permissible to speak of initiation merely because admission is accompanied by 'ceremonies'. — The second part is devoted to 'political secret societies'. As regards Europe, the Irish societies, the Macedonian *Comitajis*, and the Croatian *Ustashis* are mentioned; for America, the 'Knights of Colombus', the 'Order of Hibernians', the *Ku-Klux-Klan* (about which he says very little), Jewish societies, and various other organizations of lesser importance. — The conclusion has a 'detached' tone, indeed even a slightly skeptical one, which is rather deceptive; but on the whole it is perhaps almost inevitable that this be so for those who, under the present state of Western initiatic organizations, which have not succeeded in discovering what initiation truly is.

ANDRÉ LEBEY, *La Vérité sur la Franc-Maçonnerie par des documents, avec le Secret du Triangle* [The Truth about Freemasonry from some documents, with the Secret of the Triangle] (Paris: Editions Eugène Figuière) — This book is a collection of speeches given at the Grand Chapter-House of the Grand-Orient of France. By simply gathering them together in this way with no added commentary the author's aim was to show what constitutes the works of the high grades, and in so doing correct the misconceptions that prevail among the general public. It would be out of the question to summarize or even enumerate here all the questions this book raises, but let us just point out that among the questions the author proposes as particularly important for the study of the Workshops of the high grades is that concerning the relations between East and West. He develops some interesting points on this question, even though one may find it regrettable that his knowledge of the East, which is so indirect, led him to attach excessive importance to certain contestable Western views, such as those of Spengler and Keyserling for example, or to the statements of a few Easterners who are much less 'representative' than he seems to believe. In this connection we may add that the idea of an *entente* between different civilizations based on the constitution of a 'new humanism' stretching far beyond the narrow limits of 'Greco-Roman culture' alone, albeit no doubt very laudable, will always appear as absolutely insufficient from the Eastern point of view, just as with anything referring to elements of a purely 'human' order. — The last chapter, 'The Secret of the Temple', is a reminder to Masons, who are too forgetful of these matters today, of links that are certainly more than 'ideal' (despite what certain people might say) connecting them with the Templars. This is only an abbreviated historical outline but it is nonetheless very much worthy of interest. As the author says (and even if there may have been something else of which this was merely a consequence), there seems to be no doubt that the Templars did indeed possess a 'great secret of reconciliation' between Judaism, Christianity, and Islam. As we have already said on another occasion, is it not true that they drank the same 'wine' as the Kabbalists and the Sufis, and that Boccacio, their heir as the 'Faithful of Love', did he not assert through Melchizedek that the truth of the three religions is indisputable... because they are but one in their deepest essence?

GIUSEPPE LETI and LOUIS LACHAT, *L'Ésotérisme à la scène: La Flûte Enchantée; Parsifal; Faust* (Lyons: Derain et Raclet). *Esoterism on Stage: The Magic Flute; Parsifal; Faust.* — The title of this book is perhaps not sufficiently precise, for the three plays studied are considered (or at least such was the author's intention) from the point of view of Masonic symbolism in particular rather than that of esoterism in general. Moreover, we see something that can immediately give rise to an objection, for if the Masonic character of the *Magic Flute* is well-known and incontestable, such is not the case with the other two plays; and if we can at least assert that, like Mozart, Goethe was a Mason, the same cannot be said of Wagner. It seems that if *Parsifal* contains points of comparison with Masonic symbolism, this derives from the legend of the Grail itself, or from the mediaeval 'current' to which it is connected, much more than from Wagner's adaptation, for Wagner was not necessarily conscious of its original initiatic character, which he is sometimes even blamed for having altered by replacing it with a nebulous mysticism. In short, all the similarities the authors indicate can be explained by what they call the 'Hermetic heritage', of Masonry, which fully corresponds with what we have just said. Besides, they too often mix together vague considerations unrelated to symbolism or esoterism, but only to an 'ideology' which, even if it represents their conception of Masonry, is certainly in no way inherent to Masonry itself, even having been introduced in certain of its branches as a result of the degeneration of which we have often spoken. As for Goethe's case, it is rather complex. There is good reason to consider more closely to what extent his poem *Faust* is really 'marked with the Masonic spirit', to use the words of a critic here cited, for whom the 'Masonic spirit' was ultimately probably nothing more than the public generally believes it to be. It is surely more questionable than in the case of the other works by the same author, such as *Wilhelm Meister* or the enigmatic tale of the *Green Snake*. Strictly speaking, *Faust* as a whole is a somewhat 'chaotic' work, containing parts that show a rather anti-traditional inspiration. The influences at work on Goethe were doubtless not exclusively Masonic, and it would certainly be worthwhile to try to determine them more precisely... As for the rest, the present book contains many interesting observations, but all this needs to be clarified and put in order, and that can only be done by someone not affected, as the authors obviously are, by 'progressivist' and 'humanitarian' modern ideas that are the exact opposite of all true esoterism.

PIERRE LHERMIER, *Le mystérieux Comte de Saint-Germain, Rose-Croix et diplomate* [*The Mysterious Count of Saint-Germain, Rosicrucian and Diplomat*] (Paris: Editions Colbert). This book, published posthumously, is a rather superficial historical study which in truth sheds little light on the 'mystery' in question. Lhermier summarizes the many hypotheses which have been put forward regarding the Count of Saint-Germain; while he does not decide in favor of any of them, he nevertheless seems inclined to the view that he may have belonged to the Stuart family, or at least to their entourage. One of the reasons he gives rests on a rather astonishing confusion: 'Saint-Germain was a Rosicrucian, he writes verbatim, that is to say he belonged to Scottish Rite Freemasonry with Catholic and Stuartist tendencies. . . .' Need we add that 'Jacobite' Masonry was in no way the Scottish Rite and did not involve any Rose-Cross grade, and, moreover, that in spite of its title this grade has nothing to do with the Rosicrucianism of which Saint-Germain would have been one of the last known representatives? The greater part of the volume is devoted to an account sprinkled with various anecdotes of travels during the course of which the hero is said to have carried out various secret political and financial missions on behalf of Louis XV. Again, there are many doubtful points in all of this, and in any case, it represents only the most exterior aspect of this enigmatic life. Let us also note author's belief that certain extraordinary claims made for Saint-Germain, especially the age attributed to him, should really be attributed to an impostor called Gauve, who passed himself off as Saint-Germain, it seems at the instigation of the Duke of Choiseul, who thereby wished to discredit a man whom he saw as a dangerous rival. But let us pass over the identification of Saint-Germain with various other mysterious individuals, as also over many other more or less hypothetical matters. But we must at the very least point out that on the strength of rather vague information, a kind of 'pantheist' and 'materialist' philosophy that would certainly have nothing initiatic about it, is attributed to him! In the final pages the author returns to what he calls the 'Rosicrucian sect', in a way that seems in sort to contradict the assertion noted above, and since he invokes such 'sources' such as Mrs Besant and F. Wittemans, indeed even Spencer Lewis, *Imperator* of *A. M. O. R. C.* (not to mention a certain 'Fr Syntheticus, occultist writer whose work was law'[!]), we certainly need not be astonished at the above incredibly confused ideas above, nor at the fact that even from the historical point of view to which he wishes to adhere, what he says hardly respects the truth. This proves yet again that a measure of skepticism is not always the best protection against the danger of too easily accepting the worst of fantasies, and that traditional knowledge, even if only of an elementary order, is assuredly much more efficacious in this respect.

JEAN MALLINGER, *Pythagore et les Mystères* [*Pythagoras and the Mysteries*] (Paris: Editions Niclaus). Once we know that the author of this book was one of the promoters of the *F. U. D. O. S. I.*, which we discussed recently (issue of May 1946), certain things become clear which might otherwise have remained rather enigmatic. Thus the dedication to the memory of the chief of the 'Pythagoreans' of Belgium is easily understood; the latter, in fact, form an 'Order of Hermes Trismegistus' (a denomination which certainly has nothing specifically Pythagorean) which was one of the first to join the aforesaid *F. U. D. O. S. I.* Thus, what is normally called the 'primordial state' is here called the 'ancient and original state'; now this is no mere oddity of language, as an uninformed reader might believe, but a discreet way of referring to the title of an irregular Masonic organization of which Mallinger is one of the dignitaries. If he had belonged to another such organization, he would doubtless also say 'ancient and original state'! A curious diatribe against the 'Freemason's apron', which moreover is based on a confusion between two quite different things from the symbolic point of view, also seems due in reality to no more than a desire to make oneself stand out with regard to regular masonry... As for the very heart of the work, the properly historic part, that is to say the biography of Pythagoras according to known 'sources', all in all contributes nothing new. The facts are sometimes presented a little 'tendentiously', for example in assigning Pythagoras a very modern concern for 'propaganda', or in describing the organization of his Order in a way that makes one think that the social viewpoint was the result as it were of all the rest. The second part deals first with a question of the different kinds of mysteries that existed in Greece and elsewhere at the time of Pythagoras, and then with the Pythagorean mysteries. Here again, we suspect that to a certain extent the account is influenced by the idea that the author has formed of initiation, an idea strongly tinged with 'humanitarianism' and in which 'powers' also play an important role. And in spite of what he says elsewhere of the 'apostolic chain' [*sic*] and of the necessity of an 'immutable and traditional rite,' it is to be feared from the way he speaks of a 'return to Pythagoras' that he may still be one of those who believes a continuous and uninterrupted transmission is not indispensable to the validity of initiation. When he speaks of the 'permanence of the Order' and of 'its still perceptible heartbeat today,' we may well wonder what exactly he means, especially when we know of so many occultists who think an initiatic 'chain' can be perpetuated wholly 'in the astral'!

HENRI-FÉLIX MARCY, *Essai sur l'origine de la Franc-Maçonnerie et l'histoire du Grand Orient de France*, vol. I. *Des origines à la fondation du Grand Orient de France* (Paris: Éditions du Foyer Philosophique,). — This is a conscientious work, but makes exclusive use of secular historical methods, which particularly in such a case cannot give entirely satisfactory results, if only because of the almost complete absence of written documents. The author's cast of mind is obviously quite 'rationalist', doubtless owing to his university education. Many things escape him, especially anything pertaining to the initiatic aspect of a question, and this is undoubtedly why the bond uniting Operative to Speculative Masonry appears very 'loose' to him, as he says at the outset. However, what follows in his exposition hardly justifies this assertion, for is he not at least one of those who, against all evidence, deny the existence of a direct filiation between the two, even if he underestimates the importance of the very effective—we could even say the quite essential—link constituted by symbolism. Having voiced these reservations, we should acknowledge that within the limits of the point of view adopted, this work carries a good deal of interesting information, especially in the chapter devoted to the history of medieval architecture, more precisely that of the period from the thirteenth to the fifteenth century. A curious point to note is that the French 'masters of the work' [*maîtres d'oeuvre*] seem to have had a leading part in the construction of the great cathedrals of other countries, whence the author believes he can conclude that Operative Masonry originated in France. This is certainly only a hypothesis, but it finds confirmation in the similarity shown between the organization of the German *Hütten* and the English and Scottish *Lodges*, whereas it is unlikely they had had direct links between them. There is perhaps some exaggeration here owing to a too exclusively 'national' perspective, but it is no less true that the 'legendary' account contained in certain English manuscripts of the *Old Charges* itself seems to suggest something of this kind, while dating it back to a period well before that of the 'Gothic' cathedrals. We shall add only that, even if one accepts that Operative Masonry was imported into England and Germany from France, this says nothing as to its very origin, since according to the same 'legends' it is said to have first come from the East to France, where it would presumably have been introduced by Byzantine architects. In this connection one could raise an important question that the author does not consider, and that no Masonic historian has tried to explain: this question is that of the possible 'survival' of operative Masonry in France itself toward the end of the seventeenth century or the start of the eighteenth. In fact, given certain particularities by which the French rituals differ from the speculative English rituals and which can obviously come only from a 'source' prior to 1717, one might wonder whether they have a direct operative origin or whether, as some think, they are attributable to a Scottish importation during the closing years of the seventeenth century. Both hypotheses are plausible, and there is an enigma here that has in fact never been resolved.

The following chapter first retraces, rather too briefly perhaps, what is known of the history of Operative Masonry in Scotland and England, where its traces are at least not lost at the end of the Middle Ages as they are on the Continent. It seems moreover that to the end it remained more 'alive' in Scotland than anywhere else. The author then explains how the supremacy acquired by the 'accepted' Masons, at least in certain Lodges, leads to the Constitution of Speculative Masonry in 1717, when four London Lodges combined to form the Grand Lodge of England, the Scottish Lodges remaining alongside them together with those in England which came under the ancient Lodge of York. Here the author must be specially commended for not being duped by the way the destruction in 1720 of the documents gathered over the previous years is usually presented. He observes that Anderson 'avoids giving full particulars on the destroyed manuscripts' and that 'his explanation of the causes of the destruction is obscure.' Without expressly saying so, he obviously thinks Anderson himself, along with his 'associates' Payne and Désaguliers, had something to do with this 'act of vandalism', to use Thory's expression. As he goes on to show, it is in fact quite clear that in acting thus the aim of the founders of speculative Masonry was not to prevent 'these papers falling into the hands of strangers' as has been claimed rather naively, but to dispose of everything that could furnish proof of the changes they had brought to the ancient Constitutions. And they have in any case not entirely succeeded, for there are presently a hundred known manuscripts on which they were unable to lay their hands and which thus escaped destruction.

To return to Anderson, in announcing his death 1739, a journal in described him as a 'very facetious companion,' which can be justified by the suspicious role he played in the speculative schism and by the fraudulent way he presented his drafting of the new Constitutions as conforming to documents 'extracted from the ancient archives.' A. E. Waite wrote of him that 'he is especially very capable at corrupting everything he

touches.' Is it known that at the conclusion of these events, some operative Lodges went so far as to decide henceforth not to admit anyone bearing the name of Anderson? When we realize that this is the man whose
authority is cited by so many present-day Masons who consider him
almost as the true founder of Masonry, or accept all the articles of his
Constitutions as more or less authentic *landmarks*, we cannot help but
find a certain irony in all this… If the author has seemed more clear-
sighted than many others concerning the Andersonian falsification, it is
to be regretted that he has not been equally so regarding the origin of the
grade of Master, which, following the commonly held opinion, he
believes to be an innovation introduced only between 1723 and 1738.
Doubtless one cannot demand too great a competence for things touching directly on ritual and symbolism from a pure historian.

The final chapter contains the history of the French Masonry that
stemmed from the Grand Lodge of England, from its first appearance
around 1725 or 1726 up to the death of the Count of Clermont in 1771.
Naturally, the early days are the most obscure, and we find here an excellent explanation of the very controversial question regarding the first
Grand-Masters. Ever since the astronomer Lalande published his 'Mémoire historique' in 1773, this question became so confused that it
appeared insoluble. However, the succession seems definitely established
at last, except that we should perhaps still add another name to the head
of the list, that of the Duke of Wharton, who, between 1730 and 1735,
appears to have exercised the functions of provincial Grand-Master for
France in the name of the Grand Lodge of England, of which he had formerly been the Grand-Master. It is a pity that the author has not related
the circumstances that led the Grand Orient in 1910 to suppress the first
two names which until then had figured on the list of Grand-Masters,
when a simple correction would have sufficed. What is rather amusing is
that this suppression had no other cause than the pamphlets of a learned
occultist adversary, who particularly excelled in 'faking' historical documents to have them say all he wanted. We observed this affair rather
closely, and in spite of the time that has since elapsed, we have good reasons for never forgetting it, having ourselves had the privilege of being a
target of hostility for the same person! As for what follows in the history
of Masonry, the importance attributed to Ramsay's famous discourse is
perhaps excessive, and in any case it is certainly incorrect to say that he
'expounds Masonic doctrine.' He expresses in fact only the particular
conception formed of it by the author, concerning whom, let us note in

passing, he has given some very curious biographical details. What is true is only that this discourse subsequently exercised an incontestable influence on the formation of the high grades, but of course (and despite the fanciful legends spread in certain milieus) Ramsay himself and Fénelon had no hand in them. With regard to the high grades, we should say that in spite of the explanations given on some points, especially concerning dates, the history as a whole, which is sketched very briefly, remains confused; it is moreover extremely complicated, and it is quite possible that we may never succeed in clarifying it. Besides, when it is known that the first mention of such a grade is found in a document dated from such and such a year, are really much more knowledgeable as to its genuine origins? We shall not dwell on the other points, which are far more generally known, such as the harassment from government authorities to which the Masons had to submit on various occasions, the refusal in France to take notice of the condemnations issued by Rome, which the ecclesiastics themselves treated as non-existent, or the split brought on in the Grand-Lodge by the nomination of Lacorne as special substitute for the Count of Clermont, which leads us to the end of the period studied in this first volume. It is to be hoped that the second part of this work, which should contain the history of the Grand Orient, again brings a serious contribution to the study of these questions that have often been treated in so partial a way, in one sense or another, and sometimes also too imaginatively.

G. PERSIGOUT, *Rosicrucisme et Cartésianisme*: '*X Novembris* 1619', *Essai d'exégèse hermétique du Songe cartésien* [Rosicrucianism and Cartesianism: '10 November 1619', An Hermetic Interpretation of the Cartesian Dream] (Paris: 'La Paix' Publications) — This booklet, representing only a fragment of a much longer work, is related to a question we have already discussed (April 1938 issue, pp 155–156), in connection with an article of another author published in *Mercure de France*, and thus we need not repeat all the reasons which render inadmissible the hypothesis that Descartes received a Rosicrucian initiation. Besides, the author of the present study is not as emphatic as certain others, for he sometimes speaks merely of a 'Rosicrucian atmosphere' existing in Germany which could have influenced Descartes at a particular moment, the very one when he had his famous dream. Reduced to these proportions, the matter is surely much less unlikely, especially if one adds that on the whole this influence would have been only transitory and thereby very superficial.

However, this would not explain the different phases of the dream corresponding to initiatic ordeals, as these are matters that cannot be uncovered through mere imagination, except in occultists' reveries; but does such a correspondence really exist? In spite of all the ingenuity the author displays in his interpretations, we have to say that it is not very striking and even presents a regrettable omission, for with the best will in the world one really fails to see how the presentation of a melon can take the place of the ordeal by water.... On the other hand, it is very unlikely that this dream is a mere fiction, which in fact would be more interesting since it would at least indicate a conscious symbolic intention by Descartes, imperfectly as he may have expressed it; in this case, he would have tried to give a disguised description of initiatic ordeals under this form—but again, what kind of initiation could it have been? Strictly speaking, the only thing that can be admitted with certainty is that he had been received—as was Leibnitz later on—into an organization of more or less Rosicrucian inspiration, from which he had subsequently withdrawn (and if such was the case, the rupture must have been rather violent, to judge by the tone of the dedication of 'Polybius the Cosmopolitan'). Still, it would be necessary that such an organization had already reached a very degenerate level for it to accept so unwisely such poorly 'qualified' candidates... However, all things considered, and for reasons that we have already expounded, it is our firm belief that in terms of Rosicrucian concepts, Descartes—whom it is really far too paradoxical to wish to defend against the imputation of 'rationalism'—probably knew nothing other than the ideas then current in the profane world, and that if he came under certain influences in a different way, either consciously or more likely unconsciously, the source of their emanation was in reality something quite different from an authentic and legitimate initiation. Is it not true that the very place held by his philosophy in the history of the modern deviation is ample indication to justify such a suspicion?

LÉON DE PONCINS, *Refusé par la Presse* [Refused by the Press] (Editions Alexis Redier). — This volume is a sequel to *Les Forces secrètes de la Révolution*, which we previously reviewed here. Its title can be explained by the fact that its chapters, initially presented as separate articles to various journals and reviews, were not accepted by any of them. It would not be gracious on our part to criticize a work in which we ourselves have been quoted at length concerning the 'crisis of the modern world' and the problems pertaining thereto, and which even bears an epigraph taken from our *Theosophy*: *History of a Pseudo-Religion*. Let us only say that the author's special concerns, too exclusively political in our opinion, on occasion drive him to present passages from our writings in a way that does not exactly reflect our own intentions. Thus, in the passage he quotes on page 55, we were in no way speaking there of Masonry.... However it is no less true that these quotations, made in a sympathetic spirit, are for us a pleasant change from the insults and heinous remarks of certain other 'anti-Masons'!

LÉON DE PONCINS, *La Mystérieuse Internationale Juive* [The Mysterious Jewish International Society] (Paris: Gabriel Beauchesne). — What we recently said here concerning *La Guerre occulte* [The Occult War], of which Léon de Poncins is one of the co-authors, regarding certain exaggerations about the role of Jews in the world and the necessity of making certain distinctions, is also valid for this new book. There is certainly much truth in what is expounded here regarding two 'Internationals', one revolutionary and the other financial, that in reality are probably much less opposed than a superficial observer might believe. But is all this, which is in any case part of a far vaster picture, really under the direction of Jews (it would be more accurate to say of certain Jews), or is it not rather used in reality by 'something' that goes beyond them? Moreover, we feel that it would be interesting to undertake a rather curious study on the reasons why a Jew, when unfaithful to his tradition, becomes more easily than anyone else the instrument of the 'influences' presiding over the modern deviation. In a way, it would be the reverse side of the 'Jewish mission', and this might lead quite far... The author is absolutely right to speak of a 'silent conspiracy' as regards certain questions. But how would it be if he came directly into contact with matters that are even much more truly 'mysterious' yet and to which, let us say in passing, the 'anti-Judeo-Masonic' publications are the first to be careful never to make the least reference?

J.-H. PROBST-BIRABEN, *Les Mystères des Templiers* [*The Mysteries of the Templars*] (Éditions des Cahiers Astrologiques). For the most part the author of this volume reworks the contents of articles on the same subject which appeared some years ago in *Mercure de France* and which we previously discussed (see issue of October–November 1946). He makes every effort to define certain points and gives to the properly historic account a more 'consistent' development. And he does not seem disposed to relate everything back to questions of financial operations (perhaps this way of looking at things was above all the fact of his departed colleague), but between the role of the Templars in the East and certain modern ideas of 'colonial politics' he draws a connection that seems to us quite deplorable, all the more so since he has gone so far to recall in this connection the case of European agents who entered into contact with Islamic *turuq* in order to devote their attention more thoroughly and with less risk to what we can only consider a common and contemptible work of espionage! It is also regrettable (not to mention the rather strange transcription of the Arab words) that he has not corrected various incorrect or contestable assertions. Thus he continues to take quite seriously the famous 'secret alphabet', without noticing the grave objection to its authenticity constituted by the distinction of the letters 'U' and 'V', as we have pointed out. And we cannot understand why he persists in calling the neo-Templar Maillard de Chambure a 'disinterested author'! Almost no changes have been made regarding the alleged idols and 'Baphomet', nor have the unusual explanations of von Hammer been further clarified; we shall content ourself with returning to what we have already said on all that. A more current section which is in our opinion perhaps the most interesting in the book, concerns the relations of the Order of the Temple with the workers' guilds, both eastern and western, and especially with the building guilds. Here are things which no doubt necessarily remain hypothetical to a certain extent but which are nonetheless quite plausible, and we think there would be every advantage in encouraging more thorough research in this direction. For reasons that we have pointed out elsewhere, it is above all in the realm of Hermeticism and the traditional sciences of the same order that chivalrous initiation and trade initiations quite naturally find themselves on common ground. With regard to Hermeticism, the author explains some symbols rather superficially, and as regards the 'graffiti' of the chateau of Chinon, despite some reservations, he really gives too much importance to the more or less bizarre interpretations of Paul le Cour. However we must at least commend him for having passed over in silence a certain inscription that the latter believed he had found there, and which, as we were able to observe ourselves on the spot, was entirely imaginary… A final chapter is devoted to the real or supposed 'inheritors and successors of the Temple'; we shall not go back over what is already sufficiently known on this subject, noting only the rather enigmatic history of the 'Gentlemen of the Temple' (this designation itself sounds somewhat strange and seems rather profane), whose existence from the fifteenth to the seventeenth century is proved by the documents of various proceedings where they occurred. The fact that they were officially recognized makes unlikely the supposition that they had constituted a kind of 'third order' of authentic Templar filiation, and we confess we do not see what suggested the idea of a possible connection with the hypothetical Larmenius. Would it not simply be a question of some outer association, religious brotherhood or other, which would have been charged with administering certain goods having belonged to the Order of the Temple, and which would have taken the name by which it was known? As to the documents written in Latin and dating from the beginning of the nineteenth century of which the author had been informed, it seems quite clear to us from various details that they can only have originated from the Neo-Templars of Fabre-Palagrat (the mention of Cape Vert and other places in certain titles is pure fancy), and we do not see how there could be any doubt about it. Let us add that the initials V.D.S.A. do not mean *Victorissimus Dominus Supremæ Aulæ*(?), but *Vive Dieu Saint Amour*, the war cry of the Templars, appropriated by their alleged successors along with everything of which they could have had knowledge, in order to give themselves some appearance of authenticity. Having clearly mentioned this war cry elsewhere, how can one not see that the same thing is in question here? Be that as it may, this book certainly contains information interesting from more than one point of view, but much still remains to be done, even supposing it possible, to explain the 'mysteries of the Templars' definitively.

J.-H. PROBST-BIRABEN, *Rabelais and the Secrets of the Pantagruel.*[3] (Nice: Éditions des Cahiers Astrologiques). — Rabelais' esoterism has often been discussed, though generally in rather vague terms, and we have to recognize that the subject is far from easy. Indeed, many passages in his works give the strong impression of a 'secret language' more or less comparable to that of the *Fedeli d'Amore*, but different in kind, so that a 'key' is necessary to translate it, although till now one has not been found. This question is closely related to that of the initiation Rabelais might

---

3. Rabelais (1483–1553)was a monk, physician, and humanist, whose satirical folk epic recounts the adventures of two giants, Gargantua and Pantagruel, who are father and son. They parody the vices and foolishness of people and institutions. His humor is at times so bawdy and his criticism of the Roman Catholic church so telling that it is difficult to believe that for most of his life he was a priest. ED.

have received. That he was connected to Hermeticism does not appear to be in doubt, for the esoteric knowledge of which he gives proof obviously belongs to the 'cosmological' order and never seems to go beyond it, and so corresponds well to the specific domain of Hermeticism. But it would still be useful to know more exactly what current of Hermeticism is involved. This is a complex question, for at the time Hermeticists were divided into different schools, some of which had already deviated in a 'naturalist' direction. Without wishing to delve further into this question, we must say that opinions are rather divided precisely on the question of Rabelais' initiatic orthodoxy. Be that as it may, Probst-Biraben has shown himself very prudent, and as often happens in similar cases, one must know that his preference is not to be rushed into excessively hypothetical speculations. He has certainly not claimed to resolve all the enigmas, which would probably be impossible, but he has at least gathered many facts and evidence of all kinds in writing a book very worthy of interest.

We shall say at once that the part we find least convincing as regards the esoteric provenance Rabelais' ideas is that concerning his social ideas, for we see no clear mark of an influence of this kind, and it is possible that they derive from an exoteric source, such as his Franciscan origins, so that his views on education may very well have been inspired for the most part by his worldly relations with contemporary 'humanists'. On the other hand—and this is much more important from our point of view—there appear his writings numerous symbols clearly deriving from Hermeticism, and the enumeration thereof is most curious and could lead to many comparisons. There are also scattered allusions to astrology, but, as one would expect, especially to alchemy, without taking into account everything that made the *Pantagruel* a veritable 'repertoire of conjectural sciences.' Let us observe in this regard that if one knew precisely to which schools the various individuals ridiculed by Rabelais belonged, we could perhaps to some extent ascertain, through contrast, that to which he himself could be linked, for it does seem that behind these criticisms there must be rivalries among esoteric schools. In any case, it is incontestable that he was very well able to distinguish between the common alchemy of the 'transmuters of gold' and true spiritual alchemy. One of the most extraordinary things, but also the most openly visible, are the descriptions of a clearly initiatic nature met with in the fifth book of the *Pantagruel*. It is true that certain people claim he did not write this book, because it was only published ten years after his death, but what is most likely is that he left it unfinished and that disciples or friends completed it according to instructions received from him before his death, because it truly represents the normal crowning achievement of the entire body of work. Another particularly interesting question is that of the ties Rabelais had with 'craftsmen' and their initiatic organizations. His works contain many more or less disguised allusions to certain rites and signs of recognition, which are nonetheless quite clear to anyone who knows about these things, and which can hardly have any other provenance, for they have a very marked 'guild' character. And we shall add that it may very well also be from this quarter that he gathered the knowledge of the Pythagorean tradition, that seems to be indicated by the use he very frequently made of symbolic numbers. That he had been affiliated with some of these organizations in the role of chaplain is a very likely hypothesis, and it should not be forgotten moreover that there were always close links between the Hermetic and Craft initiations, which, despite differences of form, refer specifically to the same domain of the 'lesser mysteries'. On all such points Probst-Biraben's work contains extensive detailed information impossible to summarize here. This book will certainly not be read without great profit, and through its very moderation and the caution shown regarding rash interpretations, it should give food for thought to the university critics who deny esoterism, or at least to those among them whose prejudice in this respect is not quite irremediable.

Dr Gérard van Rijnberk, *A Thaumaturge in the* 18*th century*: *Martines de Pasqually, His Life, His Work, His Order* (Lyons: P. Derain and L. Raclet) — We gave an extensive review of the first volume of this work at the time of its publication; the second volume is on the whole a supplement deemed necessary by the author because of certain facts that subsequently came to his attention. He took this opportunity to complete the bibliography and reproduce in their entirety Martines' letters to Willermoz, currently preserved at the Lyons Library, of which only various fragments had so far been published. He cites articles in which we spoke of his book, but hardly seems to have understood our position, for he quite incredibly calls us an 'essayist', claiming that we 'strive to express original ideas and personal views'—the exact opposite of our intentions and our strictly traditional point of view. He finds 'astonishing' our remark that 'the Rectified Scottish Right is not a metamorphosis of the Elect Cohens, but really a derivation of the Strict Observance.' However, that is the simple truth, and anyone with even a vague idea of the history and the constitution of Masonic rites cannot entertain the least doubt about this. Even if Willermoz, in drafting the instructions of certain grades, introduced some ideas more or less inspired by the teachings of Martines, this makes no difference as to the filiation or the general characteristic of the Rite involved. Moreover, the Rectified Right is in no way 'Templar Masonry', as van Rijnberk says, since on the contrary one of the main points of the 'rectification' consisted precisely in the repudiation of the Templar origin of Masonry.

In another rather strange chapter the author tries to clarify the filiation of 'Martinism', which in spite of everything still remains rather obscure and doubtful on certain points. Besides, aside from a purely historical point of view, the question does not have the importance some wish to ascribe to it, for it is in any case quite clear that what Saint-Martin could have transmitted to his disciples outside a regularly constituted organization should in no way be considered as having an initiatic character. On the other hand, an interesting point is made concerning the significance of the letters S. I.—usually interpreted as 'Unknown Superior' [Supérieur Inconnu]—which in fact had many usages: we have already remarked that in particular these are the initials of the 'Society of Independents' mentioned in the *Crocodile*, as well as Willermoz's 'Society of Initiates'. As van Rijnberk says, one could provide many examples of this kind; he himself notes that they are also the abbreviation of 'Sovereign Judge', the title of the members of the 'Sovereign Tribunal' of the Elect Cohens. We may add that in another Rite of the same period there was a grade of 'Enlightened Sage', and that in the Ancient and Accepted Scottish Rite itself there is one of 'Intimate Secretary', which happens to be the sixth—which is a rather curious connection with the 'six points' (incidentally, amateurs of 'coincidences' may like to know that in the 'Strict Observance' the act of obedience to the 'Unknown Superiors' was also in six points!). But why did these two letters enjoy such privilege? The author is quite right in thinking that this is owed to their own symbolic value, which he glimpsed in reference to one of Khunrath's illustrations; but he forgot to make a distinction between two connected symbols that are nonetheless somewhat different: that of the 'bronze snake', which in fact gives the letters 'S. T.' (which are also the initials of 'Sovereign Tribunal'), and that wherein the tree or the stick around which the snake is coiled is represented solely by a vertical axis; it is this last that gives the letters 'S. I.' which figure in a different form in the snake and the arrow found on Cagliostro's seal. Since we have been led to speak of this subject, we may add that fundamentally the letter 'S' represents multiplicity and the letter 'I' unity; and it is obvious that their respective correspondence with the snake and the axial tree are in perfect harmony with this meaning. It is quite true that there is something here that 'comes from a profound esoterism,' far deeper and more genuine than the Martinist 'Holy Initiation', which is definitely no more entitled to claim ownership of this ancient symbol than of the number 6 and the Seal of Solomon!

DR GÉRARD VAN RIJNBERK, *Episodes de la vie ésotérique (1780–1824)* [Episodes in the Esoteric Life] (Lyon: P. Derain). — This book includes many previously unpublished and very interesting documents that throw an interesting light on certain Masonic circles of the end of the eighteenth century, and on the way in which many ideas and practices spread which in reality had very little in common with true esoterism infiltrated these circles, and one might even wonder if perhaps they were not launched precisely in order to divert the attention of these circles from true esoterism in just the way we have already noted, particularly regarding magnetism, which certainly played a dominant role in all this. The main section of the book consists of extracts from the correspondence between J.-B. Willermoz and Prince Charles de Hesse-Cassel, both holders of the highest grades of various masonic Rites, and who both took an active interest, in slightly different but fundamentally equivalent ways, in these things which we have just mentioned. First of all, with regard to masonic Rites, van Rijnberk's commentaries contain some inaccuracies: thus he does not seem to know that the Chevaliers Bienfaisants de la Cité Sainte [Merciful Knights of the Holy City] is the highest grade of the Rectified Scottish Rite, whose name he does not even mention (which is common to other authors who have spoken of Willermoz). Moreover, he seems to believe that Swedenborg, who in all probability was never a Mason, personally exerted an influence in Swedish Masonry, whereas all one can actually say in this respect is that some of his disciples spread certain of his ideas, and that by way of simple individual views. However, these questions have little place in the book, the most important part of which relates to magnetism, to 'revelations' by hypnotic subjects, and other things of this kind; it is naturally impossible to examine all this in detail, and we shall content ourselves with some general remarks.

Some comparisons clearly show that on many points, and especially as regards their descriptions of posthumous states, the hypnotic subjects were influenced, very likely unconsciously, by several contemporary 'mystical philosophers'. This certainly does not surprise us, for in our opinion it is rather the contrary that would have been surprising, but it is an observation that always bears noting. In addition to hypnotic subjects, and perhaps not always so clearly distinguishable from them, are what the author calls 'writer mediums', This is an anachronistic expression here, since it belongs to the vocabulary of spiritualism which only originated much later, and van Rijnberk sometimes uses the word spiritualism itself in a way that is obviously quite improper. What is true is that in a way magnetism prepared the way for spiritualism (it is even one of the reasons that renders it clearly suspect), and that hypnotic subjects were in a way the precursors of mediums; all the same there are notable differences which should be taken into account. Among these 'writer mediums', the one who no doubt played the most important role was Willermoz's 'Agent', on whom the occultists pin so many baseless legends and whose true identity Alice Joly has already discovered and made known. There were also other much less well-known cases of 'automatic writing', including that of Prince Charles of Hesse himself, which, contrary to those of Mme de Vallière, were produced independently of all hypnotic practice. Another point possibly closely connected with the former is that, according to certain passages in his writings, the Prince of Hesse admitted a kind of 'reincarnation', at least in specific cases. How he conceived this is not entirely clear however, so that it would be difficult to say whether it was really a question of reincarnation in the strict sense of the word, such as the spiritualists and Theosophists would later teach, but it is any case beyond doubt that it was at this time and in Germany, precisely, that this idea started to emerge. We shall not attempt to clarify van Rijnberk's own views on this subject, for he clearly shows the effect of 'neo-spiritualist' ideas, but we cannot help noting the rather amusing error that led him to confuse *nirmāna* with *nirvāna*! Again as to the Prince of Hesse, he performed bizarre phenomena, visions, or luminous manifestations (especially in connection with an image of Christ), to which he attributed an 'oracular' character and of which one can hardly determine to what extent they were 'objective' or merely 'subjective', to use the actual terminology.

Be that as it may, these phenomena, which seem to have been produced by 'works' accomplished according to the ritual of the Brother Initiates of Asia, call to mind rather closely the 'passes' of the Elect Cohens, among whom, it must be said, these things were also given an excessive importance. That they be taken, when they appear more or less accidentally, as outward 'signs' of the acquisition of certain results is still admissible, but what is not in any way admissible, is to consider their achievement as the very aim of an initiatic organization, for it is quite impossible to see what real interest all this can have from the spiritual point of view. There would be much to say on this, for it is quite certain that the taste for extraordinary phenomena, to which is also connected the passion for hypnotic experiments, was then and subsequently remained for Westerners one of the principal stumbling-blocks for Westerners, diverting certain aspirations and preventing them from achieving their normal outcome. We shall add only that at the home of the Prince of Hesse the phenomena in question sometimes took on an extravagant aspect that at least they seemed never to have had among the Elect Cohens. And in the same order of ideas let us again mention the conjuring performances of von Wächter, whom the more accentuated allure of 'ceremonial magic' makes more particularly suspect, not to speak of the fabulous stories surrounding them, concerning which it is hard to know what they could serve to conceal.

The second section deals with certain 'enigmatic and mysterious individuals'. One chapter is devoted to the Marchioness of the Cross, who above all gives the impression of an unbalanced person, and another chapter deals with some aspects of the life of the Count of Saint-Germain, and more particularly his relationship with Prince Charles of Hesse. The most curious chapter retraces the turbulent career of Master Bernard Müller, an alchemist (or allegedly such) who assigned himself the mission of 'mouthpiece', to use his own expression, of a fantastic 'premillenniarism'. Having won the confidence of the celebrated Professor Molitor, he was introduced into German Masonic circles. He took advantage of this to establish relations with several princes, and was for a long time protected by Prince Charles of Hesse. Then, following various misadventures, he ended by emigrating with fifty disciples to America, where descendants of this group still remained a few years ago. — Van Rijnberk's conclusion seems to call for some reservations: like him, we think that men such as Willermoz and the Prince of Hesse were serious, sincere, and well-intentioned, but when he begins to 'follow their example,' it seems to us that this example should above all serve rather as a lesson to avoid committing the same faults as they did and not to let oneself be led astray from the straight initiatic path and authentic esoterism in order to embark on the pursuit of vain phantasmagorias.

CAMILLE SAVOIRE, *Regards sur les Temples de la Franc-Maçonnerie* [Concerning the Temples of Freemasonry] (Paris: 'Les Editions Initiatiques') — This book contains chapters of rather diverse character, some being 'autobiographical', where the author notably explains how he was slowly led to modify his ideas in a direction which brought them very much closer to the traditional spirit, others being more general in tenor, where he explains his way of considering Freemasonry from different points of view. The intention behind all this is surely excellent, but from a purely initiatic and symbolic point of view the reflections developed here remain somewhat 'external'. At the end of the book are reproduced various documents meant to give a more accurate idea of Masonry than the one generally in vogue in the profane world. An appendix indicates the reasons behind the awakening of the 'Reformed Regime', of which the author is the main promoter. 'A Masonic center preserved from all political influence,' as he puts it, is surely something extremely desirable in the present circumstances, if the last remaining vestiges of Western initiation are to be saved from irremediable loss... — And we take the liberty of pointing out a rather peculiar historical error (p 282): L.-Cl. de Saint-Martin was never the 'canon of the Collegiate church' (of Lyon?), but an officer, and if he was a member of various Masonic rites, he did not found one himself. Moreover, there was never a 'Masonic system' under the authentic name of 'Martinism', the truth being that when Saint-Martin withdrew from the various organizations of which he had been a member it was in order to adopt an attitude that was much more mystical than initiatic, and certainly incompatible with the constitution of any 'Order' whatsoever.

ARTICLES

Masonic Light of Montreal

SEPTEMBER 1948–JUNE 1949 — These issues include a curious series of articles expounding a new theory on the origin of Masonry, which latter the author paradoxically relates to Solomon rather than to Moses. Basing himself largely on numerical considerations which are not always very clear (some illustrations would have been useful), he seeks to establish that the symbolism of the Tabernacle was much more complete than that of the Temple of Solomon, which, in his view, would only have been an imperfect imitation, as it were, since certain secrets had been lost in the meantime. It is of course quite natural that the Temple of Solomon should present certain links with the Tabernacle, since it was intended to fulfill the same function, but also that there should be certain differences corresponding to the transition of the Israelites from a nomadic to a settled state. But we do not see where either one can really provide grounds for disparaging it as he does. On the other hand, the Tabernacle was obviously not a stone edifice, and this alone should suffice to prevent us from speaking of Masonry in connection with it. The occupation of carpenters is certainly quite distinct from that of masons, and the ancient distinction between them, which has continued to the present day, clearly shows that any assimilation between them is impossible (see our article on this subject in the number for December 1946).[4] That the names of the principal worker engaged in the construction of the Tabernacle were introduced into certain high grades is quite another question, which has nothing to do with Masonry properly speaking. Now, if we wish to go beyond Solomon, we could with far more reason go back further still to Abraham himself. A very clear indication of this can be seen in the fact that the divine Name invoked most particularly by Abraham has always been retained by Operative Masonry. This connection of Abraham with Masonry is moreover readily understandable to whomever knows something of the Islamic tradition, as it is directly connected to the building of the *Kaabah*.

Let us also mention an article that aims to prove that there were in fact two Hirams, the father and the son, the first assassinated during the construction of the Temple and the second then completing the task. The argument is ingenious but not very convincing, and the interpretation of the biblical texts on which it rests seems to us rather forced.

Of the other articles contained in the same review, some of which are interesting from the historical point of view, we shall mention only those in which the question of a 'modernization' of Masonry is discussed. Arguments pro and con are introduced in turn, and all we can say is that those who argue for modernization only prove that from their quite profane point of view they hardly understand what constitutes the essential character of Masonry.

---

4. See chapter 5 of the present work.

Among the historical articles, we shall note one which sets forth the facts that led certain operative English Lodges between 1830 and 1840 to renounce their Masonic character and turn themselves into mere *Trade Unions*. We wonder if this might not explain what produced certain gaps in the operative rituals around this time, gaps which were later redressed, but, so it seems, done so especially with the aid of the rituals of speculative Masonry. By a curious coincidence something similar happened to the rituals of the Compagnonnage in France during the nineteenth century, and it was remedied in the same way, which might lead to some doubt as to the real antiquity of what these rituals, as they exist today, have in common with those of Masonry, which, at least in part, can only be a consequence of this reconstitution.

Also in the April issue, J.-H. Probst-Biraben studies 'Coleurs et symboles hermétiques des ancienne peintres italiens' [Hermetic colors and symbols of the ancient Italian painters]. He offers a series of interesting observations, but arrives at no very precise conclusion, perhaps because even at the time of the Renaissance certain esoteric knowledge was still frequently expressed in works that in outer appearance were purely religious. On the other hand, at the end we came across the idea of a 'Mediterranean tradition' the reality of which seems more than problematic.

In the May issue, 'Psychanalyse collective et symbolisme maçonnique' [Collective Psychoanalysis and Masonic Symbolism], by 'Timotheus', uses Jung's theories to interpret the idea of tradition and the origin of symbolism. Since in our recent article 'Tradition et "inconscient"' [Tradition and the 'Unconscious'] (July–August 1949 issue)[5] we have already shown the dangerous errors implied in these kinds of ideas, it is of no use to dwell further on the issue, and we shall only point out the following: if surrealism is linked to the action of the counter-initiation, how can one not realize that the same is all the more true for psychoanalysis?

In this issue and that of June, François Menard examines what he calls 'Le Sagesse "taoiste" des Essais de Montaigne' [Taoist Wisdom in Montaigne's Essays]. This is clearly only a manner of speaking, for Montaigne certainly knew nothing of Taoism, and doubtless never received an initiation, so that in short his 'wisdom' remains of a rather exterior order. But certain 'meetings' are nonetheless curious, and we know that others have also observed a strange similarity between Montaigne's mode of thought and that of Chinese thought, both proceeding 'in a spiral' as it were.

5. See *Symbols of Sacred Science*, chap. 5. ED.

Moreover, it is remarkable that in his own way Montaigne recognized, at least theoretically, certain traditional ideas which certainly could not have been provided by the moralists whom he studied and who served as the starting-point for his reflections.

In the October issue of the same review we note an article on the symbolism of the Blazing Star, which is especially interesting because it shows that there were many differences in the interpretation of this symbol and even in its representation. Thus, when it is said in Mackey's encyclopaedia that the Blazing Star should not be confused with the five-pointed star, this implies that it must be represented with six points, as in fact it sometimes is, and this is doubtless why it was taken as a symbol of Providence, as well as being likened to the Star of Bethlehem, for the Seal of Solomon is also designated as the 'Star of the Magi'. This is nonetheless an error, for the six-pointed star is essentially a macrocosmic symbol, whereas the five-pointed star is a microcosmic symbol. Now the significance of the Blazing Star is above all microcosmic, and there are even cases where it could not be otherwise, as when it is depicted between the square and the compasses (cf. *The Great Triad*, chap. 20). On the other hand, from the strictly cosmic point of view, the rather strange identification of the Blazing Star with the sun represents another corruption, perhaps an intentional one, for it is obviously connected with a change in the original polar symbolism. In this respect the Blazing Star can in fact only be identified with the pole star, and the letter 'G' inscribed at its center is moreover sufficient proof of this, as we ourselves have had occasion to note (cf. also *The Great Triad*, chap. 25), and as is again confirmed by the considerations noted in the study of the *Speculative Mason* mentioned above.

NOVEMBER 1949 — This issue contains an article dealing with the rule of 24 inches. There is good reason to note that the more or less recent adoption of the metric system in some countries should in no way result in modifying in rituals the indication of this measure, which alone has a traditional value. On the other hand, the author notes that this rule does not figure everywhere among the tools of the first degree. He is correct in this, but has completely forgotten to note its role in the ritual of the third degree, and this is nevertheless what shows most clearly its symbolic link with the division of the day into 24 hours. We shall also note that although mentioned in certain instructions to new initiates, the division of these hours into three groups of eight actually represents only a rather banal 'use of time'. This is an example of the 'moralizing' tendency that has unfortunately prevailed in the current interpretation of symbols; an apportionment into two series of twelve, corresponding to the hours of day and of night (as in the number of letters comprising the two parts of the formula of the Islamic *Shahādah*), would certainly lead to far more interesting considerations. Regarding the more or less approximate equivalence of the current English inch to the ancient Egyptian inch, this is doubtless rather hypothetical. The variations undergone by measures designated by the same names in different countries and ages seem never to have been adequately studied, and we must recognize that such a study would not be free of difficulties: for example, do we know exactly the different sorts of cubits, feet, and inches that were in use, sometimes at the same time, among certain peoples of antiquity?

Mercure de France

July 15, 1935 — This issue of contains an article entitled 'L'Infidélité des Francs-Maçons' [Masons' Unfaithfulness], under the pseudonym 'Inturbidus'. It offers some considerations which, while interesting, are not always entirely clear, especially regarding the distinction between sacerdotal, princely, and chivalrous, and finally craft, initiations, which generally correspond to the traditional organization of Western society during the Middle Ages and to the castes in India. It is not clear what exact place is assigned to it within Hermeticism, and it should be explained why, in spite of its craft forms, Masonry also carries the appellation 'royal art'. On the question of craft or guild initiations, the author cites at length Matila Ghyka's *Nombre d'Or*, but unfortunately the portion of this work dealing with the subject under consideration is certainly the one which calls for the most reservations, and the information it offers does not all come from the most reliable sources... Be that as it may, the question of taking the expression 'Masonic operative' in an exclusively guild sense is perhaps much too limited; the author, who nevertheless recognizes that this ancient Masonry has always admitted members who were not workers (which we would not necessarily render as 'non-operatives'), does not really appear to understand what they could do therein; does he know, for example, what a L∴ of J∴ was? In truth, if Masonry has really degenerated into something merely 'speculative' (note that we say 'merely' in order to indicate clearly that this change implies a diminution), it has done so in another sense and way than he thinks, which moreover does not preclude the correctness of certain of his reflections pertaining to the constitution of the Grand Lodge of England. In any case, by very definition Masonry, whether 'operative' or 'speculative', consists essentially in the use of symbolic forms used by the builders. 'To suppress the ritual of craft initiation,' as the author recommends, thus amounts quite simply to suppressing Masonry itself, which however he denies 'wanting to destroy,' while recognizing that it 'would thus break the initiatic transmission'— really a bit of a contradiction. We understand clearly that in his opinion it is thus a question of substituting another initiatic organization; but first why would the latter, no longer having any real link of filiation with Masonry, recruit its members from among the Masons rather than from another milieu altogether? And then, since such an organization does not invent itself, at least humanly, and cannot be the product of merely individual initiatives (even if they came from persons 'finding themselves in an orthodox initiatic chain'), this would obviously not suffice to legitimize the creation of new ritualistic forms by the latter, whence would this organization come and to what would it effectively attach itself? Brief reflection on all this suffices to show how it gives rise to difficulties that are probably insoluble. We also remain skeptical about the realization of such a project, which is really not to the point... The true remedy for the present degeneration of Masonry, and doubtless the only one, would be quite different. It would be, supposing this were still possible, to alter the mentality of the Masons, or at least of those among them who are capable of understanding their own initiation, but to whom, it must be said, the opportunity has not been given up till now. Their number would matter little, moreover, for in the presence of a serious and really initiatic work, the 'non-qualified' elements would soon eliminate themselves, and with them, by very force of circumstance, the agents of the 'counter-initiation' whose role we have mentioned in the passage from *Theosophy* cited at the end of the article, would also disappear, for nothing could then set them in action. To implement a 'reform of Masonry in the traditional sense' is not a question of 'shooting for the moon,' despite what 'Inturbidus' says, or of building castles in the air; it would only be a matter of using the possibilities at our disposal, limited though they may be to start with. But in a time like ours, who will dare undertake such a task?

FEBRUARY, 1938 — The article 'Le Songe de Descartes' [Descartes'

Dream] by Albert Shinz again raises a question that has already given rise to many more or less confused discussions—that of Descartes' supposed Rosicrucian affiliation. The only thing that does not seem in doubt is that the alleged Rosicrucian manifestos published in the first years of the seventeenth century aroused a certain curiosity in the philosopher, who, during his travels in Germany, sought contact with the authors, whom he simply took for 'new scholars', as he was not someone very 'informed'. These Rosicrucians, whoever they were (and in any case they were certainly not the 'authentic Rose-Croix', as maintained by Maritain, who published an article on the subject in the *Revue Universelle* of December 1920), appear not to have seen fit to satisfy his wish, and even if he did happen to meet someone, that person probably knew nothing. His frustration at this failure is clearly expressed in his dedication to a work entitled *Thesaurus Mathematicus*, which he proposed to write under the pseudonym 'Polybius le Cosmopolite', but which always remained an idea. It is worth translating this dedication in full in order that we may fully judge the matter:

> A work in which is given the true means of resolving all the difficulties of this science, and showing that relative to it the human spirit cannot go any further; to cause hesitation in or to ridicule the temerity of those who promise new marvels in all the sciences, and at the same time to relieve the punishing fatigue of the Brothers of the Rose-Cross, who, entwined night and day in the Gordian knots of this science, waste the fuel of their genius. Dedicated again to the scholars of the whole world and especially to the very illustrious Rose-Cross Brothers of Germany.

What is quite astonishing is that some have wished to see in this a mark of 'Rosicrucianism'. How can one not sense all the spiteful and angry irony in such a dedication, not to speak of the obvious ignorance shown by the persistence of its author in comparing the Rosicrucians to scholars and profane 'seekers'? It is true that prejudice is sometimes combined with one thing or another, but in any case to unite Cartesianism and esoterism in a common admiration or in a common hatred, is to give proof—at least as regards esoterism—of considerable incomprehension! Descartes is certainly the very type of the profane philosopher, whose anti-traditional mentality is absolutely incompatible with all initiation. On the other hand, this is not to say that he may not have been susceptible to certain 'suggestions' of a suspect character; and could not this be the most likely interpretation of the alleged 'illumination' which came to him in the guise of a rather incoherent and far-fetched dream?

AUGUST 1939–JANUARY 1940 — We must now return to the question of the Templars, for we have only now learned belatedly of a whole series of articles on the subject by J.-H. Probst-Biraben and A. Maitrot de la Motte-Capron, published in *Mercure de France*: (1) 'Les Templiers et leur alphabet secret' [The Templars and their Secret Alphabet (August 1, 1939); (2) 'Les Idoles des Chevaliers du Temple' [The Idols of the Knights Templar] (September 15, 1939; (3) 'Les coffrets mystérieux des Templiers' [The Mysterious Caskets of the Templars] (November 1, 1939); (4) 'Les Templiers et les Gardiens du Temple' [The Templars and the Guardians of the Temple] (December 1, 1939); (5) 'Le Roi de France et les Templiers' [The King of France and the Templars] (January 1, 1940).

(1) The authenticity of the 'secret alphabet' seems very doubtful to us, for it appears that no one has actually seen the ancient manuscripts where it is found, the whole of the story resting in fact on no more than the assertions of Father Grégoire and Maillard de Chambure. Moreover, we do not really see how the latter can be considered 'more serious' that the former, for if Father Grégoire received this information from the 'Neo-Templars', Maillard de Chambure was himself a member of this organization, so that the 'source' is the same and certainly hardly trustworthy. Besides, the complicated form of the cross that serves as 'key' to the alphabet in question is really that of the 'Neo-Templars', but it does not seem that it was ever in use among the true Templars. Another very suspicious detail is the distinction between the 'U' and the 'V', quite unknown to the Middle Ages, and we are amazed that the authors did not comment on this even while they were worrying about the presence of 'W', which after all could perhaps be more easily justified. Given these conditions, one might well wonder if it is really useful to engage in hypothetical 'speculation' on the symbolism of this alphabet, which doubtless has as much worth as Fabré-Palaprat's collection of 'relics'. Moreover, if it is a modern invention, it is very likely that the irregularities in the alphabetical order of the letters are in no way esoteric but have as their sole raison d'être to make the deciphering less easy. In any case, as regards the direction of rotation in which there is a desire to see 'a very marked Eastern

influence', unfortunately, if it concerns the Islamic East, it happens that this would really be the exact opposite direction. From another point of view, it is remarkable that the authors seem to want to reduce the whole mystery of the Order of the Temple to a matter of financial operations, which would hardly be esoteric. Do they not go so far as to write in the following article that 'the real idol of the Templars was international financial power'? Let us also note two historical inaccuracies: Jacques de Molay did not die in 1312, but in 1314, and there never was a papal decision suppressing the Order of the Temple, which latter was only 'provisionally' suspended by the Council of Vienna.

(2) On the subject of the alleged 'idols', the testimonies obtained during the trial under conditions hardly allowing them to be regarded as valid, are mutually contradictory; it is possible that certain histories of 'heads' quite simply relate to reliquaries. In any case it goes without saying that, whatever Western ignorance may think, idols of any sort could in no way have been borrowed from an Islamic milieu, a point on which we are in full agreement with the authors. As for the famous 'Baphomet', whose name has given rise to many hypotheses, each as unsatisfactory as the next, we can in passing provide the explanation of von Hammer's so-called *Bahumid*. It is quite true that this word does not exist in Arabic, but it should in fact be read *bahīmah*, and, if this does not translate as 'calf' (an interpretation perhaps influenced more by the enigmatic Druse 'head of a calf' than by 'the bull Apis or the golden calf'), it is at least the general designation for all kinds of beasts. Now, it is in fact unlikely that 'Baphomet' derives from the Arabic *bahīmah*, which the interrogators at the trial could not have known, it could very well be that it derives from its Hebrew equivalent, namely, the biblical *Behemoth*, and perhaps there is no need to look further for the solution to this enigma. . . . As for the four statues which, according to the same von Hammer, were found in the office in Vienna (but what has become of them since 1818?), we do not see what leads them to be considered as 'Baphomet's'. Frankly, what can be made of these statues which, from their physiognomy, lead one to being described as 'Roman', one as 'Pharaonic', and the other two as 'Persian', although all carry Arabic inscriptions, very bad Arabic moreover if the given deciphering is

really correct? It must be recognized that there is something in all this that savors of deception, perhaps even more than in the case of the caskets in question earlier... We shall not linger in detail over the interpretation of the Arabic phrases, of which the reading itself is very doubtful, but will content ourselves with pointing out a factual error. While it is true that *kenīsah* (and not *kensen*) means exclusively a Christian church (a Muslim uses this word as well as a Christian when he wishes to speak of this church, for there is no other word to designate it), but we cannot understand how it can be said that 'Maulana is never used,' for in many Islamic countries (there are others besides the Maghreb), it is on the contrary the term in current use for addressing Sovereigns, and even other respectable personages.

(3) The next question concerns the two famous caskets which figured in the collection of the Duke of Blacas (by what misfortune does it happen that they also have been lost?). As for the so-called 'Baphomets', nothing proves that they ever had the slightest link to the Templars. In the author's opinion it was simply a question of 'boxes of wild animals' used by Greek and Arab doctors. This explanation itself is quite plausible, but we shall not examine here the underlying interpretation of the figures which is on the whole as valid as any other even if it is not correct in all its details (thus, for example, we do not really see why in one place the same sign would indicate a number of ingredients, and in another a number of months or years). What is most curious are the questions that arise concerning the lid of one of the caskets. The symbolism is clearly alchemical (why do some still claim that the principal figure, which is in fact a *Rebis*, is a 'Baphomet'?), and here again we find inscriptions which, if they have been transcribed correctly, are written in an unimaginable Arabic, something that would not be too astonishing if we admit the authors' hypothesis that this cover, added later, was fashioned by Western alchemists toward the end of the Middle Ages or at the beginning of the Renaissance. The reasons for ascribing this late date to it are not clearly indicated, moreover, any more than are those for asserting that 'one does not see how a Templar could be interested in alchemy.' Quite independently of the question of the caskets, we could just as well say that we do not see why he would not be interested!

(4) The following article deals above all with the question of the possible relations between the Templars and the Ismailis, usually called 'Assassins'. The authors take needless pains to explain that it should be written *Assacine*, which does not represent a better transcription (the introduction of the mute *e*, in particular, is only a rather bizarre concession to French pronunciation); it also does not prevent the word 'assassin' from deriving therefrom rather than being a simple 'relationship through assonance'. This derivation does not of course indicate who the Ismailis really were, but merely indicates the common opinion of Westerners in their regard. The article ends with a number of contradictory assertions: why say that the Templars 'were not initiates' simply because it is unlikely they had received initiation from the Ismailis, as if they could not have had their own initiation, especially if it is admitted that they were 'Johannites'? It is also said that they had 'a profound knowledge of the symbolism of Near-Eastern and Mediterranean esoterism,' which scarcely accords with an absence of initiation, or with the wholly profane preoccupations elsewhere attributed to them. As for looking for proofs of this knowledge in the 'neo-Templar' alphabet, perhaps this is not a very solid argument despite the authors' concern not 'to exceed the limits of historical criticism.'

(5) Finally, the last article seems intended to justify everyone: the king of France, the Pope, the Templars, and the judges, each of whom would have had reasons for his own point of view. Without stressing the point, we shall be content to point out that the Templars are now presented as possessing not only a financial secret, but also a 'synarchic' secret, which is a little less grossly material (but is it really to place it in the ambiance of the fourteenth century by speaking here of a 'secular affair'?). Be that as it may, what in particular seems to result from these long studies is that it is really very difficult to know exactly where one stands regarding any of it!

Revue Internationale des Sociétés Secrètes

November 1, 1931 — This issue of the *Revue Internationale des Sociétés Secrètes* ('occultist section') consists primarily of Dr G. Mariani's article 'Le Christ-Roi et le Roi du Monde' [The Christ-King and the King of the World], and contains many flattering words about us which conceal quite false insinuations. At least for the time being, we shall not detail all the points that need to be discussed, for there are too many, but shall confine ourselves to the most important. First, after the explanations we gave in our book,[6] is it possible to seriously contend that the 'King of the World' (a very exotic term indeed, as we carefully noted) is none other than the *Princeps hujus mundi* [Prince of this world] of the Gospel? Such is not our opinion, any more than we can in good faith identify *Agarttha* with the 'Great White Lodge', that is to say the caricature of it imagined by the Theosophists, or interpret in an 'infernal' sense its 'subterranean' situation, that is, hidden from ordinary people during the *Kali-Yuga*. Besides, when the author says regarding the Hebrew texts that there are 'some Kabbalists' who give to 'their God' [*sic*] the title of 'King of the World', he betrays his ignorance of the most common Jewish prayer formulas, where the expression *Melek ha-Olam* is reiterated constantly. Better still: it is maintained that the 'King of the World' is the Antichrist (in this regard, the editor has deemed it necessary to add a note invoking the Secret of the Salette!);[7] till now, we had not been in doubt that the Antichrist already existed, or that he had existed already from the origin of humanity! It is true that this provides an opportunity to present us, in a way that is hardly concealed, as someone especially directed to prepare for the next manifestation of this Antichrist. We could merely smile at such fanciful stories did we not know only too well how likely they are to unsettle poor people who really have no need of that... Moreover, some claim to identify 'our doctrine' [*sic*] with the 'Nestorian heresy', which in fact is not of the least interest to us for the simple reason that we never look at things from the point of view of exoteric religion. Besides, those

---

6. See the author's *The King of the World*. ED.

7. The Blessed Virgin appeared to two young shepherds, Melanie Calvat and Maximin Giraud, on the Mountain of La Salette in the Diocese of Grenoble, on September 19, 1846. First, She conferred a public message to both of them; then a secret to Maximin alone; and then to Melanie, a secret message which she could publish in 1858. ED.

who are commonly described as 'Nestorians' and to whom we referred had doubtless themselves nothing to do with this heresy. It is more or less deliberately forgotten that this doctrine is several centuries earlier than Christianity, with which the world certainly did not begin, and also that the Kshatriya initiation on which the alleged 'Nestorians' apparently depended, in any case pertains only to the contingent and secondary applications of the doctrine in question. Yet we have often explained the difference between the Brahmins and the Kshatriyas, and made clear that the role of the latter could not in any case be ours. Lastly, we shall note a truly monstrous allegation against which we protest most vehemently: we have come under attack by some (citing the authority of a certain Robert Desoille, of whom we have never heard) for 'materialistic' and 'political' tendencies! Now, all our writings prove over and over again that we are perfectly indifferent to politics and to anything even vaguely connected thereto, and we are not exaggerating in the least when we say that things not belonging to the spiritual domain do not count for us. Moreover, whether one considers that we are right or wrong in this regard hardly matters, for the incontestable fact remains that this is the way things stand and not otherwise; consequently, either the author of the article is ignorant or he deceives his readers for reasons we do not wish to specify. On the other hand, we have personally received such a strange letter from Dr Mariani himself that the first of these two hypotheses seems less improbable; as the article must have a sequel, we shall come back to it should the need arise.

We also point out, in the December 7 issue of the same review, the conclusion of a long series of articles entitled 'Diana Vaughan a-t-elle existé?' [Did Diana Vaughan exist?]. In short, this conclusion amounts to saying that it is impossible that Taxil could have invented everything. It is well known that he plagiarized documents here and there, which moreover he often distorted, and also that he had collaborators such as the famous Dr Hacks. As for claiming to see in this documentation, which is as copious as it is unusual, a proof of the existence of Diana Vaughan and of her 'family papers', this is certainly not serious. It also seems that Taxil himself could not have made 'this sensational revelation that the essence of alchemy is the pact with Satan'; here, all those with even the least idea of what alchemy is cannot but chuckle!

[In the June 1931 issue of *Voile d'Isis* G. Mariani's response to the above review was published, along with Guénon's answer]:

Sir, in issue no. 134 of *Voile d'Isis*, you published a few lines by Guénon regarding my article 'Le Christ-Roi et le Roi du Monde' (*R.I.S.S.*). Since Guénon mostly likely had time to give my article only superficial attention, he has misunderstood my thinking on at least two points.

1) It is incorrect to say that I confuse Agarttha with the Great White Lodge. On the contrary, while speaking of the role played by the latter in Mme. Blavatsky's works, I quote the following passage by Guénon (p 3, n 4, sect. 3): 'If the Mahātmās were an invention, which for us is beyond any doubt, not only were they so for the sake of providing a mask to the influences that were really at play behind Mme Blavatsky, but this invention was itself conceived according to an already existing model.' This is what permitted me to write (p 9) that 'the King of the World himself holds his seat in the midst of a council of twelve wise men, which we identify as the Great White Lodge.' This identification was obviously made merely for the sake of linguistic convenience, for by its use I was able to avoid long-winded sentences and repetitions.

2) It is not true that R. Desoille and myself ever attributed any material and political propensities to Guénon. Here is exactly what I wrote following a remark from my friend (p 25): 'We are in the presence of two symmetrical traditions. One leads the spiritual, mystical destinies of this world; this Principle takes the aspect of the Christ-King in God, of whom Saint Michael is the lieutenant. The other relates to the principle directing the material, political destinies of this world. This principle takes the aspect of the Anti-christ in Satan, of whom the King of the World is the lieutenant... Guénon, with his aversion for mysticism (mysticism and not mystical speculation), with a natural tendency toward a materialistic interpretation, saw only the second tradition.' It stands out clearly from this passage that the terms 'material' and 'political' apply only to the King of the World and not to Guénon. I have not yet been so extravagant as to believe that these two personalities are one and the same. Furthermore, it is obvious that the sense of the term 'materialism' in the last paragraph should only be understood as opposed to that of 'mysticism' from the preceding line.

Finally, I draw attention to the fact that reference no. 4 (p 25), where I mention Desoille, as is there written, to the whole paragraph (relating to the double aspect of the problem, which is moreover a traditional theory), and not to the last paragraph (relating to Guénon), as my friend loathes polemic even more than I do. Moreover, I readily confess that, for want of practice, I do not know the Jewish prayers. I merely maintain that the title King of the World is not found in any biblical text accepted by Christianity and mentioned in the *encyclical Quas primas* on the Royalty of Jesus.

Sir, I ask you to kindly make this letter available to your readers and to M. Guénon. Indeed, I have as much respect for his personality as for his intellectual merit, and I would find it a pity if, instead of taking place on a purely speculative ground, this discussion were to feed a controversy unworthy of him and, I dare hope, of myself.

Please be assured, Sir, of my perfect esteem.

[Guénon's response, in *Christo regnante* Paris, March 1, 1931]:

While thanking our correspondent for the courteous tone of his letter, we must say that fundamentally it does not explain anything and is no more precise as regards his way of thinking than was his article, which, incidentally, we did read with all the attention necessary. If he spoke as he did of the 'Great White Lodge' merely 'for the sake of linguistic convenience', he was ill-informed, for a thing cannot be described appropriately by the name of its counterfeit or its parody. Would it not have been simpler to speak of *Agartha*? On the other hand, we could never have imagined that a text had to be 'accepted by Christianity' in order to be considered as belonging to authentic Judaism! Finally, on the most serious point, that is, the passage dealing with 'material and political propensities,' we note first of all that the author has a particularly low idea of the 'King of the World', which places this personage below the least of the initiates, since he attributes to him a character and preoccupations that are purely 'profane'. We further note that he uses the word 'materialism' in a quite arbitrary sense by opposing it to 'mysticism', whereas to our knowledge it has never been used in this way. Be that as it may, the fact remains that he actually applies to us the

words 'with a natural tendency toward a materialistic interpretation', and on this point we can only renew to the utmost our indignant protest. In this connection, we will point out that whereas in
all respects the 'materialistic' point of view falls short of mysticism,
ours on the contrary goes well beyond, so that mysticism itself
appears to us as something still quite 'material', as is explained in
what we wrote earlier on this subject. Dr Mariani's confusion here
simply proves once again how difficult it is for certain people to
make the necessary distinction between the initiatic domain and
the secular domain. As for the professed distaste for controversy,
we address him our most heartfelt congratulations, while asking
how this distaste is to be reconciled with his contribution to the
R.I.S.S.! In any case he may rest assured: we never acknowledge any
polemic, as we do not allow ourselves to stray from our field into
that of the adversary. As regards Desoille, we remember having
heard his name mentioned only once before we read Dr Mariani's
article, but in such a strange circumstance that when we saw it in
the note in question, we immediately put the two together. But this
is another story, which is of no interest to anybody else, and we are
not accustomed to entertain discussions with our readers on personal matters...

July–August–September 1932 — The 'occultist section' in this journal
always offers extracts from 'Master Therion' (Aleister Crowley), which
are of little fundamental interest and seem rather poorly translated.
Thus, we find the expressions 'Grand Travail' and 'Grand Ouvrage', obviously to render *Great Work*; but is the translator unaware that in French
there is something called the 'Grand Œuvre'? —Then comes an article
dedicated to an American, or pseudo-American (for its known head-
quarters is in Brussels) enterprise, entitled *The Thieron School of Life*; and
the similarity of the names Thieron and Therion leads us to wonder
whether there might not be some connection with the *O. T. O.* But this
hypothesis scarcely seems plausible, for Crowley is a much cleverer charlatan than the one who has elaborated the silliness of some examples that
we have presented here. We would more readily believe that it is a question of simple imitation of a pseudonym, intended to create a confusion
considered advantageous. Was there not once a conjuror performing
under the name *Papus*? — A certain Raymond Dulac(?), who most
decidedly seems to have inherited the succession of the 'Mariani fire',

continues to attack us. it seems that we incorrectly attributed a quotation This can happen when one is not a 'scholar' and does not have at hand the means to verify everything, and moreover in the present instance this would change nothing fundamental, which alone is our concern. Be that as it may, he must be truly demonic to describe such a slip as a 'fraud'. But there is an much graver error in his review: where has he ever seen us speak of 'esoteric groups'? Besides, we are in no way a 'philosopher', and we really make fun of philosophy, as of all kinds of profane knowledge. And what is this ambiguous phrase where he alludes to 'Jews of the socio-logical school,' as if it was not quite well-known that we had only con-tempt for university theories and that we are also as thoroughly 'anti-evolutionist' as it is possible to be? Who is he trying to deceive by such gross cock-and-bull stories? Finally, what can we make of the claims of someone who not only 'demands proof' (something worth about as much as undertaking to prove the existence of light to a blind man) but 'waits for one to point out the contents and the depositories of the Tradi-tion'? Who does he take us for? We are neither a spy nor a traitor, and we do not intend to make ourselves in any way an accomplice to the nasty work of these gentlemen. What is more, it is not for such worldly-minded people as these that we write!

The Speculative Mason

OCTOBER 1932 — This issue contains an article that considers the rela-tionship between Operative and Speculative Masonry in a way contrary to current opinion, for it suggests that not only have both coexisted since remote times, but that Operative Masonry is even only a dependency as it were of Speculative Masonry. There is much truth in this thesis, although the terms in which it is expressed are not safe from all objection. If by 'speculative' is meant a 'doctrinal' Masonry directing or inspiring the work of craftsmen, this agrees precisely with what we ourselves have often pointed out regarding the strictly initiatic origin of the arts and crafts. Doubtless this is basically what the author wished to say, for he recog-nized that this so-called 'speculative' Masonry was in reality 'operative' in a higher sense. But for precisely this reason it is improper to use the word 'speculative', which we do not believe was in use formerly, and indicates rather a kind of degeneration—a Masonry become exclusively 'theoreti-cal' and therefore no longer working effectively toward any 'realization', either spiritual or material. Moreover, some of the assertions contained in the said article are questionable. In particular, why consider seriously the 'Egyptological' fancies of Dr Churchward. In any case, there are many other points meriting closer examination, such as the orientation of the Lodges and the place of the officers, the use of the name *al-Shaddai* in operative Masonry, and also the role played by 'polar' symbolism, which is in reality of a much higher order than 'solar' symbolism, and at the same time nearest to the origins, as all those will easily understand who have some true idea of the 'Center of the World'.

OCTOBER 1949 — After giving a general summary of the contents of the manuscripts of the *Old Charges*, of which almost a hundred are now known, and having noted the evidence found there regarding secret information that obviously could not be very explicit in written and even 'semi-public' documents, it examines in particular the question of the name given to the architect of Solomon's Temple. Remarkably, this name is never Hiram; in most of the manuscripts, it is either *Amon* or some other form that really appears to be a corruption thereof. It would seem therefore that the name Hiram was only substituted for the former later on, probably because it is mentioned in the Bible, although in fact the position of architect is not attributed to him, whereas the question of Amon does not arise. It is also odd that in Hebrew this word has precisely the meaning of craftsman and architect, which leads us to wonder whether a common name has been taken for a proper name, or if on the contrary this designation was given to architects because it was first the name of the one who built the Temple. Be that as it may, its root, whence derives also the word *amen*, expresses in Hebrew as well as in Arabic, ideas of stability, steadfastness, faith, loyalty, sincerity, and truth, which agree very well with the character attributed by Masonic legend to the third Grand-Master. As for the name of the Egyptian god *Amon*, although identical in form, it has a different meaning, that of 'hidden' or 'mysterious', although it is possible that among all these ideas there are really more connections than may appear at first sight. In this respect it is at least curious to note that the three parts of the word *Royal Arch* to which we have referred in one of our studies ('Paroles perdue et mots substitués' [Lost Word and Substituted Words], in the issue for October–December 1948),[8] and which are considered to represent the divine

---

8. See chapter 3 of the present work. ED.

names in the Hebraic, Chaldean, and Egyptian traditions, are in Operative Masonry related to Solomon, Hiram king of Tyre, and the third Grand-Master, respectively. This leads us to think that perhaps the 'Egyptian' connection suggested by the ancient name of the third is perhaps not purely accidental. Another interesting point is that it has been assumed that since what is given as an Egyptian divine name is in fact the name of a town, it was introduced there only through a confusion between a divinity and the place where that divinity was worshipped. However, if we take into account the uncertainty of the vowels, it really enters in a scarcely different form into the composition of one of the principal names of Osiris said to be his 'royal name'. What is odder still is that it actually means 'to be', as does the almost homonymous Greek word, which according to some may also have contributed to the confusion. We do not wish to draw any conclusion from this, if not that in such questions one cannot without close examination put confidence in those solutions that seem simplest.

Another interesting article is entitled *The Tables of King Solomon and King Arthur*. The 'tables' in question have a similar astronomical symbolism, and here priority is claimed for that of Arthur, because it is identified with the archaic zodiac of Somerset, whose origin would have been far earlier than the time of Solomon. In truth, the question of priority seems to us to lose much of its importance if, as we think it does, the issue concerns, representations derived from the same prototype but without any direct filiation from one to the other.

Symbolisme

JUNE 1933 — This edition of *Symbolisme* has an article by Oswald Wirth with the excellent title 'L'Erreur occultiste' [The Occultist Fallacy], which is the one we ourself considered using for a book that would have paralleled our *The Spiritist Fallacy*, but which circumstances have prevented us from writing. Unfortunately, the title offers more than is delivered by the contents of the article, which amount to vague generalities that prove nothing, except that the author has an idea of initiation which, while different from that of the occultists, is not much more accurate; he even goes so far as to write that 'the first initiate must have initiated himself,' evincing complete ignorance of the origin and 'non-human' nature of initiation. — Remarkably, he weakens his own case in his following article (July issue), entitled 'Le Virtu des Rites' [The Virtues of Rites], where he states quite clearly that 'initiation is human and is not conferred as a divine institution'; and in order to show even more clearly that he does not understand the first thing about the subject, he says again that 'the initiatic rites are secular'(!), which however does not prevent him a few lines later from adding without concern for contradiction, that 'priestly initiations played an important role in the past'. Furthermore, he thinks that the 'Great Mysteries' of antiquity were 'those of the beyond', which looks a little too much like spiritism, and that, at Eleusis, it was a matter of 'greeting the soul after death', which, without even speaking of the anachronism of the expression, is solely the affair of exoteric religion. He again confuses magic and religion, two things that are in no way connected, and also seems to confuse 'priesthood' with 'clergy', which after all is perhaps his best justification. . . . We would like to stress even more that what is said of initiatic transmission and of 'spiritual influence' shows a lack of understanding that it would be difficult to carry further; there are negations which are truly terrible . . . but only for their author. In reading certain phrases on the 'secular rites accomplished' (we willingly translate: 'accomplished by the ignorant', which, alas! would also conform to the truth of the original meaning of the word), we cannot stop ourselves from thinking that Homais is not dead!

DECEMBER 1946 to MAY 1947 (excepting that for March, which is entirely devoted to the memory of Oswald Wirth) — These issues of *Symbolisme* include serialized segments of the study 'Le Triangle et l'Hexagramme' signed 'Maen-Nevez, Maître d'Oeuvre'. These include observations of uneven importance, the most interesting in our opinion being those that deal specifically with both Operative symbols and those of the Compagnonnage. The author reproduces a stone cutter's mark found at Vitré that depicts the 'quatre de chiffre' [sign of four] which we have discussed elsewhere,[9] but he seems to have made no attempt to delve deeper into its meaning, although he takes this mark as a starting-point for discussions, of which some relate only indirectly to the matter at hand. However, he has at least succeeded in 'placing' the mark in question on one of the graphic 'grids' employed for that purpose by the ancient guilds of builders. We should also point out that the reflections set forth in the course of this work on construction in wood and stones, especially in

---

9. See *Symbols of Sacred Science*, chap. 64. ED.

Nordic architecture, are comparable to what we ourself have said here on this subject with reference to other traditions (*Maçons et charpentiers*, in the issue for December 1946).[10] Concerning 'Trinitarian' symbols, there is a curious picture deriving from the Compagnonnage formerly reproduced in a special issue of *Voile d'Isis* (November 1925). That this figure resembles the three-headed Gaelic God is incontestable, but the author, who is evidently interested in a most particular way in Celtism, wishes to draw too many conclusions. In any case, there is something else rather strange in the picture, which we do not believe anyone has ever noticed: the design in question is exactly similar to certain paintings from Mount Athos (except that in the latter the inscriptions are naturally Greek instead of Latin), which, it seems, are used by the Greek monks as a support for contemplation. This fact that could perhaps throw an unexpected light on certain 'affinities' of the Compagnonnage. From another point of view, we should mention a slight inaccuracy: it is not *Shiva*, but *Brahmā*, who is represented with four faces in Hindu iconography; in contrast, there are figures of *Shiva* with three faces (in connection with the 'triple time'),[11] which would have been more appropriate to mention in this connection. The remarks on the hexagram which follow are inspired largely by the works of Matila Ghyka and call for only one observation: it is quite true that the right-angled triangle and the inverted triangle correspond respectively to fire and water, of which, moreover, they are the alchemical symbols; but this is only one application among many others, and the author envisages it much too exclusively. We are not acquainted with the work of R.-J. Gorsleben to which he refers, but judging from the citations he gives, it does not appear that it can be used without caution, for it is to be feared that his interpretation of symbols contains some rather fanciful 'modernizations'.

Symbolos

JULY–NOVEMBER 1947 — These issues contain a long study by François Ménard on 'The Hermetic Virgin', that addresses rather diverse questions, all however relating to the cosmological order as this is envisaged more particularly in traditional Western forms. The symbolism of the

---

10. See chapter 5 of the current work. ED.
11. See *The Great Triad*, chap. 22. ED.

'Hermetic vase', which corresponds to a certain aspect of the Virgin, is examined first; the author then seeks to explain the meaning of the 'Hermetic Wisdom' of Khunrath, drawing the conclusion that 'the Virgin is the essential principle of Hermeticism,' but that 'this aspect is nevertheless orthodox, that is to say that it is linked to the metaphysical domain which, as we know, is that of the supreme Principle', this link moreover corresponding to that which normally exists between 'royal art' and 'sacerdotal art'. Then, with regard to the Virgin as 'Light of Glory', we find a kind of scientific fantasy on the 'coronal light'. This is regrettable in our opinion, first because things of this kind have only a rather hypothetical character, and then also because, like everything inspired by profane science, they really have nothing in common with traditional data, Hermetic or otherwise, but on the contrary recall rather too much the kind of speculation dear to occultists. We could say almost as much about 'the cycle of nitrogen and the web of the perceptible world,' although here the author has at least taken the precaution of pointing out, with regard to the force of which the different modalities constitute this 'web', that 'Hermeticism has the considerable advantage over modern science in knowing this force from the inside as it were, of having identified it with the light that is in man, and that it has recognized that, to a certain degree, his well-directed will can act on it and so obtain definite results, through a sure technique'. We for our part will say more clearly that in these two cases, Hermeticism and modern science, the knowledge involved is not in fact of the same order. The next question is that of the 'zodiacal Virgin', like the myth of Ceres to which it is related as a 'sign of earth'. This is followed by an outline of the different stages of Hermetic realization according to Dante's symbolic description in the *Divine Comedy*. In wanting to 'elucidate the hieroglyphic mystery of *Hokmah*,' the author has unfortunately committed a grave error: he has confused the final *he* with a *heth*, which, naturally, entirely distorts his calculation and his interpretation. As for his conclusion that 'the Hermetic Virgin, insofar as she is found to be in contact with sensible and material things, is the form of the Goddess (that is to say, of the *Shakti*), the best suited to the West and to our age of extreme materialism,' let us say that it seems somewhat in contradiction with the fact that, in the modern West, the traditional sciences are completely lost.

INDEX

Lightning Source UK Ltd.
Milton Keynes UK
UKHW042228050720
366006UK00003BA/44/J

9 780900 588518